Cupid's Knife: Women's Anger and Agency in Violent Relationships

Much domestic violence literature has called attention to the fact that women's material needs for shelter, daycare, employment, and legal protection may render them helpless to leave toxic relationships. Yet, even with the provision of these, many women remain tightly wound in their abusers' embrace. In *Cupid's Knife: Women's Anger and Agency in Violent Relationships*, Abby Stein draws on the gripping narratives of physically and emotionally abused women to illuminate how splitting off their own aggression undermines women's agency, making it almost impossible for them to leave violent partners. Psychology, with its focus on "managing" men's anger in violent relationships, has had little to offer in the way of substantive critical work with women on the identification, integration and constructive use of a range of darker emotions typically labeled as antithetical to the norms for female behavior.

In this book, Abby Stein shows that although a number of psychological processes that contribute to the intractability of abusive relationships have been identified – such as trauma bonding and learned helplessness – their recognition has offered no clinical pathway out of the abyss. Stein suggests that our attention to other aspects of the internal world, the relational framework, and the cultural context in which both operate, may be more useful than current interventions in determining individual treatments that break the oft-cited "cycle of violence." More globally, *Cupid's Knife: Women's Anger and Agency in Violent Relationships* jumpstarts a provocative conversation about how female aggression can be repurposed as a catalyst for social change. It will be essential reading for psychoanalysts, psychologists, psychiatrists, sociologists, criminologists, students and the lay reader with an interest in clinical treatment, interpersonal psychoanalysis, domestic violence, gender roles, dissociation and aggression.

Abby Stein is Associate Professor at the John Jay College of Criminal Justice and post-graduate faculty at the Manhattan Institute of Psychoanalysis. She is the author of *Prologue to Violence: Child Abuse, Dissociation, and Crime* (Analytic Press, 2007).

PSYCHOANALYSIS IN A NEW KEY BOOK SERIES

DONNEL STERN
SERIES EDITOR

When music is played in a new key, the melody does not change, but the notes that make up the composition do: change in the context of continuity, continuity that perseveres through change. Psychoanalysis in a New Key publishes books that share the aims psychoanalysts have always had, but that approach them differently. The books in the series are not expected to advance any particular theoretical agenda, although to this date most have been written by analysts from the Interpersonal and Relational orientations.

The most important contribution of a psychoanalytic book is the communication of something that nudges the reader's grasp of clinical theory and practice in an unexpected direction. Psychoanalysis in a New Key creates a deliberate focus on innovative and unsettling clinical thinking. Because that kind of thinking is encouraged by exploration of the sometimes surprising contributions to psychoanalysis of ideas and findings from other fields, Psychoanalysis in a New Key particularly encourages interdisciplinary studies. Books in the series have married psychoanalysis with dissociation, trauma theory, sociology, and criminology. The series is open to the consideration of studies examining the relationship between psychoanalysis and any other field – for instance, biology, literary and art criticism, philosophy, systems theory, anthropology, and political theory.

But innovation also takes place within the boundaries of psychoanalysis, and Psychoanalysis in a New Key therefore also presents work that reformulates thought and practice without leaving the precincts of the field. Books in the series focus, for example, on the significance of personal values in psychoanalytic practice, on the complex interrelationship between the analyst's clinical work and personal life, on the consequences for the clinical situation when patient and analyst are from different cultures, and on the need for psychoanalysts to accept the degree to which they knowingly satisfy their own wishes during treatment hours, often to the patient's detriment.

Vol. 19
Cupid's Knife: Women's Anger and Agency in Violent Relationships
Abby Stein

Vol. 18
Contemporary Psychoanalysis and the Legacy of the Third Reich: History, Memory and Tradition
Emily A. Kuriloff

Vol. 17
Love and Loss in Life and in Treatment
Linda B. Sherby

Vol. 16
Imagination from Fantasy to Delusion
Lois Oppenheim

Vol. 15
Still Practicing: The Heartaches and Joys of a Clinical Career
Sandra Buechler

Vol. 14
Dancing with the Unconscious: The Art of Psychoanalysis and the Psychoanalysis of Art
Danielle Knafo

Vol. 13
Money Talks: In Therapy, Society, and Life
Brenda Berger & Stephanie Newman (eds.)

Vol. 12
Partners in Thought: Working with Unformulated Experience, Dissociation, and Enactment
Donnel B. Stern

Vol. 11
Heterosexual Masculinities: Contemporary Perspectives from Psychoanalytic Gender Theory
Bruce Reis & Robert Grossmark (eds.)

Vol. 10
Sex Changes: Transformations in Society and Psychoanalysis
Mark J. Blechner

Vol. 9
The Consulting Room and Beyond: Psychoanalytic Work and Its Reverberations in the Analyst's Life
Therese Ragen

Vol. 8
Making a Difference in Patients' Lives: Emotional Experience in the Therapeutic Setting
Sandra Buechler

Vol. 7
Coasting in the Countertransference: Conflicts of Self Interest between Analyst and Patient
Irwin Hirsch

Vol. 6
Wounded by Reality: Understanding and Treating Adult Onset Trauma
Ghislaine Boulanger

Vol. 5
Prologue to Violence: Child Abuse, Dissociation, and Crime
Abby Stein

Vol. 4
Prelogical Experience: An Inquiry into Dreams & Other Creative Processes
Edward S. Tauber & Maurice R. Green

Vol. 3
The Fallacy of Understanding & The Ambiguity of Change
Edgar A. Levenson

Vol. 2
What Do Mothers Want? Contemporary Perspectives in Psychoanalysis and Related Disciplines
Sheila F. Brown (ed.)

Vol. 1
Clinical Values: Emotions That Guide Psychoanalytic Treatment
Sandra Buechler

Cupid's Knife: Women's Anger and Agency in Violent Relationships

Abby Stein

Routledge
Taylor & Francis Group
NEW YORK AND LONDON

First published 2014
by Routledge
605 Third Avenue, New York, NY 10017
4 Park Square, Milton Park, Abingdon, Oxon OX14 4RN

Routledge is an imprint of the Taylor & Francis Group, an informa business

Library of Congress Cataloging in Publication Data
A catalog record for this book has been requested

ISBN: 978–0–415–52786–6 (hbk)
ISBN: 978–0–415–52787–3 (pbk)
ISBN: 978–1–315–86746–5 (ebk)

Typeset in Times New Roman
by RefineCatch Limited, Bungay, Suffolk, UK

Cupid Chastised

Of course, Mars is angry. That's his nature.
And Venus should divert his anger with love.
Poor Cupid was only doing his job, to move
Desire; mischievous, but not misbehavior.
Consider, the boy inflames the God of War
Towards the Goddess of Love, his mother.
Yes, some uproar among the gods ensues.
Venus and Mars are derided, labeled fools.
Did Cupid intend another sister or brother,
Or to soften the eternal wrath of Mars
By ambush, with a lover's show of arms?
He didn't count on being struck to the floor,
Or a Mars invulnerable to a Venus' alarm.
Each god must despise the thing he stands for.

Christopher Guerin

Contents

Acknowledgments *x*

1 An ill-fated introduction 1

2 The utility of contempt 29

3 Engendered self-states 52

4 Masochism as medium 77

5 Theater of judicial absurdity 105

6 Venus with arms 134

Epilogue *162*
References *165*
Index *179*

Acknowledgments

I wish to thank my friends and colleagues at the John Jay College of Criminal Justice, most particularly those in my feminist theory reading group: Katie Gentile, Kyoo Lee, Allison Pease, Leeza Yukins, and Erica Burleigh, an interdisciplinary group of scholars who have opened my mind and enriched my repertoire, sometimes a bit against my will. I also want to give a shout-out to the Interdisciplinary Studies Program, my base of operations, where I have learned to teach, think, and write from a variety of perspectives, and to the Anthropology Department, which offered me a second loving home within the college. Thanks to John Jay College for the start-up funding that got this project off the ground and to the Professional Staff Congress of the City University of New York which funded the research that forms the backbone of the book.

Probably no group of people has played a larger part in the development of my ideas for this book than my colleagues at the William Alanson White Institute for Psychiatry, Psychoanalysis, and Psychology. Within the Institute, I am especially indebted to the core members of the Sexual Abuse Service, including Julie Marcuse, Richard Gartner, Sondra Wilk, Alison Feit, Sarah Stemp, Daniel Gensler, Karen Marisak, Ernesto Mujica, Eric Dammann, Gail Harris, Helene Kafka, Martin Walkler, Jill Bellinson, Robert Akeret, and Milt Zaphiropoulos. Betsy Hegeman is, luckily for me, a colleague at both the White Institute and John Jay College; there is nothing better than running into her in the hallways of one institution or another and knowing my world is of a piece.

Finally, Donnel B. Stern, my editor and a brilliant psychoanalyst and scholar, has been a presence in my intellectual life now for many years. He has been a guiding light and a real mensch in matters both great and small. I am honored to know him and incredibly fortunate to have benefitted from his remarkable insights about the human condition.

Author's note: Support for this project was provided by PSC-CUNY Awards in 2010, 2011, and 2012. Awards are jointly funded by The Professional Staff Congress and The City University of New York.

Grateful acknowledgment is made to the following for permission to reprint:

"Cupid Chastened" – permission granted by Christopher Guerin, Cupid Chastened from his "Brushstroke" sonnet series, Zealotry of Guerin http://christophergeuerin.blogspot.com/

"Anger is much more powerful and reassuring than anxiety, which is the antithesis of power." Harry Stack Sullivan, originally published in Sullivan, H. S. (1950), The illusion of personal individuality. *Psychiatry: Journal for the Study of Interpersonal Processes, 13*, 317–332.

The Ballad of Francine Hughes by Lyn Hardy and Donna Herbert. Lynn Hardy, www.lynhardy.com, and Donna Herbert, www./fiddlingdemystified.com. Copyright © 1986 by Swinging Door Music. Used by permission. All rights reserved.

Permission is granted to use parts of the chapter "Utility of Contempt" which originally appeared in Stein, A. (2011), The utility of contempt. *Contemporary Psychoanalysis, 47*(1), 80–100.

Permission is granted to reproduce the chapter "Engendered Self-states" which originally appeared in Stein, A. (2012), Engendered self-states: Dissociated affect, social discourse, and the forfeiture of agency in battered women. *Psychoanalytic Psychology, 29*(1), 34–58. Doi: 10.1037/a0024880. Copyright © 2012 by the American Psychological Association.

"Abuse is merely a dyadic notion. Aside from the abuser and the abuse, there is also an enabling environment." Permission granted by Asaf Work.

"You Fit into Me" by Margaret Atwood. In Canada this selection appears in *Selected Poems 1964–1984*, published by Oxford University Press.

Excerpt from "You Fit into Me" from *Selected Poems, 1965–1975* by Margaret Atwood, by permission of Houghton Mifflin Harcourt Publishing Company. All rights reserved.

Excerpt from "You Fit into Me." In the United Kingdom this selection appears in *Eating Fire: Selected Poetry 1965–1995*, published by Virago Press/Little, Brown Book Group.

Excerpt from "You Fit into Me." Reproduced with permission of Curtis Brown Group Ltd., London, on behalf of Margaret Atwood. Copyright Margaret Atwood © 1971.

"The only cure for contempt is countercontempt," excerpt from H. L. Mencken, *Minority Report*, published by Borsai/Knopf, 1956. Reproduced with permission of the publisher.

Excerpt from *Masculine Shame: From Succubus to the Eternal Feminine*, by Mary Ayers, published by Taylor and Francis Group LLC Books, reproduced with permission of the publisher.

Excerpt from from *The Rebel* by Albert Camus, translated by Anthony Bower, translation copyright © 1956 by Alfred A. Knopf, a division of Random House, Inc. Used by permission of Alfred A. Knopf, a division of Random House, Inc. Any third party use of this material, outside of this publication, is prohibited. Interested parties must apply directly to Random House, Inc., for permission.

Chapter 1

An ill-fated introduction

> Anger is much more powerful and reassuring than anxiety, which is the antithesis of power.
>
> (Harry Stack Sullivan)

> Slowly, slowly I got up and went out to the shed
> I grabbed a can of gasoline and I poured it around his bed
> And I lit a book of matches and I threw it at his head
>
> (From *The Ballad of Francine Hughes*, by Lyn Hardy and Donna Herbert)

I am a veteran in the field of violence. Over 20 years, I have worked with assaultive and homicidal men and women and the victims of their attacks. I have been around a lot of angry and aggressive people although, surprisingly, they have rarely recognized themselves as such. For perpetrators, cyclically subordinate to an incapacitating tension, rage erupts like an overdue visitor, but goes unrecognized as the instigator of unquantifiable suffering. *I am just not an angry guy, wouldn't hurt a fly, not me.* For the victims of interpersonal violence, anger seems equally impossible to access. They, too, live with an overwhelming anxiety that neuters agency, their anger classically turned inward, finding expression mainly at the end of the other person's fist. *I'm not angry, not me. I just want it to stop.*

For some women, like Francine Hughes, an abused wife whose cautionary tale of suppressed anger became legend with the publication of *The Burning Bed* (McNulty, 1977), split-off rage is conveyed in a stunning forensic finale that appeals to our sense of vigilante justice. In fantasy, we valorize such agency, but the majority of women who kill their abusers – unlike Hughes, who was acquitted on grounds of temporary insanity – do long hard time for their crimes and return to an inimical world. Of course, cases of women killing their batterers or causing them grievous injury are extremely rare. For the majority of female victims of domestic violence, aggressive feelings stay underground, where the inability to recognize, experience, process, and appropriately exercise a continuum of negative emotions has a destabilizing influence on their perception of agency in their relationships. It is my contention that abused women are enslaved as much by this narrative of passivity as they are by their partners' suffocating control and the seeming randomness of their attacks.

Psychology, with its focus on "managing" anger in violent relationships, has had little to offer in the way of substantive critical work with women on the identification, integration and constructive use of a range of darker emotions typically labeled as antithetical to norms for female behavior. Psychoanalytic models that foreground trauma and dissociation come closer but, in shying from the political context of violence against women, miss an opportunity to link women with a constituency of empowerment. It is my hope to make the case for enlisting the tools of critical consciousness – which have already been used successfully in group work around intimate violence – for an expanded, more personally and politically mindful way of doing interpersonal psychoanalysis. First, let me tell you how I arrived at this place.

Writing about child maltreatment as a precursor to adult criminality in an earlier book, *Prologue to Violence* (Stein, 2007), introduced me to the quality and impact of family violence. Although my focus in that work was on the youngest victims of domestic violence, rather than their mothers, I could not help but notice the paradox of adult women who, despite the brutality of their partners, were often unable to tear themselves away from corrosive relationships. My thoughts remained as background noise until, years later, my frustration with a private client – mired in a series of destructive love affairs – both amplified and fine-tuned those reflections. My experience in helping that client navigate a path out of the abyss inspired the larger research project that informs this book.

The client, Phoebe, whose story is woven throughout the book, seemed at turns oblivious, apathetic, and, finally, curiously incapable of becoming angry – or even mildly indignant – in response to the manipulations and abuses of her lovers. She would often insist that she had "no right" to protest her treatment at their hands. Growing to know Phoebe more fully, I was surprised to encounter not only the usual set of internal obstacles to change but also an immersion in post-feminist notions of supposed gender equality that seemed to me profoundly *disempowering* for Phoebe, like settling for being "friends with benefits" with the men she desired romantically or "manning up" rather than complaining about physical abuse. Because of this particular layering of her defenses, over time I found it necessary to transcend the usual conversational boundaries of clinical dialogue and engage broader cultural issues surrounding men, women, violence, servitude, control, romance, desire, humiliation, power, and retribution. Watching Phoebe's evolution toward greater agency and esteem included the unfurling and eventual integration of her dissociated rage, through techniques that expanded the usual site of psychological work into the larger landscape of gender and politics, and forced us to do psychoanalysis "with culture in mind" (Dimen, 2011).

What I was learning with Phoebe moved me to speak with other women, women who had been in even more dangerous relationships than she. I designed and received funding for a study that enabled me to spend a summer interviewing women who had been in long-term relationships characterized by verbal and emotional abuse as well as extremely serious physical violence. Embarking on the study, like most witnesses to domestic assault, I wanted to know what kept women from asserting themselves at the nascent signs of abuse: a partner's unfounded jealousies, his controlling manner, the reckless shove across a crowded room. What kept women there, year after year, long past any hope of change? What had to happen for women to leave? Were abusive relationships that never became overtly violent different in quality or only quantity? My own informal conversations with friends and colleagues suggested that women, rather than accidentally stumbling upon them, were often drawn to men who mistreated them. Others persevered in rotten relationships for no reason that outsiders could fathom. Every psychoanalyst's client roster has its share of women seeking help specifically because they feel abused, in some way, by romantic partners. What was the connection between these more pedestrian relational disasters and those of the women in my sample?

The scholarly work done on the subject is considerable but contradictory, owing to differences in sample size, subject characteristics, and methodology. The published clinical work is no less confusing in its kaleidoscopy, brokering almost immediately anachronistic snapshots of popular locales in the geography and history of attitudes toward women; here an hysteric, there a masochist, everywhere a post-traumatic survivor. Indeed, there is enormous difficulty in documenting the human struggles with attachment and aggression that register as timeless but whose particular expressions are indeed time and culture specific. It becomes a giant game of whack-a-mole to move among personal and collective inducements and encumbrances, private damage and shared injury.

So, in addition to acutely attending the personal stories of women, I have mined a burgeoning literature on the cultural contribution to unconscious life, particularly as it concerns refractory states of violence. These literatures are disharmonious too, at least in emphasis. The domestic abuse literature consistently underscores how the lack of access to employment, suitable housing, and daycare inhibit women's flight. Available feminist narratives concentrate on how the dictates and practices of patriarchy set the stage for female tragedy. Social psychologists liken a battered woman's plight to that of a hostage, foregrounding the eerily reflexive nature of her submission under extreme conditions. When I spoke to women who had emerged from situations of abuse, most did indeed exemplify some of these stereotypical attributes of victimhood. But each theoretical strike, in naming a solitary cause for female trouble, rang hollowly against the cupola of reality. The truth of what women endure and how they respond is idiosyncratic, multifaceted, and deeply paradoxical. It involves the visible world of legal procedure, psychiatric codes, busted noses, and scripted narratives that make manifest an invisible world of attachment, humiliation, love, power and sundered identity.

Cupid's knife

Much as women clamor to discuss, dissect, and even monumentalize their stories, there is often a terrible incapacity to affectively register what has transpired in their homes or to cognize the impact of their interior world on its material counterpart and vice versa. Many of the women I interviewed reminded me of Phoebe: well put together, highly functional, all cool detachment as they reported perverse invasions of autonomy, incessant shaming, sexual debasement, corporeal blows. I quickly learned that the flatness of their affect signaled neither equanimity nor grace under pressure. Each woman's tale was simply two tales: the one they admitted to themselves and the one they completely dissociated. Again and again, the analysis of their narratives revealed a psychic splitting between event and symbolization, between actuality and affect, between memory and knowledge. Although recent writing about repression, splitting, and dissociation suggests that "knowing" (in its most pregnant sense) is not by itself as mutative in clinical work as was once believed (Stern, 2010), telling the tale that refuses to be told is still central to psychoanalysis, qualitative psychological research, and the understanding of both love and violence.

With intimate abuse, the task of finding and naming what has happened is hard but the job of enumerating what one *refused* to see, hear, taste, or feel is even more arduous and important. It is these unattended viscera that most ardently concoct the practical world of pain where batterer and battered intersect. It is the yielding spot where Cupid's knife gets stuck. In real life, a Cupid's knife is a concealable switchblade, easily purchased in many jurisdictions. The knife's danger lies in its retractable blade, which pops straight out the front so that the victim cannot see it coming. In the online gaming world, the Cupid's Knife has been re-imagined as a torture device designed to cause pain to a victim whenever they think any negative thoughts about their abuser, forcing them to feel only love. Both descriptions resonate with the emotional circumstances of the women I interviewed and, more generally, epitomize the paradoxical attachments that women form in conditions of oppression.

Defensive attachments

In *The Ghost Sonata*, August Strindberg (1907/2004) constructs a spectral world of betrayal, filled with Gothic horrors, to represent the family, which he elsewhere has called "the home of all social evil." Although the staple of much art and psychoanalytic theory, the apparent verisimilitude of such anti-family sentiment is easily outweighed, even in this jaded age, by the testimonials of familial love and loyalty that line bookstore shelves and social media sites. Without making a judgment about the value of such contradictory tribute, it seems commonsensical to observe that, although love and hate coexist in all relationships, it redounds to our defensive benefit to recognize the good in those to whom we are attached more than their malignity. Thus, it is common to minimize or even deny family members' aggression toward us even as we craft (unconsciously) a defensive maneuver that obviates its impact.

Here is a greatly simplified example that captures the broad outlines of how aggression is integrated (or not) into our being: a father always demands a large bite of his young son's ice cream despite the boy's cries that "you are taking too much, Daddy," to which the Daddy replies that, since he was the one who paid for the ice cream, he is entitled to the bite. When the boy is a little older, he saves his allowance to buy his own ice cream but, still, the Dad insists on his share, making the boy feel powerless and trapped. Frustrated and enraged, he sobs to his mother but her condolences are little comfort or guidance in a world dominated by the shadow of an unjust giant. By the time the boy is grown, he has developed a habit that others might find lovely: he offers those around him a taste of his food before he commences eating. By becoming its stage director, the man suavely and unconsciously masters the boyhood "trauma." While he may or may not recall the formative incidents that triggered this latter behavior, chances are that, even in remembering, the man will not associate the antipodal phenomena directly. His own feelings will be retroactively demoted from betrayal and rage to a mildly stinging lesson about power differentials. (One wonders how similar behavior by a mother would be internalized.) Even if the man does recollect his own tearful affect when Daddy snatched the ice cream, he may only remember the father's behavior as pushy, maybe obnoxious, but certainly not hateful or abusive. The memory may even be turned into a humorous family anecdote about a parent's eccentricities. That is no doubt a useful turn of events but it is also fairly dissociative. (One wonders whether similar behavior by a mother might escape scrutiny in so predictable a way.)

For the most part, unless he is unusually self-reflective (or goes into a psychodynamic therapy) these two facts of his life – the precipitating trauma and the contemporary narrative defusing it – will remain peripheral and unconnected to the man's general sense of self. This is because, as long as family members' malevolence is relatively transitory and minimal, we grow up not *too* dissociative and not *too* prone to destructive enactments. On the other hand, if the ice cream incidents are part of a larger menu of humiliation in a boy's life, the effects will not be so benign. Maybe the boy will grow up to grab his own son's ice cream, repeating the trauma, or maybe he will rob ice cream trucks for a living. Or eat so much ice cream, and grow so fat, that he dies of a heart attack by 40. Depending on a large variety of contextual and temperamental variables, the boy could (whether aware or unaware of the precipitating trauma) conceivably grow up to own a frozen treat empire or kill a man whom he wrongly perceives to be coveting something he owns. My forensic experience suggests that the harsher, more chronic, and earlier the bad treatment, the greater the likelihood of a catastrophic denouement.

If we make the child in the most extreme version of the anecdote a daughter rather than a son, it is less likely that she will become either a mogul or a murderer. She may develop a touch of anorexia or a tendency toward eating others' leftovers, because those behaviors are more culturally encrypted for women. In romance, she might seek a man who takes her stuff as if it is his right and ignores her reactive entreaties. The worse her treatment in childhood, and its reenactment in adulthood, the more dissociated she will likely become, as such states build upon one another. Both male and female are apt to master trauma through unconscious repetition (van der Kolk, 1989) and, like the boy, the incentive for the girl (or woman) to not notice what is being done, to her and by her, grows in direct proportion to its toxicity. Unlike the man, the woman will probably refrain from mastering trauma through perpetration. She will instead engage in repetitions with herself as victim. Indeed, among the women with whom I spoke, there was a wide range of toleration for mistreatment at the hands of intimate partners, with women who had been physically maltreated as children leading the pack in adult indices of experiencing abuse. Having honed dissociative defenses early on, they were adept at ignoring serious violations in adulthood.

Physically abused women may sever the tangible evidence of what they have suffered (bruises, broken bones, vaginal tears) from what the conscious acknowledgement of those traumatic experiences might activate: terror, horror, repulsion, fury. Harry Stack Sullivan (1956b) long ago identified these "uncanny" emotions as threats so overwhelming to the integrity of the self that people would sooner disengage than emotionally process them. To varying degrees, the women I interviewed most meticulously dissociated the very emotions that normally instill a sense of integrity and agency, and motivate survival behaviors in the face of threats to the self. What is perhaps women's best defense against abuse – a righteous indignation signaling "you can't do this to me" – was not available to either forewarn or rescue most of the women from brutal relationships.

A fair number of women saw violence as evidence of their partner's passion; her own capitulation standing as testimony to the strength of their connection as a couple. Often a woman's private history simply drove her to define deviance downward: derogatory treatment was tolerated because she had no prior experience of more pacific love with which to compare her current situation. On the other hand, the larger social world she inhabited did little to discourage that destructive inveterate meaning. Even though we may be reluctant to admit it, the romantic terrain in which violent relationships are rooted mimic the best and worst of our collective idealizations about love and devotion. While some women stayed mainly because of logistical concerns, others got stuck for more socio-cultural reasons, including a strong investment in performing "normal" heterosexual behavior within their families or particular community.

When working with women in very abusive relationships it is easy to treat their conditions as anomalous when, in fact, they exemplify a strand of behavior characteristic of many romantic relationships. Many couples share the idea that possessiveness and control are the hallmarks of strong chemical attractions; they believe that love is measured in decibels and the louder the shouting, the more intense the commitment. This idea is commonplace among both violent and non-violent couples but is often discounted by clinicians, who consider the pattern so dysfunctional that they may assume there is no "real" love in the abusive relationship. Treatment providers should not ignore the very genuine affection and commitment that a woman may feel toward her partner, even when her clinical presentation highlights the intensity of their problems, or when it seems to us that a dangerous situation dictates her immediate exit. In any case, interventions narrowly aimed at separating couples often backfire, as outside attacks make them draw even closer to one another (Goldner et al., 1990). Stoically entrenched women are the focus of a book by Erin Pizzey and Jeff Shapiro who, while working with women who were "trapped for lack of an escape route," came across a distinct second group of women who, having been raised in highly dysfunctional homes, as adults kept "recreat[ing] situations of violence and pain, for those situations stir the only feelings of love and satisfaction the person has ever known" (1982, p. 7). The frustrations of work with women and couples like this were reflected upon in a focus group I ran with psychoanalysts who specialize in abuse cases. Their observations are recounted in the book.

I met fiercely enmeshed women in my study, too. Despite their self-justificatory rants during high-voltage arguments at home, and the poignant presentation of their suffering to me, at the end of the line the women seemed more interested in defending their partners than themselves. Although these women did express anger, they undid it just as quickly. Sometimes women simply could not stomach the terror and guilt involved in recognizing their own power to hurt the abuser by standing up to him, or leaving. Only when they reclaimed the mantle of fault for themselves – a silent agreement between the partners that she deserved her bruises – was homeostasis restored. Anger morphed into guilt. Punishment could begin anew.

It is very important to underline that not all women become totally consumed by an unacknowledged mise-en-scène around dissociated anger and its explosion; not all that I interviewed were "stoically entrenched." Some women, less fragmented cognitively and emotionally, were instead able to rationalize quite consciously about the price of self-expression; speaking up only when it felt safe, physically and emotionally, to do so. Living under the reign of what one researcher called "patriarchal terrorism" (Johnson, 1995), these women strategically refrained from any appearance, not only of anger, but of contrarian thinking; ideas or actions that might be (mis)interpreted as threats to their partner's control or masculinity. The non-expression of anger was a *choice*, not a sentence meted out by the unconscious. While just as persecuted as their sisters, they were more successful in retaining a sense of their separate identity, even in the face of maltreatment. Anna Quindlen (1998), in the novel *Black and Blue*, captures the unnerving mindset of such women. Her self-aware protagonist, Frances Ann Benedetto, insightfully speaks about the emotional cost of living so constrained an existence with the man who has most recently broken her nose, even noting how the object of her rage has incrementally changed from the abuser to herself: "Not just hating Bobby, but hating myself, too, the cringing self that was afraid to pick up the remote control from the coffee table in case it was just that thing that set him off" (p. 11). By this point, much of Fran's sense of herself has been seared off, leaving only exposed nerve endings and some lame vestige of conjugality. She dissociates but not completely. Though she has fallen prey for many years to her husband's remorseful apologies after innumerable senseless beatings, Fran never denies the reality of her injuries or the necessity of her eventual flight. The character's agentic self stays intact enough to design and implement a secret plan to escape her tormentor. I met women like this in my study, too. Often their flight plan began at the moment of their lover's first abusive trespass.

A final group of study subjects brooked no violation of their autonomy or integrity by the men they had chosen. They were righteously angered by such attempted incursions and said so, plainly and often loudly. While these women were not necessarily less likely to get into bad relationships, they were quicker to recognize the warning signs of abuse, understand their significance, seek help, and leave the relationship before intimate violence exacted a steep price. They did not split off, compartmentalize, suppress, or dissociate the negative. They were able to get mad, and to use that emotional condition to pole-vault out of their relationships. They were natural examples of the integration of aggression and its use as a springboard for agency.

A part of me would like these self-possessed women to be the heroines of the book, rising from the ashes in the inspirational "stories of deliverance" that Janice Haaken (2010, p. 88) deems irresponsible distillations of complex interrelational phenomena. Haaken is right, though: such heroic apocrypha only work on paper anyway. In real life, the heroines paid a fine for their precocious agency *after* leaving violent mates. Some lost their children. One has a price on her head for dishonoring the family. Yet not one expressed that she would have changed her decision to stand up for herself in the way that she did. These valorous survivors' ongoing struggles with the nuclear fallout of anger and exit remain a cautionary note in my promotion of agency for battered women.

Engaging anger

Research has shown that women who are assertive with their anger are less likely to suffer from depression and anxiety and are more likely to foster conditions of mutuality in their relationships. Yet, while controlling the anger of male batterers is seen as the acme of psychological intervention for domestic violence, no models exist that systematically address the *lack* of expressed anger in female victims. Theoretical paradigms have focused strongly on the rage, pity, and contempt of male perpetrators as instrumental to their sense of entitlement and power, but there are virtually no research studies examining the role of similarly negative affects in the behaviors of female victims and survivors of domestic abuse. My conversations with women, culminating in over 1,000 transcribed pages, were aimed at investigating the role of dissociated anger in the development of victim self-states – not just as a product of interpersonal trauma, but in the broader context of cultural demands for women to dissociate feelings that have been labeled antithetical to accepted gender norms for heterosexual behavior. Chapter 3 describes how victim self-states – the repository of dissociated aggression – develop, but I will highlight some ramifications of that psychological neutering here.

The more detached from their anger the women were, the more sadistic their partners tended to be, and the longer the unions seemed to last. The data showed that women's inability to feel and express a range of aggressive emotions, rather than keeping the relationship's temperature under control, as they believed it would, only made it more likely that those feelings would rise in their partner, unbidden and unregulated, and do extraordinary damage. Consequently, disowning anger was both a defensive reaction to massive threat and, in some cruel way, its courier. Over and over again, women's muscular dissociation of aggressive affect *increased* the odds that something terrible would happen. Doris, for example, after many years of marital rape and assault, ended up severing her husband's jugular vein. When interviewed about her feelings prior to the homicide, Doris turned out to be the *least* enraged of all the women I surveyed. Ileana, who suffered maybe the cruelest blow of all – the loss of a child due to a beating she suffered in pregnancy – even two decades later has trouble expressing malevolent feelings toward the man who meted it out. It was clear to me, when learning their back stories, that Doris and Ileana had been trained to split off their anger in early relationships with abusive caregivers, where any returned rage would almost guarantee a catastrophic comeuppance. Later, in adulthood, the root of their inability to leave batterers seemed to lie in this renunciation of their own aggression.

Doris and Ileana split off and externalized rage and contempt, choosing men who instrumentalized those affects, to chilling consequence. Despite the fact that masochism is derided as a mythological construct in feminist scholarship, there are no words that better describe the quicksand of their affiliations better than sadomasochistic. Problems surrounding the use of masochism as a diagnostic label are discussed in Chapter 4, along with a discussion of why its nuanced application may be both theoretically sound and clinically useful. As Elizabeth Howell (1997) noted over a decade ago, the removal of the term masochism from the *Diagnostic and Statistical Manual of Mental Disorders* in 1987 "threw the baby out with the bath water, implicitly leaving a large and important realm of psychopathology underemphasized by its omission" (p. 240).

Looking back to women's childhoods, it became obvious that the dissociation of so called "negative" emotions was both interpersonally and socially fashioned. Women's passivity was largely supported by family, community, church, law, and medicine, cultural institutions that promote and police binary gender roles. Even more troubling was the observation that dissociated aggression and enactment played a large role, not only within women's intimate relationships, but in the structural violence meted out by the institutions with which battered women interacted. I found that I had to move beyond just examining the ways that early messaging inside and immediately outside the home might delimit women's affective scripts; ultimately I recognized the nexus formed when the subject, thus limited, faces identical traumas – not just in her intimate relations, but also in the broader institutional world where, in a parallel process, her dependency is conclusively inscribed.

Just as domestic violence against women recapitulates cultural invective, cultural institutions often reinforce interpersonal gender inequality. Often they do so in the guise of a kind of "benevolent sexism" (Glick and Fiske, 2001), like designating a woman as mentally ill as a result of abuse only to later use this as a justification for curtailing her rights. Or by instituting practices that masquerade as gender neutral, such as arresting both parties at the scene of domestic violence (even if the woman has sustained great injury and the man only defensive or minor wounds) thereby ignoring perfectly sound reasons for differential treatment. These institutional practices suggest that police, clinicians, and jurists, mirroring the values of their society but dissociating their own traumatic reactions to women's involvement in violence, have become blindly complicit in perpetration.

The data

As part of a research paradigm called the Emotional Empowerment Project, funded by the Professional Staff Congress at the City University of New York, I interviewed women who had been in lengthy relationships that included verbal and psychological abuse as well as exceptionally grave physical violence. After interviewing those research subjects, I reanalyzed the clinical material I had collected over the years of working with Phoebe, spoke informally with female friends and colleagues about the nature of our romantic and sexual relationships, and ran a focus group with fourteen psychoanalysts on the topic of sadomasochistic attachments.

The research interviews and the focus group proceedings in this book were audiotaped and excerpts from them appear verbatim. Informal conversations, clinical material, and my own reminiscences were recorded in notes either during or immediately following personal exchanges. All identifying material has been removed for the sake of confidentiality, including identifiers for anecdotes from my own life that are unrelated to my role as researcher or practitioner. Although some findings are numerically aggregated for the sake of creating a statistical profile of battered women's states of mind, every effort has been made to present each woman qualitatively within her unique context. For this reason, there are no composite characters or stories in the text. Each story stands as its own testimony to the psychological complexity of intimate abuse and the logistical challenge it presents to those who wish to understand its massive infiltration of the heart.

Theoretical considerations

In order to transliterate my data into multiple discourses, I drew on many different kinds of theories, all of which highlight the impact of trauma, splitting, dissociation, and enactment on the "feeling of what happens" and how that impacts consciousness, decision-making, and action (Damasio, 1999).

It is with Harry Stack Sullivan's insights that I began my investigation and analysis. Sullivan, a psychiatrist who did talk therapy with seriously mentally ill patients when few in the field believed they could be helped by such interventions (with the recent ascendance of biopsychiatry, most medical practitioners once again do not), pioneered a branch of psychoanalysis that joined psychiatric work with the social sciences. Enriching his clinical theories with the insights of anthropologists like Edward Sapir and Ruth Benedict, and the political psychologist Harold Lasswell, Sullivan created models that provided the "intellectual roots of the community mental health movement" (Sharfstein, 1998, p. 852).

Sullivan characterized mental life as occurring within distinct and overlapping fields, comprised of real and imagined relationships and experiences, all cultivated in the amniotic fluid of culture. More than many other traditions, interpersonal psychoanalysis very early on took seriously the gravity of the human surround in the articulation of individual personhood. Because of this, interpersonal theory is flexible enough to incorporate more critical and postmodern notions of subjectivity and agency, a necessary elasticity when deconstructing narratives about gender and power.

Deserting Freud's drive theory for more relational pastures, Sullivan maintained that what he called "the self-system" was a composite reflection of the appraisals of significant others, a way of organizing experience that directed the fledgling human to behave in ways that would keep the extreme anxiety induced by others' disapproval to a minimum. This was accomplished through a series of adaptations and somewhat strenuous dissociations, all engineered on behalf of saving the baby from the unbearable frustration of being so utterly dependent on a fickle mistress: his mother. Insofar as the caregiver's sourness was a personalized reproduction of the punitive character of her culture, the infant was getting a continuing education about the world outside the nursery door. Sullivan might say that, if the full-time job of a baby is to learn to anticipate her caregivers' bad moods, she is doing formidable preparatory work for a lifetime of similarly adaptive gymnastics. This is poignantly expressed in the lives of battered women, who meticulously monitor and manage the moods of the men in their lives through rapt attention to the slightest shift in their visage or manner. If the actions of the childhood caretakers of an adult woman were what Sullivan termed "particularly incongruous" (p. 170) with her needs – as was often the case with the battered women I interviewed – she likely developed a greatly heightened vigilance around them and twisted herself into pretzels to receive their good will. If they were outright perverse, or brutal, those distortions of human feeling were internalized as affective models and templates of interaction that foretold something about incendiary processes in later romantic attachments.

Sullivan intuited that, because the reactive rage parental cruelty engenders in the child has no value in negotiating a truce between them, the child is likely to divert anger to safer objects: imaginary companions, smaller children, toys, and animals, or to repurpose anger in anarchic tantrums blithely aimed at arousing ever greater levels of frustration and aggression from the parents. Women and men who find themselves in adult relationships that replicate this power differential may behave in similar ways, dissociating anger against their partners or choosing ways of expressing agency that undermine their own and others' safety. That interpersonal space, with its arousing disquisitions, becomes an arcade of personifications of both child and parent and, later, woman or man and mate, personifications being somewhat like caricatures of the contradictory aspects of self: the good, the bad, and the completely unrecognizable. This splitting into unambiguous categories is one reason that narratives of intimate violence so easily devolve into cliché (Haaken, 2010).

However, far from the foregone conclusions that clichéd tales reach, the engagement among the various self-states of two people is a precarious dance with an uncertain outcome, one whose intricate routine is almost impossible to master. Not only is the abused girl or woman protecting herself from the monstrousness of others, she must also shield herself from the knowledge that the grotesquerie resides in someone on whom she is dependent, and also from the consciousness of her own capacity for destruction. This last is especially pressing in the context of womanhood, as the suppression of negative feelings, particularly aggressive ones, is an intensely penetrating demand of the social surround, one that may circle back, ironically enough, to the original culturally proscribed circumstances of her splintering into "good me," "bad me," and "not me" as a child. The greater the threat to selfhood, the more ferociously the "not me" is enjoined. When strong emotions like terror or rage cannot be identified as belonging to the self, they are externalized. It is in this way that girls and women come to disown their anger, most often relegating it to fester in occult ways that later manifest just as surreptitiously through highly choreographed attacks on the self that use other people, usually romantic partners, as the instrument of self-destruction. Less often, women unleash their rage in colossal enactments from which there is no return.

The Emotional Empowerment Project

Twelve subjects responded to an advertisement posted on a listserve distributed to members of a large urban resource and support center for battered women. Early enrollees were paid $10.00 for their time and travel. Subjects who enrolled later were the beneficiaries of increased funding for the project and received $25.00 for their participation. Women were interviewed in my university office for approximately two hours, although some interviews were lengthier, and in one case there was opportunity for a follow-up interview. One woman withdrew from the study prior to data analysis, and so her responses are excluded from this analysis. Subjects ranged in age from early 20s to mid-50s. They came from a variety of ethnic backgrounds: African-American (4), Caribbean (3), Hispanic (1), Arab-American (1), Jewish (1), and Irish-American (1), and included both legal (1) and illegal (2) immigrants. All of the women were in heterosexual relationships at the time of the abuse. Some women had only recently left their abusive situations, while others had been out of the battering relationship for decades. One woman had served a three-year prison sentence for killing her husband in the midst of a battering incident.

Interview method

Women's stories were elicited using an unstructured interview format that schematically educed material in five areas: (1) the emotional context of early childhood relationships; (2) historical information about significant adult relationships; (3) affective experiences related to having been abused verbally, physically, or emotionally; (4) the degree of emotional dissociation from painful experiences and consequent cognitions and affects; and (5) the examination of emotions that a subject felt enabled her to detach from the abuser and, ultimately, to leave the battering relationship.

Many of the life history questions were based on an interview instrument used with juveniles that I helped develop in the 1990s with forensic psychiatrist Dorothy Otnow Lewis and psychologist Catherine Yeager (Stein et al., 1993), and which has been adapted over the years for work with a variety of populations. While the style of the interview used in this particular study was unstructured and allowed for twists and turns based on the information being brought forth by subjects, I also made sure to cover all topics relevant to the particular research questions being investigated.

The interview technique was clinical in nature, based on psychoanalyst Harry Stack Sullivan's (1970) notion of the "detailed inquiry." It was Sullivan's belief that an "interview, in order to be significant, has to be exceedingly far from a conversation made up of correct answers to clear questions." This is because defensive operations on the part of the person being interviewed conspire to deform communication, often in the direction of offering a kind of window dressing that hides self-revelations experienced as potentially humiliating. "How does one get the data one needs despite the interviewee's anxiety?" Sullivan asked (p. 100), and his recommendations comprise the foundations of my own interviewing style: an attention to the constant refinement of my initial hypotheses through gaining greater specificity in the material that subjects are producing, by asking for clarifications, pursuing subtle nuances, and calling attention to inconsistencies in the narrative. My manner of research inquiry closely hews to clinical methods of investigation preferred by interpersonal psychoanalysts who embrace the idea of dichotomous states of consciousness. Accordingly, my interviews attempted to elicit information about different self-states rather than either pervasive charactological data or symptom complexes, per se.

Of course, the detailed inquiry – for all its prying – must not feel like an interrogation. Thus, I found myself moving back and forth between periods of laser-like focus on small experiential moments that seemed to encompass great expository power and more expansive forays – often dressed with humor – that invited a subject's critical faculties into the conversation, to keep company with her less accessible selves.

The interview was psychoanalytically informed in a theoretical, as well as methodological, way. By this I mean that any narrative produced during the interview process was conceived of as a product of the dynamic between me and the subject, rather than a simple recitation of facts from the subject's life. Bromberg (1994) has explicated this interactive position in the course of ongoing therapy.

> "Speaking," in psychoanalysis, is thus not simply a process of delivering content. It is also a relational act that shapes the content of what is spoken about. For patients dealing in a primary way with dissociative experience, this point comes into particularly high relief because words themselves feel more or less meaningless. . . In the interplay of silence and words, a patient can, at least potentially, force the analyst to give up his attempts to "understand" his patient and allow himself to "know" his patient – to know him in the only way possible – through the ongoing intersubjective field they are sharing at that moment.
>
> (p. 524)

As Sullivan (1970) noted, the interviewer is a participant-observer whose early impressions form hypotheses about the interviewees, which are then methodically tested through the meticulous collection of information, both verbal and non-verbal. In addition, transference and countertransference information gleaned during the process acts as a guide for narrowing the focus or expanding the purview of the interview, as noted above, as well as being an important tool in the data analysis.

People bring to all interpersonal interactions not only the presenting self, often relatively intact and functional, holding at least the illusion of unitary consciousness, but also an array of unitegrated selves based on profoundly alienating past experiences which have never been fully digested. Thus does the past backlight the present interaction in a transmogrifying way, distorting one's observations of – and reactions to – others. Sullivan (1956a) called these "parataxic distortions" the "basic warp of personality" (pp. 200–201) and suggested that "if the possibility of their existence is ignored, some of the most important things about the [. . .] interview may go by default" (1970, p. 25). While transference reactions are less reasonably adduced in the short-term couplings common to research situations than in ongoing therapeutic dyads, I have generally found that a keen alertness to the parataxic distortions that invade even more circumscribed conversations offers keys to unlocking the meaning behind utterances (by both halves of the dyad) that, in retrospect, seem comically or tragically off course, or impregnated with ulterior agendas. The degree to which such attention can be brought to bear during the interview, rather than in its wake, will often determine the depths that the interview is able to plumb.

As is the case for clinical interventions, in this research, my foremost consideration was in providing a safe atmosphere for the revelation of difficult material, and an open forum in which subjects could explore states of consciousness around the particular events of their lives without feeling threatened that such states would be aroused but insufficiently processed. Thus, no matter how dramatic certain interviews became, to my knowledge no one left my office in an emotional place they felt incapable of handling. The majority of women indicated that they found the interview helpful, even liberating. In addition, a list of free and low cost mental health clinics was given to the women at the conclusion of our time together.

Domestic abuse

The domestic abuse section was subdivided into four categories: physical abuse, verbal abuse, emotional abuse, and sexual abuse. All of the subjects had endured at least one of these kinds of assault. In only five cases did women call the police for help. In four of these cases, the men were arrested. Three of the men arrested were convicted of assault and served some time for their crime.

Physical abuse was coded in three levels, which were: (1) for pushing, shoving or biting; (2) for simple assault and battery, where the intention was to place the victim in fear of bodily harm; and (3) for aggravated assault and battery, where the intent was to cause grievous bodily harm or death. Ninety percent of women suffered some type of physical abuse.

Nine of the women experienced at least a low level of violent interaction. Sometimes the violence occurred during a fight in which both parties resorted to physical attacks. Other times attacks seemed to come out of nowhere, stunning the recipient of a slap or punch, who was later told that she was being punished for some infraction of a rule she hadn't known existed. Many incidents involved drug or alcohol ingestion by the batterer. For example, one woman described being surprised by an assault that seemed to have no trigger:

> So he's at my house on a Friday night and he got so completely trashed drunk, drinking I'm not even sure what. He got stupid, stupid, scary drunk and started pulling my hair and pushing me around while I was sitting on the sofa. And it was frightening.

Eight women experienced a simple assault and battery at the hand of their partner. One woman described a premeditated attack against which she defended herself successfully:

> Except I just remember him hitting me and having me, he was about to hit me again and his, he was holding my face so he could get a good shot at me and I bit him. And then he stopped. And by that time, he had ripped a new bathrobe that my grandmother had given me for Christmas in half.

Another woman remembered locating her husband after he had disappeared with the children.

> He was dragging me by my hair, but my hair comes out. I'm trying not to make too much noise because the kids are downstairs. I picked up my hair on my way out and went to the police so there would be evidence.

Yet another described a strangely harrowing episode where, "during lovemaking, he started pinching me and weird pinching and punching and doing weird things, leaving bruises all over me. All over my face, all over my arms, all over me."

Six women experienced a level three assault – the most serious kind of physical abuse, where the batterer intends to forcibly rape or maim, shows indifference to the likely outcome of an potentially murderous assault or, worse, purposefully tries to kill the victim. The same woman who had endured the pinching episode later had her collarbone broken by her husband; then when he visited her in the hospital as she was recuperating, "he put his hand down my throat and tried to rip my throat out from the inside." After she left him, he came to her new apartment, jumped her, cracked her jaw, broke the orbit of her eye, and tried to smother her with a pillow. She came for the interview with a cane, her limp a remnant of the long ago beatings. Another woman was thrown down the stairs while she was pregnant with twins and subsequently lost one of the babies. Others in the study reported being thrown from moving vehicles or having their partners try to run them over with a car.

Verbal abuse has no established definition in the scholarly literature. For the purposes of this research, I considered threats, yelling or badgering with the intent to intimidate, shame, or harass, and direct name-calling, to be verbally abusive. Eight women were verbally abused by their batterer. Often, the men suspected that women were cheating on them and kept them at a suffocating closeness:

> He would call me a pig. He would call me all the bad names that people would consider bad. And, you know, if I did talk to someone that he didn't approve, any coworker, he will start calling me names, accusing me of [infidelity].

Another woman offered that:

> He'd say stuff like, "You're a woman, like a shoe. You see this shoe? That's what you are" . . . And at that point, he started calling me a "bitch," "slut," you know, American girls are always "hos," you know, like we're easy.

Emotional abuse was defined as a pattern of hostile verbal and non-verbal behaviors aimed at putting the targeted person in fear or manipulating them into compliance. All of the women were emotionally abused by their batterer. The theme of emotional abuse was often very gendered, with men demeaning women's bodies or sexuality, or heavily surveilling women's activities to assert their domestic ownership. At other times, the emotional abuse consisted of constant threats of physical violence punctuated by occasional beating or more subtle methods of control, like refusing to have a woman's name on the deed to the house or not allowing her to make phone calls to friends or family.

Children were often used as pawns, with men insisting that women beat their children or threatening to beat the children themselves unless the women complied with their demands. Other times, men threatened to take the children away, either by kidnapping them or through pursuing legal custody. Indeed, one of the most disturbing things I learned during these interviews was that an effective strategy used by men to get women back who had left them was threatening to file for custody of the couple's children, or actually doing so. Women knew that the courts often rewarded custody to the father – as long as he had not hurt the children physically – because the father was likely to be more financially stable than the mother, and because he often appeared the more cool-headed party during court proceedings. The pursuit of child custody was a very useful threat toward many women I interviewed, who feared losing their kids to their batterers more than they feared losing their lives. Four women I interviewed did lose their children this way and continue to fight for their return.

Sexual abuse was divided into the following levels: (1) for infection with sexually transmitted diseases, (2) for sex through coercion or threat, and (3) for violent or forcible rape. Almost half of the subjects suffered some type of sexual abuse, about evenly distributed as to type.

Three women were given sexually transmitted diseases by their partners, who then would blame them for the infections. One woman was subjected to examinations to reassure her husband that she was not cheating on him:

> I could see he was totally twisted [that my bus was late]. He said "Go over there and take your clothes off. I'm going to make sure you ain't cheating on me." And before I could get to the bedroom . . . he ripped the rest of my clothes off. He stuck his fingers in me. He smelled me. And then he shoved me on the bed and started choking me.

Five women were either raped or were coerced into sexual activity, including anal sex without lubrication or vaginal intercourse where they were not allowed to use birth control despite pleas that they did not want to become pregnant.

History of childhood maltreatment Seventy-two percent of women in the study were physically abused while growing up, with the mother being the most frequent abuser. Punishments ranged from being made to kneel on rice ("ridiculous but very painful" said one woman) to being switched or beaten ("I can't remember the worst . . . that was the life . . . we were just used to it") to being intentionally burned ("I remember I hated cigarettes"). One woman reported not being fed when she went to live with relatives ("After three months, I stopped demanding food and things like that").

Five women were sexually abused by immediate and step-family, more distant family members, friends of the family, or clergy. Molestations – with or without penetration – happened to children as young as seven, although most incidents occurred during the pre-teen and early teenage years. All sexual abuse perpetrators were male. Rarely did the girls tell anyone of their plight, even when sexual abuse was ongoing.

Dissociative signs and symptoms Fully 100 percent of this sample evidenced signs or symptoms of dissociation, either during childhood abuse, adult victimization, or both. Dissociative symptoms included flashbacks and intrusive thoughts (for example, a woman who had been repeatedly sexually molested in childhood said "They diagnosed me with migraines when I was eight. But I really knew it was thoughts because whenever I had thoughts in excess, out of a certain boundary area, then there's just this giant pain happen in my head"), time loss, automatisms ("I was just like a robot"), and flat or inappropriate affect when describing scenarios in which they had been brutalized.

The peculiar dissociation of any feeling attached to what they had suffered was notable. For example, I queried one woman about her cool demeanor as she related terrible personal events and she replied: "I haven't had, you know, even as you ask me questions, feelings. I don't really feel too much. There's just something else that I do, but I just don't feel." Another explained a similar lack of feelings this way: "For me, it [the abuse] was like nothing. It's like just something happened. Things happen, you know, in life. Things happen."

Some of the subjects referred to their "old selves," the ones who had suffered abuse, in a mildly dissociated way, such as, "I didn't like who she was" or "I didn't like what I saw in the mirror; I didn't want to be her anymore." Some women even had a name for that victimized part of themselves or the other, stronger part who had helped them survive. Only one of the eleven subjects evidenced more serious identity confusion, and personality alteration suggestive of a dissociative disorder. When I followed up on disparate names she had used in written correspondence to me, the woman explained how she perceived the replacement self who had arisen to escape her husband's assaults:

> Sondra didn't have it right at all, you know . . . Now I'm Katherine. We still have Sondra. But now Katherine did what it took to get it together and this is why she's the winner she is. Sondra didn't have that opportunity. Katherine had it.

Apparently, this woman's son had tried many times to explain to her that Sondra and Katherine were the same woman. While Sondra had an inkling that this might be true, Katherine – who had by now happily assumed most executive functions for Sondra's life – was not, as far as I could tell, in any hurry to return the reins to her weaker sister.

Emotional range

The emotional repertoires of my subjects were in many ways similar to those of any people who have undergone substantial trauma over long periods of time. Women's narratives were replete with examples of how profound feelings of isolation, pervasive sadness, crippling anxiety, immutable guilt, helpless dependence, and longstanding shame propelled their actions or, more often, truncated them, making even the private fantasy of action a terrifying leap. This slate of feelings correlates with the high rates of depression usually found in meta-studies of battered women, rates between 50 and 80 percent (Holtzworth-Munroe et al., 1997). Many of the feelings are also indices of post traumatic stress disorder, another common diagnosis in this group (Holtzworth-Munroe et al., 1997).

On the other hand, some very positive emotions colored women's memories. Subjects could still recall moments of intense intimacy with their partners, and an almost overwhelming sense of security with them that translated into feeling loved and happy. These positive feelings often overrode more logical cognitions about the fruitlessness – and even danger – of remaining in violent relationships. Dutton and Painter (1993) have explained this "paradoxical attachment" by calling attention to two features of abusive relationships: the power imbalance between the partners and the intermittent nature of violence (p. 105). In the former construction, women in subservient roles may borrow some sense of power from their dominant partners, identifying with their aggression and even basking in a partner's manliness and attention. In the latter, an abusive relationship cycling through the typical stages – mounting tension, violent eruption, contrition, and loving reunion – becomes entrenched because of its schedule of shifting reward and punishment. At each pacific juncture, relief and hope combine to dim the memory of traumatic wounding and make possible anew the fantasy of relational unification. As I said in the beginning of this chapter, because of stark power differentials, partners in abusive situations often need one another to find homeostasis.

The women I interviewed seemed to derive great joy from the status their relationships conferred; to be married, especially, made public the acknowledgment of their desirability. Most came from homes where having a husband was held in high regard, whether or not there had been a committed man in the home during their own upbringing, and this was reinforced by both their immediate social groups and the culture at large. Many women were prideful to a fault and refused to seek help because they felt humiliated about the failure of their relationships. Over and over again, I heard that they were too embarrassed to call for help, seek medical attention, or reach out to friends. When beaten, they simply went to the drug store for cosmetic cover-ups.

Paralyzing projections about future shaming derived from women's fears that their own parents would blame them for the break-up of a marriage, even in cases where the men had been arrested for beating them. Women's worst fears were often borne out when, arriving at their mothers' doors, suitcases in hand, they were told to return to their abusive husbands and try to work things out ("my mom put my stuff in a garbage bag and said 'you're not staying here'"). Or, as was sometimes the case with immigrants, women were beaten by family members – male and female – for having disgraced them.

Most women averred that they had stayed in the relationship because they still loved their partner. They hoped that things would improve, or remained out of a sense of familial obligation or because they feared the social stigma of divorce. Another, smaller group gave as their primary reason for staying financial dependence or worries about the effect that a break-up might have on their children. A few women stayed because they had been told by their partners that leaving would bring a death sentence. As the majority of women killed by their intimate partners are killed after leaving their batterer, or while attempting to leave (Chewter, 2003), ostensibly these women made the right decision to bide their time.

The cultural and institutional surround

Women account for 85 percent of the 2.2 million victims of intimate partner violence in the US (Bureau of Justice Statistics, 2003). Indeed, about one in four American women will experience domestic violence in their lifetime (National Institute of Justice, 2000). Incredibly, domestic violence is the *leading cause of injury* to US women between the ages of 15 and 44; more common than automobile accidents, muggings, and cancer deaths combined. And yet, compared to women in the rest of the world, we have it pretty good. Many of the immigrant women I interviewed spoke with unmistakable envy – and some irritation – toward their Western sisters who have the "luxury" of calling 911 for assistance when a partner performs an act that is criminal in the US but considered merely a male privilege in their country of origin. Even when relocated to the United States, immigrant women import their countries' perils with them, as many fear that a call for assistance with a domestic assault will result in deportation for them or their partner. Wherever they are from, women suffer a disproportionate share of private and public violence. Charlotte Bunch (1997), a leading advocate for women's rights, reminds us of the gross inequities that plague women from Dumbo, Brooklyn to Darfur, Africa:

> Imagine a people routinely subjected to assault, rape, sexual slavery, arbitrary imprisonment, torture, verbal abuse, mutilation, even murder – all because they were born into a particular group . . . Such a group exists. Its members comprise half of humanity. Yet it is rarely acknowledged that violence against women and girls, many of whom are brutalized from cradle

> to grave simply because of their gender, is the most pervasive human rights violation in the world today.
>
> (p. 1)

Domestic violence does not occur in a vacuum. Whether in the United Arab Emirates – where beating one's wife has been declared by the high court to be within a husband's rights to discipline his spouse – or in Sweden – where charges may be brought against a man who seriously and repeatedly violates a women's "integrity" with or without physical assault – all partner abuse should be understood not only in terms of the interpersonal dynamics of couples caught in its destructive grip but in the context of the institutionalized norms that promote and maintain gender inequality. Attorney Bonita Meyersfeld has observed the immutable connection, writing that "systemic intimate violence against women is not a case-by-case peculiarity, but often a manifestation of social views, perceptions, priorities, and customs" that maintain existing arrangements between men and women (Meyersfeld, 2008). As Sweden has demonstrated with its broadened definition of offenses against women in intimate relationships (Nylen and Heimer, 1999), the amelioration of gendered violence may be at least partially contingent on changes to traditionally patriarchical arrangements in law and culture. Sweden, considered progressive on issues of gender equality, has substantially lower rates of domestic violence than even its most liberal Western counterparts (Peter, 2006). Stateways *can* change folkways, William Graham Sumner's famous dictum notwithstanding.

Formal law and institutionalized regulatory systems (such as psychiatric diagnoses) both consciously and inadvertently shape interpersonal agendas, even in the most private of spaces. Groups in power reflexively construct things in a way that upholds their authority and keeps unempowered groups marginalized. Nowhere is this truer than in areas that involve the distribution of power between men and women, where it has long been observed that it is easy to ignore the signs of oppression when one is sleeping with the enemy (de Beauvoir, 1952).

Chapter 5 examines the link between personal and institutional experiences. I consider how making gender-blind arrests, psychiatrically evaluating women so that the sequelae of violence is held against them, or awarding custody of children to the abusing parent becomes an extension of domestic assault. Many women with whom I spoke were retraumatized by doctors, police, lawyers, and judges, the very people to whom they appealed for help. Indeed, a therapist would need a really large office to treat all the players implicated in just one woman's experience of domestic violence, or really long sessions to parse out the multiple introjects fueling destructive enactments.

Interpersonal psychoanalysis and political consciousness

How can we synthesize contemporary psychoanalytic models of multiplicity with an even more critical and libratory conceptualization of therapeutic goals? In addition to the more traditional goals of psychotherapy, libratory work with abused women also contextualizes private pain within a wider ethos and articulates the different levels of oppression – many covert – which women must navigate. This broadened perspective affords clients both personal and political channels for examining the contradictory nature of their desires and the multiplicity of their identities – some which accept domination and others which resist it: "The process of raising critical consciousness presupposes that when we transform ourselves, we simultaneously transform our relationships with others and the communities that embrace us" (Almeida et al., 2008, p. 25). The very concept of political consciousness aligns with the goal of any interpersonal treatment: to do what we do with more awareness, psychological integrity, and relational reciprocity. These conditions comprise not just mental health, but an authentic sense of agency. It is felt agency that allows one to speak truth to power.

When feminist theorist Gayatri Spivak (1988) famously asked "Can the subaltern speak?" she was wondering aloud whether marginalized people (including women) had any narrative other than the one that had been given to them by their oppressors. Spivak used the extreme example of women who had engaged in sati, the practice of self-immolation following a husband's death, to illustrate how society translated and interpreted actions on behalf of the voiceless (actually, in this case, the dead) in a way that maintained binaries and inequality, first for the Hindu government and then on behalf of British colonialists. She began a robust exchange in the academic world about whether women (as the most powerless among the powerless in a colonized society) even had access to an autobiography not constituted by imperialism.

Spivak's analysis is writ small on the faces of abused women. In the course of speaking with women, I recognized how firmly the forfeiture of agency was bound to the muting of their own aggressive voice; it was as if, without aggression's propellant properties, women could find no energetic center from which to launch their self-concept. Dissociation dictates that someone else is furious; someone else is frightened; someone else bears or delivers the violence. The depleted self has no face or voice, save that of its master: the battering mate, the judgmental parent, the parentified judge, or an even more disembodied moral authority.

Simultaneous with Spivak's political conversation about the internalization of voices that make the subordinate complicit in their own oppression, a particularly rich vein of psychological theorizing opened up with the publication, also in 1988, of Jessica Benjamin's *The Bonds of Love: Psychoanalysis, Feminism, and the Problem of Domination,* which applied similar thinking to the analysis of gender relations. Benjamin interpersonalized the advent of domination, situating it as a byproduct of love and attachment, and saying that she "above all" wanted to "understand how domination is anchored in the hearts of the dominated" (p. 5). Until Benjamin, only a small group in the psychoanalytic world had really explicitly tied these kinds of global inequities to the essential conditions under which most men and women love. Benjamin recognized that "the center of male domination lies not in direct expressions of personal violence (rampant though they are) but in the social rationality that may or may not be defended by men" (p. 216).

Benjamin, and Chodorow (1974) before her, had argued that, given the constitution of the contemporary family, men's power was seeded in the separateness and rationality forged through Oedipal crisis, while women's subordination relied on the supposedly impoverished (or castrated) need for psychic continuity with others. In that context, subverting the cultural discourse is ultimately more generative than handcuffing individual assailants.

As Lynne Layton (2007) suggests, it is the hierarchical arrangement of people according to their sex that "push[es] us to split off part of what it means to be human, thereby creating painful individual and relational repetition compulsions" (p. 146) that mimic the social inequalities they were designed to defend against in the first place. Goldner (2002) agrees that only "resistance to the normative construction of gender polarities and hierarchies" (p. 87), as they adhere in present day families, will render the psychic splits experienced by family members less dramatic and irremediable. To put it in Sullivanian terms, more flexible gender roles may produce fewer "not me" moments for women, particularly around the experience and expression of aggression and self-determination.

The difficulty in reconciling feminist and psychoanalytic perspectives has been to find a way to drill down into the explanatory power that a cultural critique provides without eclipsing personal experience and human agency; how to highlight the structural drivers of women's renunciation of agency without sacrificing an honest portrayal of the highly idiosyncratic and deeply psychological ways in which women absorb and reflect cultural demands in mediating their own aggression.

At the level of praxis, the challenge is to keep content and process "experience near" without decontextualizing them from a larger narrative of status and power. Although many psychoanalysts have been vocal about recognizing the mutual impact that psyche and culture have in producing the gendered subject, the implications of this view for technique have been slow to evolve. Virginia Goldner (1999), explicating the work she pioneered with violent couples in the 1980s and 1990s, was one of the first clinicians to note the importance of working multi-modally. Reviewing paradigms that emphasized either a feminist/socio-cultural or a psychoanalytic approach, she concluded that each one, used in isolation, was inadequate to address violence. Although Goldner, in a critique of the state of treatment for relational violence published in 1999, expressed confidence that "the field may be prepared to move into a more sophisticated phase of its inquiry without having to reiterate all the old arguments every time" (p. 327), a decade later, Janice Haaken (2010) is still bemoaning the split between movement activists and those who wish to integrate feminist perspectives with more nuanced psychoanalytic views. Political activists tend to believe that psychologists "blame women and make excuses for men" (p. 62) while psychologists assert that a static feminist narrative ignores the wide variation in the ways individual men and women respond to cultural messages about gender and violence.

Here I believe we can again return to Sullivan's (1965) common sense notion that, while individual and cultural pathologies are basically coextensive, "understanding comes neither from the conventionally far too narrow field of exploration nor from a schizophrenically universal search" (p. 24). Even though it is embedded in systems, culture is unconsciously transmitted through people: mother, husband, sister, landlord, doctor, lawyer, deacon, bully.

> Almost from the moment of birth onward the factors of prime significance in the integrated total situations are other people, and other people go on being rather beyond the grasp of intellectual processes, as does the self.
>
> (p. 23)

Culture's regulation of the psyche can never be directly sensed, but is always inferred. The ways in which it transforms us likewise go unnoticed, like the infinitesimal growth spurt of a sleeping adolescent, until of course we change so much that there is no way to return to our original form. Sullivan saw the evolutionary potential of this, as influences can be charitable as well as malignant. Like Robert Jay Lifton (1999) who, after a lifetime of writing about the destructive capacities of the multiple self, embraced its protean possibilities for resilience and connection, Sullivan (1950) saw the heart of his psychiatric enterprise as vital to making a better world, through "elevating to lucid attention" the disjunctive dynamisms that impede effective collaboration among people (p. 315).

Despite the postmodern turn that Sullivan's theories presaged, he always held fast to the belief that the self, while largely an imaginary installation, was still anchored in real events with significant weight and shaping power (Lionells, 2000). In presenting the real experiences of women, I try to keep alive the important distinctions between the particular ways in which individual woman have adapted to violation and the universal toleration of violence against women, without losing sight of how irrevocably they are bound.

It is in this regard that I became interested in the work of Paulo Freire (1970/2000), the author of the seminal *Pedagogy of the Oppressed*, and its application to interpersonal psychoanalytic work in the domestic violence field. Freire, who taught literacy to indigenous groups in South America, emphasized how interpersonal relations were shaped by sociopolitical circumstances. He believed that personal reflection, enhanced by cultural awareness, could not only lead to a greater understanding of individual predicaments but might also engender collective action to shift the oppressive environments that fueled so much individual pathology. Almeida and Durkin (1999) have adapted many of Freire's ideas for psychological work with couples and families mired in intimate violence. If Almeida's schema is by no means complete by itself, at times promoting a purely cultural critique in place of a distinctive personal exploration, it still may offer a strong complement to existing models of psychoanalytic intervention.

Freire's insights have given rise to the potent discourse between politics and theater that is alternately called analytical theater, theatrical anthropology, or legislative theater, the most enduring of which has been Augusto Boal's (1996) "Theater of the Oppressed," which facilitates personal and social change through a public offering of private psychodrama. Psychodrama itself was identified as a therapeutic method in the early part of the twentieth century by J. L. Moreno.

Like Sullivan, Moreno was quite radical for his time. Although he did not embrace a philosophy of dissociated multiple selves in the way that Sullivan did, all his interventions were created with the idea of the "multi-role personality" (Moreno, 1987, p. xiv) and the need for developing facility and flexibility within those roles. Moreno catalyzed what an interpersonalist would term a dissociated enactment through the use of various psychodramatic techniques, as a way of turning thoughts and affects into actualities. I have found this a useful technique with women whose agency is highly intangible, particularly as it encourages experimentation with both authentic and fantasied expression within a safe space. As Moreno said, the technique at its best is capable of producing "social revolution on a microscopic scale."

A third useful construct for work that connects battered women to the larger social context is "social dreaming" (Lawrence, 2000). Social dreaming utilized in interpersonal psychoanalysis allows the listener (the practitioner or members of a therapy group) to associate to the dreamer's images in ways that implicate the collective nature of unconscious material. A clinician working with the method might give freer rein to her own associations around gendered or aggressive content in a patient's dream; she would associate to the dream as if it were her own, rather than interpreting it according to things she knew (or thought she knew) about the patient. In contrast to more traditional dream interpretations, which are idiosyncratic and targeted, social dreaming methods try to highlight meanings as reflecting shared frustrations, worries, affects, and values (Lippman, 1998).

> The varied experiences in dreams may be thought of as continuously exploring, portraying, rehearsing, commenting upon, criticizing, adding to, varying and improvising on aspects of the socially shared characteristics of a people . . . in the deepest privacy of dreaming, the culture's ways are being developed, tested, explored, and reinforced.
>
> (pp. 203–204)

Hence, the final chapter of this book explores how clinical sensibilities and techniques might raise political consciousness in ways that feel organic to the nature of psychoanalysis. These include a detailed inquiry about the rituals, values, and rules in one's family and community, the clinician's recognition of his own participation in cultural systems of oppression, an openness to collective interpretations of unconscious life, and a willingness to play out in the consulting room fantasies of powerbroking, revenge, and even gender swapping (one patient called this "putting on our pants" although, ironically, we were both already wearing them). Joining the detailed inquiry and participant-observer models of Harry Stack Sullivan, the psychodramatic techniques of Freire, Boal and Moreno, and social dreaming methods offers a powerful triumvirate model of treatment. All of these theorists emphasized action among people in the process of change rather than just isolated reflection or verbal catharsis.

Transtheoretical models of change in psychotherapy have already unearthed many successful strategies that transcend any single school's perspective or techniques. Consciousness raising and social liberation are two higher order processes demonstrated to facilitate movement from contemplation to action for many troubling behaviors (Prochaska and DiClemente, 1982, 1994). As part of a psychoanalytic repertoire, they can become catalysts for change in both analyst and analysand. When techniques accelerating critical consciousness are used in work with women in abusive relationships, they can expedite the moment of readiness for change that Bowkers (1983) deemed most crucial: a woman's irrevocable decision that, no matter whether she stays or goes, abuse must end.

It is remarkably useful for women to understand the continuum of social behaviors that impinge upon women's rights and security so that they can contextualize their own situations. This knowledge changes their view of struggle from a strictly individual one, to an interpersonal and even communal one. It lessens their aloneness, increases mutual recognition and identification with treatment providers and others, and offers multiple ways in which to engage agency. Moreover, because women who have been abused are forced to psychologically navigate within institutional settings that range from helpful to hostile (doctors, lawyers, judges, police, and psychological evaluators may control their access to tenable solutions), the psychoanalyst's grasp of the institutional context in which the patient navigates becomes critical to understanding how they may construe (and perhaps counter) power and violence in their lives and in themselves. Finally, work that is expansive in this way encourages clinicians to mine the points of identification between themselves and patients rather than finding a lazy solace in the fantasy that they themselves would never love so fruitlessly.

My research project has led me to write a great deal about how practitioners and educators can work with women on helping them to assert themselves in an appropriate but determined way early in relationships, rather than being passive in the face of mounting assaults on their integrity and autonomy. Importantly, this work is just as applicable to women in abusive relationships that have *not* included actual physical violence. The hope is that if women can create interpersonal limits, for both their own and their partners' speech and actions, they will be less likely to overlook incremental escalations of offending behavior. They may be more likely to leave before the going gets rough or, perhaps, will find a voice that manages to install greater equality in the relationship.

Still, any menu of female empowerment is always happening within a wider world that may undermine its goals. For example, when we tell women to own their anger we also must teach them to judge the safety of the situation in which they are expressing it. If we work to strengthen a woman's resolve to leave her batterer, we had best be aware that we are greatly increasing the probability that she will be injured or killed. About 75 percent of the visits to emergency rooms by battered women occur after separation. Moreover, women are seven times more likely to be killed or seriously injured after they end their relationship with the abuser (Stark and Flitcraft, 1988). Empowerment on an individual level, even if it is desirable, is a high risk activity. It is with that cautious reminder ricocheting in my head, that I write my prescription.

Intimate partner violence in the United States

2.2 million people are physically assaulted by an intimate partner annually in the United States. Women account for 85 percent of the victims of intimate partner violence (Bureau of Justice Statistics, 2003).

About one in four women will experience domestic violence in their lifetime (The Centers for Disease Control and Prevention; National Institute of Justice, 2000).

Domestic violence is the leading cause of injury to women between the ages of 15 and 44 – more common than automobile accidents, muggings, and cancer deaths combined.

Recent research on college women suggests that up to 40 percent of women experience intimate partner violence (Gentile et al., 2007).

Women aged 20–24 are at the greatest risk of non-fatal intimate partner violence (Bureau of Justice Statistics, Intimate Partner Violence in the U.S. 1993–2004, 2006.)

Forty percent of girls age 14–17 report knowing someone their age who has been hit or beaten by a boyfriend (Children Now/Kaiser Permanente poll, December 1995).

The risk of violence increases with co-habitation. Some research has found that half of all women will experience some form of violence from their partners during marriage, and that more than one-third of married women are battered repeatedly every year.

Women of all races are about equally vulnerable to violence by an intimate partner (Bureau of Justice Statistics, Violence Against Women: Estimates from the Redesigned Survey, August 1995).

People with lower annual incomes (below $25k) are at a three-times-higher risk of intimate partner violence than people with higher annual income (over $50k), although the figures may represent low-income women's greater reliance on the public service systems that supply data to reporting agencies. (Bureau of Justice Statistics, Intimate Partner Violence in the U.S. 1993–2004, 2006.)

Even given the possible income disparity, violence is the reason stated for divorce in 22 percent of middle-class marriages (EAP Digest November/December 1991).

Women are at the greatest risk after they leave their batterers, being seven times more likely to be killed or seriously injured; about 75 percent of the visits to emergency rooms by battered women occur after separation (Stark and Flitcraft, 1988).

About 1,200 women every year are killed by their intimate partners. Intimate partner homicides accounted for 30 percent of the murders of women (Bureau of Justice Statistics Crime Data Brief, Intimate Partner Violence, 1993–2001, February 2003; Bureau of Justice Statistics, Intimate Partner Violence in the U.S. 1993–2004, 2006).

Chapter 2

The utility of contempt

> Two souls dwell, alas, in my breast
> Each would from the other split;
> One clutches, in its dullish lust
> Tight to the world with its organs' grip;
> The other raises itself forcibly from dust:
> High ancestral fields are its quest.
> (Goethe, *Faust I*, lines 1112–1117)

> Sometimes the only cure for contempt is countercontempt.
> (H. L. Mencken)

That contempt is primitive can be seen in the way it attaches to the physical self. Racists usually exaggerate and denigrate the physical attributes of their victims. Sex murderers partialize their prey into discrete body parts (e.g., eyes, tongues, nipples), reflecting the way that their own internal world consists of broken parts of objects rather than whole human beings. Contempt *in facie curiae* – contempt in the face of the court – may result in your sorry ass being carted off to jail. The process of contempt relies on this kind of elemental distillation to the crude and concrete. Whereas facial expressions of anger and rage have been shown to be later stage acquisitions based on experience, the contemptuous look is present from birth (Basch, 1976). The sneer, the upper lip raised Elvis-like, poised to reject: you, it, all. The face of contempt is hardwired but, of course, we must develop the interpersonal skills to know how to use it, and on whom.

In a compelling example of the corporeality of contempt, a client in marital counseling insisted continually that his wife's breath stunk, although in repeated visits to dentists and their hygienists she had always been informed that her breath was fine. After finding no medical validation for his claims, the man began insisting that his wife chewed in a disgusting way, with her mouth open. Although this could neither be confirmed nor disproved with certainty, the wife was a professional woman with many admiring friends and ample lunch dates, so it seemed unlikely that if, as her husband said, it was impossible to watch her eat without wanting to throw up, she would not have suffered some professional repercussions – or at least would have been advised by one of her closer colleagues to be more careful.

But I digress precipitously. The point has nothing to do with the veracity of the claim but its maiming intent. Even if a lax jaw and consequent drool had dominated the dental terrain, there might have been a less contemptuous, less wounding way of broaching the subject. The husband's choice to articulate things in the way he did demonstrates how he weaponized his words for maximum destructive impact. That is a contemptible behavior appropriately met with equivalent opprobrium. But does hurling contempt back and forth serve any purpose save the moral diminution of the pitchers? Why would an interpersonalist want to educate someone in such dark sport?

As far as I know, Sullivan (1956b) never spoke specifically of contempt in the interpersonal repertoire. He did remark that repulsion, often twinned with fascination, asserted itself in interpersonal affairs in which one party was being taken advantage of by another and that it was "an unhappy addition to self-awareness," as opposed to being a distortion invited by dissociation (p. 360). I interpret this as meaning that, in certain circumstances, contempt is a signal that one has awakened from a dissociated sleep and reintegrated emotions that veered toward the uncanny: terror, dread, all the feelings that may accompany the subtle disintegration of trust in one's perceptual and memorial capacities. Broadening the perspective, Jaggar (1989, p. 145) recognizes the political usefulness of integrating negative emotions like contempt, saying that less typically female emotions "may lead us to make subversive observations that challenge the status quo" and help us realize that what we took as the natural order of things has only masked our intentional subordination. This is a transitional contempt that removes the scales from one's eyes, facilitates action, and – perhaps most important – diminishes significantly once its object is abandoned or otherwise disempowered.

For example, when the woman with the supposedly stinky breath shifted the focus away from the accuracy of her husband's claim and became conscious of his cruelty, she was able to become contemptuous of his treatment of her. The shift was partially facilitated when she fully took in the husband's own stained and crooked teeth and realized the nature of his projection. Thus, contempt may, at least as a transitional affective state, let someone perceive another's flaws in an educative and empowering way. Knowledge that fuels insight can have clinical value, and even presage behavioral change.

What does it mean for contempt to be repurposed in this way? Can contempt be seen as catalytic, in a positive sense? I would raise the same question that Buechler (2008, p. 170) does in broadening her discussion of anger in the analytic dyad: "More generally, can we be strengthened by the assertive force of anger without being disabled by its destructive power?" Likewise, I wonder: Can you titrate contempt enough to cure without killing?

The analysis of taped interviews I did with battered women suggests that such a goal is certainly worthy, and my clinical experience with my client, Phoebe, demonstrates that it is attainable. Too often, women in my sample only seemed able to access their aggressive emotions after suffering grievous injury, or when long dissociated contempt finally exploded in the perpetration of their own deadly assault. Phoebe, even after so much work, still struggles with disowning her outrage, feeling entitled to it only in the smallest of doses, following the largest of insults. But she is ever more capable of using it to change her circumstance.

The case of Phoebe

Phoebe refers to her boyfriend, quite contemptuously, as a "man whore." In its specificity, the phrase implies that whoredom, or even the more frivolous whorishness, is really the province of females. After all, no gender declamation need be attached when a girl whores around, as my client's mother often accuses her of doing, adding that Phoebe must "think she has a penis" to stay out so late. Both the "man whore" and plain old "whore" slurs simultaneously enshrine and explode – so to speak – the power of the penis. In contemporary social discourse, each term signifies an enslavement to sexual need that is masculine but also engenders a social opprobrium historically reserved for females. In Phoebe's case, the moniker slung by her mother did not quite fit (she had had only three lovers by her mid-20s). But, as Phoebe told it, you couldn't be in her male friend's house without picking up the whiff of other women; "stained sheets and used rubbers in the garbage" – a reminder of his predilections for free sex and costly (at least for Phoebe) relationships.

Every time Phoebe said "man whore," I liked it, in spite of myself. It named the problem and emasculated her sadistically provocative boyfriend with derogation sharp as a machete. Yet, when she said it, she seemed almost beatific: lids heavy, a smile playing across her lips. The same face she probably wore when answering her religious mother's damning barrage: "Yes, mom, I *am* sleeping around. Yes, that's right. I take money for it, too." Close to deadpan, blithely dissociated, that beatific mask hid a smug self-possession that was outside her usual victim's repertoire. Watching her, I immediately thought of Sullivan's (1956b) conception of the "not-me" self – in Phoebe's case, the exiled self that contained both her sexuality and her mother's condemnation of it – and the way that it flourished despite its banishment to the outskirts of awareness.

Phoebe's presenting problem was the fear that her romantic involvement might precipitate a desperate depression. The situation with her current boyfriend was similar to an earlier affair that had triggered a depressive bout. Although the first relationship had included physical violence, abuse in the second seemed to operate on a more abstract plain. The narrative of her relationship was thick with examples of sexual manipulation, verbal assault, and a slippery kind of emotional exploitation wherein the boyfriend credited Phoebe with being the architect of her own victimization, a not uncommon strategy of perpetrators, particularly those who target women. As if to boldface her own paralysis, or the fear that she was crazy, or maybe the need to be held, Phoebe often slid her arms into the sleeves of her hooded sweatshirt backwards as we spoke and crossed them, fashioning a makeshift straightjacket.

The young man described himself as a "friend with benefits," which is contemporary parlance for no-strings-attached sexual friendships, which *in vivo* rarely redound to the woman's benefit (Bisson and Levine, 2009; Hughes et al., 2005). Phoebe referred to both the current and previous relationships as "circles." A circle meant that part of the deal was that she would agree to tolerate a relationship that included another woman with whom the man slept, and to whom she would relate as a second wife in a polygamous marriage. Although occasionally she might make out with the other woman, this seemed more for the man's pleasure than her own.

Phoebe described past and present players in these triadic performances in terms of their relative status at any given moment; she talked about being "privileged" over the other women at times, although now she had been "completely demoted," and had fallen into a depressive compliance with the boyfriend's assessment of her value. I gathered that she had been downgraded, not because she had had a two-night fling with someone (the circle arrangement demanded no fidelity), but because she had not revealed her affair with sufficient speed. Because she committed this "sin," she could no longer retain her "privileges" (such as they were) of being treated as a person rather than just a whore. The language of hierarchy she used had a militaristic rigidity; when I would query her silence in the face of the boyfriend's baiting, she always said that she had lost her right to any protest when she violated his trust (a trust that was one-sided anyway).

This type of relational structure, with relative rights and the concessions to status they impose, ends up looking like a Venn diagram with contempt at its intersection. As David Franks (1989, pp. 160, 164) suggests, "status deprivation" is one of two critical components of coercion, the other being "noxious stimuli," such as physical violence. The obsession with status is "hardly vanity but [is] motivated by the harsh fact that one's very emotional 'realness' to others (and eventually one's self) is socially bestowed." I am sure that Sullivan would agree: his notions of consensual validation recognize the shaping power of external attributions in our developing sense of (in)authenticity. Hence Phoebe's persistent fantasies of herself as deanimated, and peripheral in her lover's world. According to Franks (p. 164), the perception of our position in the social hierarchy provides a kind of translation between "private emotion" and "public arrangements." The humiliation Phoebe experienced when she was excluded from her boyfriend's life – in some circumstances he insisted that their relationship not be publicly acknowledged – served as a constant reminder of her existential nothingness (Laing, 1959).

For Phoebe, the obsession with her status (relative to significant others in both her family of origin and her romantic *ménages*) was interpersonally central and symptomatic of a cultural pandemic that disproportionately afflicts women. When women experience status deprivation and physical violence at both personal and political levels, there is a mutual reinforcement of their worthlessness and a kind of repetition compulsion that ratifies continuing degradation. In this vortex, "normative unconscious processes" (the conflicted internalization and expression of social norms) "pull us to repeat affect/behavior/cognition patterns that uphold the very social norms that cause psychic distress in the first place" (Layton, 2007, p. 149). For battered women, power differentials in the outside world make them even more vulnerable to internalizing their abuser's derogatory views of themselves, and assuming agency only in the sense that they take responsibility for causing their own abuse. Forte et al. (1996) point out the defensive function of such mental fusing with the abuser, which allows the victim to anticipate his response, thereby averting danger.

> In oppressive social situations, role-taking is asymmetrical . . . the more powerful person is unlikely to take the role of the subordinate and is not motivated to attune himself or herself to the other's subjective experience. The less powerful person, on the other hand, frequently uses role-taking and tries hard to accurately understand the partner. [. . .] In oppressive situations, adaptive role-taking used by subordinates to cope with their superiors can be transformed into a maladaptive fusion with the aggressor. This fusion diminishes the ability to retain an independent point of view.
>
> (p. 60)

In the current imbroglio, Phoebe said that she had "no say" in her boyfriend's extra-relational sexual escapades, which were allegedly numerous, although I could never quite separate the boyfriend's promiscuous reality from his false, but nevertheless provocative, assertions. Nor, for that matter, could I discern which stories of infidelity came from the boyfriend and which were products of Phoebe's self-punishing, almost delusional, jealousy.

In interactions with the boyfriend Phoebe seemed bereft of intentionality, empty of indignation, and incapable of an agentic response. In fact, she described herself as a "twist toy" in his pocket, something that he spun for amusement when he was anxious, or "worried" like Greek *komboloi* beads. At other junctures, she spoke about his monopolization of the spotlight, whereas she was relegated to being "wallpaper." As Layton (2007) has argued, relational bargains are struck between players – in this case lovers – who are always fine-tuning who will be objectified and who will be allowed to function as a subject with agency and autonomy. The portrait Phoebe offered of her relationship suggested that it was devoid of the conditions that would allow her to negotiate either position. She despised the zero state that objectification imposed but hungered for the desirability it implied. She craved the power that subjectivity might confer but, at the same time, feared the demolition it might invite.

But a psychoanalytic perspective allows us to see that the real distinction between men's and women's aggression is probably not the amount of aggression but access to it. Women too rarely make clear distinctions between agency and destructiveness, excitement and damage to others, competition and a feeling of or wish to murder (Harris, 2002).

Only in her jealousy or envy could Phoebe work up a head of steam with me, slinging accusations around the room in nasty gendered word bundles, e.g., "man whore," "fucking bitches." The sessions seemed reminiscent of that scene in *The Exorcist* (Friedkin, 1973) in which innocent little Reagan, in full devil tilt, first taunts Father Damien with sexually explicit language. I found Phoebe's accusations an incredibly dissociative performance for a woman who usually was so shy about sexuality that she could not even say the word "horny" aloud, preferring to show me a cellphone message where her boyfriend had texted the word when summoning her to his apartment. I found myself pursuing this disdainful rage, intuiting that the key to her agency was lost in the seismic split between aggression and attachment.

Aggression and attachment

Phoebe was highly functional, not violently predisposed, with a background of trauma, but not, as Shengold (1989) would say, with soul murder. I knew she felt that her contempt occurred in a social matrix that supported her male friend's provocative actions and left her scant recourse. Like Phoebe's more classically battered counterparts, she had learned to swallow fear and at least partially dissociate resentment. *Expressed* aggression and the sexuality with which it seemed infused would unsettle the relational hornet's nest. Instead, all that passion and anger was reflexively tucked away, like a stray wisp of hair behind her ear. That is why I coveted her aggressive enactments. I wanted the expression of anger to feel safe in my office, in a way that perhaps it could not be with her boyfriend or, more broadly, in the culture at large.

It is true that a woman who makes her anger or contempt known may be singled out for a special kind of discounting by those to whom she expresses it. She may be called a "shrew" or "hysteric," her accusations may be called baseless, she may be infantilized and told her anger is "cute," or that she suffers from being too needy. The more ubiquitous the social dictates, the more they limit the available scripts for female behavior; passivity is reinforced, whereas aggression is disowned and projected onto men (Layton, 2007). The transgenerational transmission of this wider ethos feels inseparable from the personal experience of both autonomy and attachment that predisposed my patient toward exalting the latter, even at the risk of decimating the former.

Phoebe, who had forfeited most of her mother's attention when her older sister was diagnosed as schizophrenic, told me she had suffered during childhood from a particularly acute fear of not being heard. Her defense against it was to remain silent (as a child she had been so totally unresponsive to her parents' constant query: "Phoebe, what's your name?" that they had her undergo cognitive and aural testing). As an adult, her speech defense was more echolalic: she robotically repeated what her mother or boyfriend said to her ("Yes, I am a whore"), although, in sharing the stories with me, she did betray a smidgen of affect, often inappropriate. Terrified of abandonment, bad attention was preferable to none at all. But she feared that if she made her need for more positive attention known it would be perverted by the listener and used against her. In relational matters, Phoebe remained voiceless.

Despite the antipathy Phoebe harbored toward her mother, she remembered that, as a child, she became hysterical whenever her mother left the house. Phoebe's separation anxiety was so dreadful, her panic that her mother would abandon her or commit suicide (as she sometimes threatened to do) so paralyzing, that when her mother was asleep, Phoebe would check her breath for signs of life. She both feared and loathed her sister, whom she described as haunting the house, padding on feline feet, present but absent: "completely crazy." In the displaced way that a clinician looks through the window at such scenes, it seemed a bit Hitchcockian.

About a year into our work together, I found out that, in addition to being beaten with 2×4s and extension cords, one of the ways Phoebe had been punished as a child was by having a wet rag stuffed in her mouth, terrifying her. Phoebe reported this to me in her usual affectless way. Without thinking, I blurted out "You were waterboarded!" She looked at me blankly and said "What's that?" and I, regretting my impulsive comment, but not knowing how to back off, said quietly "It's been in the news a lot lately. It's a kind of torture used on political prisoners." "Oh," she said, unmoved. Reflecting on my "gaffe" later, I recognized that I had accidentally established what I thought about her treatment at her mother's hand and made us allies in a way we had not been when I was in stricter listening mode. Over the next few months, the transference changed dramatically, as I increasingly became the placeholder for the part of her that could not feel indignant at her mother or her abusive boyfriends. Rather than mirroring her perceptions, I began to actively suggest alternative takes on her experience. This met with increased resistance.

Phoebe sometimes did not show up and often came late (once with only ten minutes left in the session). She paid a low fee because she was not earning much; she paid cash because she did not have a checking account. She paid after each session instead of monthly. When she did not show up, I would still charge her and she would pay for the session, saying "no problem" in a deadpan, dissociated way. When opportunities presented themselves, I would call attention to the missed sessions. I would wonder aloud what I might have done to anger her, or whether I had hurt her in some way she could not express. She would have none of it; confrontation for Phoebe was still too dangerous to be engaged head-on. "Well then," I finally said, "it's so curious. I wonder why you want to pay for something you aren't getting."

She ignored me. She counted out the fee, sometimes dollar by dollar until I felt angry and humiliated but completely at odds about what I could or should say. Usually, I said nothing. There was only the silent seesaw of power relations, with Phoebe and I both anxiously anticipating the tipping point.

During such scenarios, I increasingly felt that I was (unfairly) enduring the brunt of Phoebe's sadistic withholding and aggression. The way she counted out the money made me want to cry "Just give it to me, it's mine!" and her missed appointments – which usually followed the rare instances in which I had asked to reschedule her hour – often made me feel like an innocent victim, unfairly harassed or ignored, but strangely devoid of anger and unable to stand up for myself, ironically silenced by my own psychoanalytic design: an elective mute. Reflecting on my projective identification, I grew to understand how Phoebe felt.

In the second year of our work, I began to share more of those feelings with Phoebe, along with some observations about her passive aggression. Most often she denied her anger and pretended she had not heard the articulation of my own felt shame. This had an oddly invigorating effect. The more she denied me and my shame, the more integrated my anger became until I was able to break the impasse around our mutual enactment by more clearly calling attention to our dance and, in not so many words, insisting that we untangle our feet. In meticulous detail, we began to deconstruct the moments between us and decode the nuances, including what it meant to "get something you're not paying for" and, conversely, what it might mean "to pay for something you're not getting."

With the renewal of the kind of detailed inquiry that had marked our first year of work, I found out, to my surprise, that Phoebe – a Latina with skin almost as light as mine – was acutely aware of her color, particularly in contrast with that of white people. (This came up in a dream of Phoebe's – and she brought dreams rarely – in which her boyfriend, during a *ménage-à-trois* composed of her boyfriend, herself, and a white woman, preferred the white woman.) I was able to discern more about the genesis of her status concerns, particularly in regard to her mother's religiosity versus her friends' more secular homes, and her discounted position in the family: neither male like her brothers nor "special" like her sister. This thrust us into a heightened sense of paying attention, and an increased feeling on her part that she was being attended to and heard in ways she did not experience outside the room, such as at home with her parents or in rendezvous with her boyfriend.

At the end of the summer Phoebe got a job and moved into her own apartment, a huge breakthrough. But she was still dating the abusive boyfriend, who berated her publically, humiliated her privately, and – if feeling generous – fucked her without a condom, *as a reward* (she often had nostalgic reveries about the good days – before she had "ruined everything" – when they had sex without the rubber between them). Phoebe shared that she had never had an orgasm with him. It was this late-revealed snippet that probably frustrated *me* the most (Phoebe claimed not to care all that much). I knew that she had been very orgasmic with her first abusive beau and she had portrayed the second man as quite a Casanova. In my own fantasy, I had assumed that good sex had linked the two lovers, furnishing at least a partial reason for Phoebe's inability to leave him. I wondered how her lack of satisfaction might be connected to "paying for something you don't get." Faced with the obstinacy of her connection to him, I felt worn down, even insufficient.

I demurred when, perhaps picking up on my feelings of inadequacy, she lumped me in with her self-negation, saying that "all women were nothing but cows": too dumb to protect themselves from slaughter. Indeed, on occasion, she proposed that my entire ability to understand her stemmed from my own pathetic femaleness, although sometimes she would change course and say petulantly that she imagined that I had a man whom I led around by a nose ring. I challenged her stereotyping and engaged in some psychoeducation: I was neither of those women – although I sometimes felt like each – and those sadomasochistic representations did not describe the range of ways that women and men could be together. I felt this educational component to be very important, not because Phoebe did not already know these things on some level but because she could not give herself permission to engage a different personal narrative. Over time, she would repeat things about women that I had said to her in our conversations, seemingly oblivious to the origin of her insight. Even though the words began as an external imposition, I believe they eventually became not just internalized but elaborated in productive ways. Occasionally, when she spoke of her first boyfriend, I would cajole her into role-playing what she would say and do to him if he were in front of her in the moment. I borrowed from Moreno's (1987, p. 54) work on psychodrama, premised on the belief that "however relieving an analysis of situations may be for the patient, for a final test [s]he must go back onto the stage in a real life situation." Because Phoebe seemed to lose her facility with language in situations with domineering men, becoming confused and incapable of stating her position, I found that practicing getting angry was not an altogether bad thing. She said that I was her "corner man," like in boxing, sending her out for round after round until she "manned up." The masculinization of the attitude of aggression was not lost on either of us.

Then, Phoebe expressed real anger for the first time. She came in fuming because her boyfriend had refused her Christmas gift: earrings that cost nearly as much as a year's worth of appointments with me.

At first I thought her purchase masochistic; a pandering for his love and then, almost immediately, I saw the arrogance in it, and the aggression: this attempted procurement of a "man whore." She was one-upping him on the contempt scale. Her own disavowed aggression bubbled up; she had a name for her boyfriend and it was not flattering. I thought at that moment that it was the closest she had come yet to recognizing her own capacities as a willfully angry narrator of situations, a potential author of endings.

And what did it mean between Phoebe and I, her declaration of his worth in stark contrast to my own? Contempt was not a laser, after all, it leaked around the edges, and I too was now caught in its spreading light. More happy at her anger at him than angry at her contempt for me (how layered these things are!) I decided in the moment to forgo a discussion about us, and just listened to her rage against the man's sadism, and, eventually, her mother's, too.

The more open she became, the more willing she was to share the fetid air of her childhood apartment, the less distanced and more woozy I felt peering into what she called "the emotional bowl of vomit" that was her family. Although no longer mute like her sister, Phoebe still had "no say" in her relationships, romantic or otherwise. Therefore, it was with great interest, and some surprise, that I learned about the denouement of Phoebe's first relationship.

As noted above, although I had mostly thought of contempt as a destructive emotion, I found it remarkable to see the ways in which its development seemed a necessary precursor to Phoebe's empowerment, a way of polishing the moral lens through which she viewed her two boyfriends' actions. I had heard about her paralysis in the face of the first man's rejections, her suicidal gesture, her self-contempt over the offer of her virginity to keep him. As we returned over the next two years to how she was able to leave the first abusive man, she would catalogue the evidence of his intolerableness: scrawny, low, grimy, wearing white briefs ("He looked like a 12-year-old; it *disgusted* me. Wear *boxers*, for God's sake!"). She was adamant that, because he was so stupid (he mispronounced "whopper," ordering a "whooper" from the cashier at the local Burger King), she could feel superior to him, and it was this disdain that had opened the door for her escape from his abuse. Occasionally, Phoebe would lapse into a voice that sounded like the cartoon character Bullwinkle, and she would mock the "retarded" way her former boyfriend spoke.

Then, one day she blurted out that she had only been able to leave the first man after listing all his characteristics, good and ill, in her spiral notebook and encountering the visual representation of the "bad" list, which took up three pages. I asked her what things were on the list, expecting to hear about the time he threw her out of the car, the time he burned her with a cigarette lighter, the sexual infidelities, the various cruelties he had inflicted. Instead, Phoebe said, "I couldn't look at his feet." "*Really?*" I hummed. "What was it about them?" "They were just too flat. I couldn't look at them anymore. I told him: 'just put on your socks.'" The disgust in her voice completely nullified his membership in the human race. She had inhaled Ambrose Bierce's (1911) description of contempt as the feeling that someone prudent has for an enemy too formidable to be safely opposed.

Phoebe mustered the courage to leave the man shortly after this concrete finding. Her derision ballooned when she told me the story about his feet; all certitude, it crowded out any possibility of retreat from the confrontation. She had *dismissed* him and his flat feet. His feet enabled her to walk away. I had researched a case once where the female perpetrator had chopped up her wandering boyfriend, starting with his feet. Phoebe and the chopper shared a kind of cool detachment once their decisions concerning feet were made; they both rode their anger to the edge of massive enactments. It seemed that only an instrumental contempt could precipitate their exits. We will return to Phoebe's narrative of escape and recapture shortly.

Theories of contempt and other negative emotions

Rozin et al. (1999, p. 374) have written that "the condemnation of others . . . is a universal and essential feature of human social life." They find that the same contempt, anger, and disgust ("the CAD Triad") that fuel toxic engagements may also act as a compass for the moral violations of others. According to them, along with internal assessments of our own actions that may produce shame, guilt, or embarrassment, the CAD triad – or what Izard (1977) more memorably called the "hostility triad" – forms the emotional foundation for moral judgments. Anger (rooted in goal frustration) and disgust (a primal defense against contaminated food) begin as rudimentary somatic defenses against threat but are then elaborated culturally and interpersonally, although they never seem to have shaken their animal associations.

I see contempt in much the same way Kohut (1972, p. 361) saw narcissism: that it need not be "a product of regression or defense" thus giving it a "pejorative connotation." Although, for people with early and severe narcissistic injuries, adult adaptations might be marked by extreme grandiosity and the infliction of similar injuries on others, Kohut believed that narcissistic rage might be transformed in "mature aggression." As with narcissism, I believe that contempt in response to the invalidating aspects of an abusive relationship may be personally and socially advantageous.

In emotionally and/or physically violent relationships, the abusive partner dismantles the identity of the victim. He may reduce her self-worth by disparaging her looks, her brains, even her perception of the abuse. The victim in such a diminished state – often mystified about the causes or nature of attacks – seems disqualified from a moral universe in which an appreciation of the abuser's contemptible nature and acts can ever take root. Humiliated into a subservient crouch, she is truly in no position to judge her abuser.

As Sullivan (1956b) suggested, identity itself can be dissociated through the sheer force of such invalidation. In this reduced state, a woman learns exactly which emotions are allowed to see the light of day and which must be disowned. Contempt in particular may go underground, tied as it is to elements of disgust and outrage. Sullivan points out that in romantic relationships there can be a kind of "hateful integration" composed of mutual humiliations (p. 375). Kant (1797), in *The Metaphysics of Morals*, inveighs against contempt specifically because of its potential to undermine human dignity and trigger dispositive acts of violence.

On the other hand, some contemporary philosophers believe that contempt is not only useful but justifiable when appropriately focused: "[the defense of contempt] offers a general challenge to the view that an enlightened morality must be a gentle morality" (Mason, 2003, p. 236). Mason argues that contempt is "not necessarily a retributive emotion," like revenge, because contempt is just as likely to cause withdrawal from an object as an attack on it. She asserts that contempt in personal relations should be considered moral whenever we can consider the object of our contempt a "free, responsible moral agent" not only in the matter at hand, but in his or her mode of being in the world: narcissistic, arrogant, uncaring, hurtful. Indeed, contemptible.

Contempt can be regarded along with what feminists have called "outlaw" emotions, such as anger. However, in addition to being a rejoinder to real or imagined injustice (as anger or even rage are), contempt is also an expressed assessment of someone's moral standing (Bell, 2005). When the contemptuous reaction is to something real, such as a partner's mistreatment, the emotion is a highly specific relational transaction. Contempt imposes an interpersonal moral hierarchy, elevating the contemptuous subject in status even as it deflates the contemptible object. Although interpersonal expressions of contempt can be as hot as a lynching or as cold as a mother who leaves no forwarding address, the feeling itself always involves a form of personal alienation. "This psychological distancing is a way of expressing one's non-identification with the object of one's contempt and it precludes sympathetic identification with the object of contempt" (Bell, 2005, p. 84). Distancing may serve an important purpose for victims of abuse, who often empathize with their batterer's troubles to the detriment of their own safety.

Of course there is no end of examples of the mushroom cloud that contempt can initiate in its more toxic forms. At the extreme end, such distancing leads to a depersonalization of others whose only logical outcome is annihilation: think of the broad contempt toward groups or classes of people, which is usually preceded by more elaborate, paranoid constructions. Contempt in its purest form is a defensive contraction to such overpowering feelings of humiliation – as opposed to terror and pain – that it may signal a final step in a person's identification with the non-human realm: a hospice from the world of potentially annihilating attachments (Searles, 1960). This is the kind of contempt we see operating on the side of the perpetrator of violence: it is hard, if not impossible, to return from that edge.

But what if we consider the victim's narrative instead of the oppressor's? Might we then allow a transitory, liberating notion of contempt, more akin perhaps to the kind of contempt that fueled slaves' uprising against their owners, or ghettoized Jews' armed resistance in World War II Germany? To paraphrase Spelman (1989, pp. 266–267), contempt gives a person the right to set up a code of conduct and judge whether someone has violated it; this capacitates agency in the subordinated person. For victims in abusive relationships, the realization that their tormentor does not own the moral high ground and, in fact, may be inferior to them, can be the first step in recognizing inequity and repackaging the relationship – or discarding it entirely.

As childhood trauma so often sets the stage for this dissociation of affect, it is no surprise perhaps that the most critical emotions for self-preservation – those that signal "you can't do this to me" – are unplugged early, making women even more vulnerable to potential victimization. I cannot help but feel that an intact early warning system, replete with a full complement of negative emotions, might have saved Phoebe and her sisters the secondary trauma.

Work with Phoebe, middle stage

I gave an early draft of this manuscript to Phoebe, after asking her for permission to write about her story for possible publication (parts of this chapter were originally published as an article in a psychoanalytic journal). I had hidden her identity but not the complexity of my feelings towards her or my assessment of her issues. My head was filled with worries about privacy, betrayal, and the tiny slice of her I had magnified in the article, as if it were all she was. But Phoebe insisted that she was happy with the manuscript; she said that "I totally got her," and thought it was "cool" that I wanted to publish her story.

In the following months she started to break away from her boyfriend and speak more frankly about her negative feelings towards him, sometimes in words cribbed from my manuscript. One day, looking flush and 14, she crowed about a new lover and even gloated over her impending liberation from the unsightly construction of her sexual identity that her ex had imposed. But soon enough, the old boyfriend called her "a cheat," "a whore," and "a booty call"; Phoebe, devastated, completely agreed. She came to a session and sat down, announcing "I'm a liar" so loudly it startled me. This was not the Phoebe I knew who, even after hundreds of sessions, still struggled poignantly to begin a conversation. The conviction of her "badness" filled the room in the booming voices of her many disparaging internal objects, covering her own fledgling one.

Many months passed. Then she suddenly announced it was over, and told a story of going to his house and screaming that he should "give the fucking earrings back," as he dumped around her all the things she had bought for him and said to take them all. I held my breath, imagining her sense of elation and entitlement. This was clearly my projection, because she – far from celebratory – bitterly recounted staring longingly out the bus window in the ensuing days, desperately hoping to see him, although she said she knew that she "had ruined it for good now." Inside, I was furious that she seemed still unconvinced of his worthlessness and her superiority, and upset that I had allowed my agenda (Get angry! Get contemptuous! I'm even writing an article about it!) to become (briefly) more valuable to me than her own.

Over time, Phoebe admitted that life without him was much improved and, in one meeting, recounted all the ways in which she had grown and changed, saying at the door that it had been "a really, really good session." She met someone else, who seemed wonderful. He listened to her, they exchanged Yuletide gifts, and in her telling he seemed kind and gentle. And just as I was feeling good, in that self-satisfied way clinicians can when a client seems happy and inherently *different*, Phoebe inadvertently reminded me of Bromberg's (1998) clinical wisdom about staying the same while changing. She broke the news that there was a complication in the new relationship that she had neglected to tell me about. There was another woman with whom her new boyfriend had been involved and with whom he was going to vacation over the holidays. (Many months later, I found out that Phoebe had known of the other woman all along. That woman was the man's girlfriend and I guess the correct language would indicate that it was Phoebe herself who played the role of the "other woman.") I asked Phoebe if they had discussed it. She said that she "didn't have the right" to ask about it, but allowed that maybe she should anyway. I felt such sorrow for her at that moment, and such pain, but also contempt, anger, and disgust. How much came from me and how much I was holding for her, I cannot answer. I was still struggling with whether we could turn our integumentary "hostility triad" into something more conscious and potentially generative – or even empowering – for us both.

As we hit the three-year mark, Phoebe became more cognitively integrated and much more likely to speak up for herself, even with men. She has even rejected a few of them, a far different situation than when she felt obligated to be with almost anyone who wanted her just because they had asked.

Nevertheless, Phoebe is affectively dissociated; with all of the hurt she had endured and discussed, Phoebe has never cried in my presence. Sometimes I joke with her about it, such as when she gloms a handful of tissues for her allergic sneezes and I observe that I owe them to her because she has not yet used up her clinical allotment of tissues. In a recent session, she indulged in a long reverie about her relational history. There was much more affect than there had ever been in her usual recitations. It was as if she had suddenly recognized the depth of her mistreatment and the rage she harbored as a result; her monologue on the injustice of it all squarely brought her, I felt, to the doorstep of disparaging the intentions of those who had hurt her. Nodding in support of her conclusions – really her awakenings – I found myself incredibly sad. When the session came to a close, Phoebe said, "I almost cried," and I answered, "Yes, I know." After a long pause, I said, "I almost cried, too." Phoebe said, "Yes, I saw that," and smiled shyly at me, a co-conspirator in matters of the mind and heart. I felt no more contempt for her then; she had finally begun to take it for herself. I see that contempt as a kind of way station between anger and assertiveness. As the doctor said to Portnoy at the end of his blistering complaint: "Now we can begin" (Roth, 1969).

The moral imagination of the abused woman

The philosopher Rudolf Steiner (1894) was intrigued by the conditions that promoted freedom of thought and action. He preached the integration of subjective nature, which includes our drives, feelings, and ideas, with the objective realities of the world that so often constrained it. Steiner conceptualized the moral imagination as a place where we could form highly individualized ethical responses to pressing circumstances and, in this radical moment of invention, become free to act with integrity. No longer seduced by the short stick of our immediate needs or stifled by the truncheon of their denial, we might expand our perception of situations, intuiting new solutions to old problems. This feels like an enormous conceptual leap to ask of women who have been battered, that they imagine a moral universe where they are equal to, or even better than, the mates who have completely de-moralized them (Both moral and morale come from the Latin *moralis*: a custom or mood of morality). On the other hand, it is what psychoanalysts *always* ask of patients, that they relitigate experience as a way of straining the seams of their straightjackets enough to allow a realignment of limbs . . . and maybe the possibility of escape from their bonds.

The aesthetics of psychoanalysis resonate with Steiner's belief that we should wean ourselves from "excessive dependence on fixed patterns and forms, preparing [. . .] instead for dealing with the flowing and extremely complex reality characteristic of living beings" (Dahlin, 2009, p. 550). Because psychoanalysis offers a counterproposition to mainstream psychiatry and psychology, which too often marry an essentialist ideology to normative goals, it is uniquely situated to take up issues of freedom and agency among individuals compromised by excessive regulation in personal and political spheres. Interpersonal and relational analysts in particular understand poverty of content and restriction of affect in extremely nuanced ways that highlight "the repudiation of mentalization in an attachment context, the disruption of the psychological self by the emergence of the other within the self, and the vital dependence on the presence of the other as a vehicle for externalization" (Fonagy et al., 2002, p. 198). With these understandings, psychoanalysts can access the inner world through a dyadic play mode whose acquisition has been considered an estimable gauge of health (Winnicott, 1971).

> What is playing? Playing, says Winnicott, is first of all something that happens in the interface between our inner world and external reality. Taking place neither strictly in our imagination, nor in the truly external world (ie. all that is out of our control), playing happens in that space where our imagination is able to shape the external world without the experience of compliance, climax, or too much anxiety.
>
> (Alexander, 2010)

Phoebe had been deprived of the opportunity for this kind of play in her childhood, where so much was imposed in the way of rules and regulations and moralistic caveats. As a result, her imaginative capacities were stymied. According to Winnicott, if caregivers, rather than allowing the space between themselves and the child to potentially fill with products of the child's imagination, dominate the space with their own thoughts instead, the environment feels persecutory and, because of parental omnipotence, inescapable. The child's creativity is shut down. Grown up, she does not know how to inhabit interpersonal space lightly, with flights of fancy, with novel attempts at meaning making. In an adult treatment, it may be difficult for the psychoanalyst to encourage her analysand's imagination without becoming similarly, unwittingly, persecutory (Winnicott, 1993). Yet she must try.

Retrospectively, I can see that much of my charge was to open up a space for Phoebe where vitriol and slander and all manner of murderousness could be expressed without an actual death taking place, where she might pretend to be an agent in relationship to others, even if the confrontation felt unbearable and even if I feared slipping off my neutral perch to fully engage the *enfant terrible*. I wanted her to form a gun with her thumb and forefinger, as a child might, without real consequence but to have it be, all the same, "a metaphor that is meant"

(Bateson, 1972, p. 141), one reified just enough to change her perceptive and communicative style.

> The resemblance between the process of therapy and the phenomenon of play is, in fact, profound. Both occur within a delimited psychological frame, a spatial and temporal bounding of a set of interactive messages. In both play and therapy, the messages have a special and peculiar relationship to a more concrete or basic reality. Just as the pseudocombat of play is not real combat, so also the pseudolove and pseudohate of therapy are not real love and hate. The "transfer" is discriminated from real love and hate by signals invoking the psychological frame; and indeed it is this frame which permits the transfer to reach its full intensity and to be discussed between patient and therapist.
>
> (Bateson, 1972, p. 147)

At the beginning, the rigidity of Phoebe's responses to the men in her life and the hierarchical structure she imposed on interpersonal interactions seemed to me impenetrable. (I cannot help but think of that hoodie, backwards; a restraint that symbolized a life lived niggardly and too narrow.) To play seemed for her impossible; she simply could not trust enough to fall backwards and know that I would catch her. Worse, I could not always trust myself. Every time I pursued a rare moment of spontaneity, or presented an opportunity for Phoebe to fantasize or role play, I wondered whether I had engineered the outcome in a way that replaced her imagination with my own becoming, in effect, Winnicott's prophesied persecutor. I tried to be vigilant in this regard, awaiting the day that she might be able to tell me when I had crossed a boundary, and redeem the territory as her own. But the conundrum lay in the fact that her interpersonal repertoire centered on the forfeiture of her brain to another and, so, it seemed particularly easy to be pulled into enactments where I became too directive, too insightful, too powerful, allowing her to outsource agency, relieving her of the very thing she so muscularly disavowed: the rumblings inside her own head.

Disavowal is a refusal to accept the reality of a perception because of the harrowing associations it might invoke. Pheobe, for example, disavowed her own thoughts and feelings because to embrace them would call into question the perceptions and intentions of significant others, including her mother and a series of boyfriends, risking loss on an annihilative scale. Hence, the loud announcement "I'm a liar" was a disavowal (of her lover's cruelty) and a negation (the fulfillment of a wish for union with her lover through agreeing with his negative assessment of her) rolled into one.

Freud (1918) first used the term *Verleugnung* (in English, "disavowal") to describe how the knowledge of something could be accepted in one sphere of the mind while simultaneously being refused in another. Disavowal does not makes ideas disappear any more than repression erases affect, it just renders them incomprehensible or irrelevant. Disavowal forecloses an accurate perception of reality, which interrupts the judicial function of the ego. An example Freud had earlier articulated (1908) was the way that little boys held fast to the notion that everyone had a penis like their own, despite being confronted with incontrovertible evidence that at least some of the people they saw naked did not. Thus, at the same time, boys could both know and not know about sexual difference. They could know, yet still refrain from thinking about, the fact that their mother (according to classical Freudian theory) lacked what was so obviously needed to be potent, authoritative, and admirable: a phallus (De Mijolla, 2005).

Ironically, Freud (1925) also noted that for some girls the wish to obtain a penis, to be like a man, persisted despite its impossibility and "became a motive for strange and otherwise unaccountable actions" (p. 253). Freud had concluded that boys had a stronger superego (moral compass) than girls at the culmination of the Oedipal crisis; one wonders if the "strange actions" to which Freud referred included the kind of agentic assertion of moral equivalence that Phoebe had struggled to express. After all, had not Phoebe's mother gone on and on about how Phoebe must have thought "she had a penis" to stay out late and fraternize with men? Phoebe's mother clearly shared Freud's critique of gendered prerogatives. Freud's broadside, thoroughly absorbed by the culture and still reflected in contemporary gender stereotypes, was robotically internalized by Phoebe, causing her to split off her own rebellious, aggressive self. In this way she could, by dissociative turns, both embody and disown her mother's assertions about her "strange actions," her itinerant penis, her moral turpitude. During the day, Phoebe abided by all the despoiling social contracts she had signed. At night, Phoebe abrogated the shame of those exploitations by becoming a bit shameless, though rarely as much as I might have hoped.

An antidote for shame

The Jungian analyst Mary Ayers (2011) chose Cézanne's painting *Eternal Feminine* (c.1877) as the cover art for her book. The canvas shows a naked woman lying on a white sheet, bloody holes where her eyes have been gouged. She may be giving birth or at least her parturient position suggests this. The woman is surrounded by men: popes and trumpeters, rapists, doctors, and grim reapers. An artist off to the side is painting her portrait. At first, the crowd appears to be admiring her but then, confoundingly, it seems that their eyes too are pecked out. The "worship" is blind and thus unlinked to any gesture that might alleviate her nakedness or pain: "indeed in his depiction of all the men around her with closed or even missing mouths, vacant eyes, and no ears, Cézanne seems to be saying that all mankind has dulled their most vital senses to the Eternal Feminine" (Ayers, 2011, p. 115). In Jungian psychology, the Eternal Feminine is the unintegrated, contrasexual side of man: his dissociated female self. In Freudian psychology a similar notion is exemplified by the Oedipal mother who is similarly repudiated in favor of "the higher aim of identification with the father" (p. 42).

> Maternal femininity is the carrier for shame, and so the oppression of women provides the archetypal fuel, so to speak, for shame's annihilating capacity to create non-existence.
>
> (Ayers, 2011, p. xii)

Ayers notes how the image of the woman's exposure, and the paradoxically heightened yet insensate arousal of the men, becomes a metaphor for shame that is transferred from perpetrator to victim. Abusive behavior is often about a man's perception of his own feminization under the (supposedly) alluring gaze or taunting tongue of a woman, and his attempt to throw off that humiliation through projection and violence. The jarring image of Nazi Amon Goeth in Spielberg's film *Schindler's List* springs to mind. Goeth beats his Jewish slave, Helen Hirsch, because he is ashamed of his desire for her:

> I would like so much to reach out and touch you in your loneliness. What would that be like, I wonder? What would be wrong with that? I realize that you're not a person in the strictest sense of the word, but, um, maybe you're right about that too. Maybe what's wrong, it's not us, it's this. I mean, when they compare you to vermin, to rodents, and to lice. I just, uh, you make a good point. You make a very good point. Is this the face of a rat? Are these the eyes of a rat? "Hath not a Jew eyes?" I feel for you, Helen. [leaning to kiss her] No, I don't think so. You Jewish bitch, you nearly talked me into it, didn't you?

Sadism in some instances is a kind of counter-masochism, a protective device that shields the sadist from experiencing the crushing directives of an internal moral inquisitor, a harsh superego. Looking back at Phoebe's mother, I see sadism in the guise of religious fervor, illusory prophylaxis, ascendant morality. As each attitude reconstituted its antipode – devotion and disdain, virtue and vice, desire and disgust – Phoebe received the contradiction in the only way she could: through splitting the information (about both her mother and herself) into separate silos. However, in trying to make meaning of this illogic – I love you but I humiliate you – there was also a repetitive attempt to fuse the irreconcilable forms, a cohering of love and debasement. In my time with Phoebe, those affects were continuously blown apart, patched together, sundered, and knit again, their attraction as preordained as iron filings to a magnet.

A similar dynamic took hold when Phoebe's boyfriend convinced her that she was at fault for his abuse. He only did these awful things because she had "ruined it" and then, the more abuse she took, the more ashamed she became. When I suggested that perhaps the boyfriend should be ashamed of himself for such ugly behaviors, it was rejected out of hand. Her dissociation on the matter was active and intense: her choosing not to "spell out" alternative scenarios suggested that she could not imagine an alternate interpretation (Stern, 1997, p. 121). She believed that he was only doing what came naturally, within a context that Phoebe invariably assumed responsibility for creating. Men could not be held accountable, in general, she thought. They were all dogs, just as all women were fated to be cows. Phoebe's moral universe was rigidly arranged but seriously out of order.

> The cultural and psychological expectation creates a remarkable and profoundly tragic distortion: it is shameful to suffer violence yet it is a source of pride and honor to be the one who dispenses violence to others.
>
> (Ayers, 2011, p. 116)

Women's traumatic experience is filled with dissociated outrage and seeming inability to muster contempt, or even indignation, toward the men who bully them, as they earlier could not risk implicating caretakers in maltreatment. One of the hallmarks of traumatic dissociation is the disavowal of a range of appropriate feelings toward the abuser, often right through the relationship's concluding moments:

> Although retrospectively, it can be seen where her defenses against denial of her anger at being an abuse victim are unraveling, the women do not have any conscious awareness of those feelings. Their descriptions of the final incident indicate that they separate those angry feelings by the psychological process of a dissociative state and, thus, do not perceive them.
>
> (Walker, 2009, pp. 135–136)

Yet this splitting defense, rather than de-escalating dyadic attacks by forestalling retaliation, instead triggers reciprocal cycles of shame and guilt. These cycles only solidify the primitive enmeshment of abused with abuser, and drive suppressed or dissociated rage to new heights (Scheff, 1987; Lansky, 1999). This is a common trajectory in abusive relationships: women dissociate the more negative affects that might catalyze agency and potentiate escape, and instead are paralyzed by states of helplessness and shame. Women's humiliation is catnip to the abuser: violence escalates, he feels guilty, she (disowning anger) forgives, which shames him, leading to more anger and abuse.

The leitmotif of Phoebe's story is the appearance and disappearance of the affect of contempt. As her narrative illustrates, the ownership of negative feelings is an important component in women's decisions to leave bad relationships; given this, clinicians might put greater emphasis on strategically working toward their integration and expression. Phoebe does not have as violent an abuse history as many of the research subjects I have interviewed. Yet, Phoebe's psychological dynamics seem remarkably similar to theirs. The stories, taken together, illustrate the dire consequences of not accessing and integrating one's darker side. Such integration, I believe, is best achieved in an environment where it is safe to express potentially annihilating thoughts without fear of total affective dysregulation (Bromberg, 2008). Therapy provided this "safe space" for Phoebe.

My experience with Phoebe suggests an approach to treatment that might be useful for work with abused women in general. Although the foundation of the model rests on the broad idea of working psychoanalytically toward the integration of dissociated affect, as suggested in the work of Sullivan (1956a, 1956b) and, more recently, Stern (2003, 2009) and Bromberg (1998, 2006), it adds a more specific elaboration for work with those currently living in situations of domestic violence: (1) psychoeducational work to help the client recognize the inequality and abusiveness in gendered relations; a raising of "critical consciousness" (Almeida and Lockhard, 2005); (2) psychodramatic work to help the client recognize and express negative affects (Moreno, 1987); and (3) cognitive-affective work to help the client develop the capacity for moral evaluation, even as the client passes through a stage where contempt for the abuser is made manifest.

I hoped that, for Phoebe, therapeutic freedom would present as the willingness to engage anything, including the ugliest parts of others and the most aggressive parts of herself, the parts that avoided the mirror most strenuously. To be an agent she would have to use all those parts as tools for navigation and negotiation. What has contempt to do with this beauteous rhetoric of freedom?

It may have something to do with awakening, as Sullivan observed, with facing the reality that Steiner thought a necessary prerequisite for the moral imagination. For example, the wellspring of contempt for Phoebe, in one instance, had been the making of a list of a man's bad intentions. Seeing in black and white what she had previously disavowed, despite ample evidence to the contrary, put the brakes on Phoebe's fantasy of fusion and offered a moral resolution to her entanglement. Layton (2012) sees such disavowal as the "perverse core of every repetition compulsion" because individuals cannot accept that the person who is supposed to care for them, instead hurts them. In discussing a clinical case presented by Feimberg (2005), Layton describes the patient as "oscillating between helpless longings to be taken care of by the other" and a "contemptuous disdain for the other," allowing that the latter is a grandiose kind of defensive maneuver that "signals self-sufficiency." My time with Phoebe helped me recognize how the contemptuous part of self could be leveraged as a bulwark against self-recrimination and diminution of the ego and, defensive as it partly was, facilitate a break in certain dissociative processes.

To me, it seemed that, in some ways, Phoebe was only capable of constructing reality in an agentic way when she gave full throat to her contempt, which belonged to the more aggressive self that she equated with masculine privilege. That aggressive self was a site of pleasure when she gave herself over to its libidinous hum, but also a place of terror when she realized where it might take her. In those moments, overpowered by her own potential to annihilate, Phoebe gave the job of thinking "bad" thoughts to me. I exterminated all these men, in turn, on her behalf.

What makes the idea of confrontation so unthinkable for most women, what triggers their dissociation, is the relational asymmetry represented by the role positions they internalize, positions that encourage the "person with structural sources of status and power" to "remain imperceptive to the needs of the less powerful person" (Forte et al., 1996, p. 61) and the less powerful person to shelve any needs they have. Expectations and actions are selectively shaped by the frame of reference the couple has developed around the primacy of his needs and her acquiescence to them. A critical reflection about the disjunction of what is and what ought to be – a problem sometimes called "Hume's guillotine" by moral philosophers – cannot be engaged. Hence Phoebe's robotic reliance on the hierarchal distribution of rights within a romantic relationship, the inability to imagine alternative distributions of power, indeed the sense of only being able to discern her own worth relative to another woman vying for her lover's attention, all conspired to rob her of an independent autonomous way of interacting. In this, she may be Everywoman.

Phoebe redux

Each session with Phoebe feels like a cliffhanger to me. It is not anything like the teasing of a borderline, whose life of emergency renders superfluous the best intentioned intervention. Nor is Phoebe like the patient who releases a bomb with their hand on the doorknob when it is time for goodbye. It just takes her ages to "warm up"; she usually hits stride about 40 minutes in, which causes me time and again to suspend the frame on pain of interrupting what finally feels like connection. Her withholding sometimes feels sadistic and other times like a shy seduction. But Phoebe never fails to touch me in those final minutes, and leave me hungry to reconvene, only to find myself in the next session, again estranged. The next session always unfolds in a triplicate dissociation: she seems not to remember how she has left things, she seems unplugged from any affective force, she does not surmise how or why one session might continue to another. She never speaks but sometimes makes a face or looks at me beseechingly until I feel that I must be the sadist for expecting speech when she wants to re-enact her childhood muteness. Sometimes I say that it would be fine to not speak, to just be in the room together, but in saying those words, I have already relieved her of the pressure of going first and she can begin: "Nothing is happening," she says. She rarely takes off her coat or jacket or sweatshirt – whatever the season dictates – although she does, incongruently, sometimes take off her shoes. For ages, I continued to be perplexed about her issues with men's flat feet, convinced there must be a story behind it, but eventually giving up that psychoanalytic conceit and chalking it up to nothing more than an "innate" preference. This was not the only time I forsook deep thinking around Phoebe: another enactment.

Phoebe now comes on time, or even early, for most sessions, although there are still occasional last minute cancellations. She briefly dated a man who seemed nice at first but ended up taking advantage of her; she ended up playing nursemaid to the crushing anxieties that curtailed his capacity to give. Once, when his elderly grandfather showed up unannounced, Phoebe was asked to hide in the bedroom because the grandfather was racist. She "could not believe it" but did as she was asked. Finally, she broke with the man in dramatic fashion, yelling at him in the street and walking away. Some weeks later, though, Phoebe became embroiled in a strange series of crude text messages where the man so disparaged her, in such a sexual way (as she spaced out, robotically replying), that I finally asked, with what I hoped came off as playful curiosity rather than the impatience I was struggling with, "what would he have to say for you to hang up on him?"

She said she did not know. She was mad at me for not recognizing what a "good job" she had done by not going over to "blow" him, although he had requested it (more of this story in Chapter 4). No one gave her any credit apparently, least of all me, who had said many times that I understood how difficult it was for Phoebe to stand up for herself. I felt the weight of my own disillusionment and judgment. I did not know what to say next. If Phoebe was a thinker without thoughts, I was a mass of thoughts without a thinker. We left it that way. A few weeks later, she mentioned that she had blocked the man from her Facebook account and phone. Was that hard to do? I wanted to know, but she did not have much to say about it. Change had crept in on little cat feet,[1] sat on silent haunches. By the time she articulated it, Phoebe had already moved on from the relationship.

Toward the end of a session, she told me a story about the years when her mother had tried every religious remedy, save exorcism, for her older sister's schizophrenia. Phoebe was most often dragged along to various high priests and healers who laid on hands and channeled the savior as she, maybe four or five years old, slept in the corner or watched sideways out of slit eyes. She remembered this one time when, suddenly, the minister took her up in his arms and swung her wildly around, proclaiming that Jesus would "give her arches." I knew that she had grown to be a non-believer, pretty much, but I wondered what she made of the whole thing. "I don't know," she said, momentarily embracing the magic, "but I do have nice high arches. I am the only one in the family who does." I wondered if there was some conflating with another childhood memory of her mother's picture of the archangel Michael, hung high near the door. Saint Michael's job, in Catholicism, is to rescue souls from Satan at the hour of their death. Phoebe was indeed the saved child. Of all her siblings she was the only one who survived into adulthood without disease or infirmity or mental illness . . . or, evidently, flat feet. There was plenty of survivor's guilt but also a constant sense that the God of carnage (Reza, 2009) might be lurking close by.

She joined a gym and bought a bike.

She met a man who seems very nice. It's been going on for a while.

She no longer spends all her time with me reliving the humiliations of hundreds of hours spent with men she hoped to please but could not. She talks about an array of things: her work, her goals, her clothes, and also their sex life, which is good. "Very eventful" she intimates. Sometimes she is even the event director.

One day she tells me how she suddenly blurted out to him something she feared would be taken the wrong way and become ammunition for his rejection of her. Although it was something really quite droll and not at all antagonistic, she heard her own voice as a harridan's. She even inserted an expletive when she told me what she had said although, upon further questioning, she admitted she had not actually cursed at him. She only feared that he had glimpsed the obscenity of her aggression. At first she asked me if she had done something awful but then reversed course. "See," she said, "I can't confront anyone." I pointed out that she had confronted him, quite spontaneously, and that nothing terrible had happened.

There is hope that Phoebe's communication might portend a future ability to better engage what Bromberg (2003) calls "safe surprises," candid interactions that can be distinguished from their traumatizing counterparts. You cannot learn from severe trauma because it triggers massive dissociation but you can learn a lot from the milder anxieties that punctuate human interaction, if you can come to tolerate them (Sullivan, 1956b; Bromberg, 2008).

For Phoebe, shame may someday abdicate its throne. As self-contempt recedes, contempt for others might become a useful expression of appropriate outrage, employed only sparingly, but to great effect. Rather than the two-edged sword that pierced the armor of her dissociation, a subversive catalyst for change, contempt might become simply a healthy sense of entitlement, riding shotgun, just in case.

Note

1 Thank you, Carl Sandburg.

Chapter 3

Engendered self-states

> Abuse is not merely a dyadic notion. Aside from the abuser and the abused, there is also an enabling environment.
>
> (Asaf Work, personal communication)

In my work with Phoebe, I explored the curious absence of aggressive affects in a woman experiencing partner abuse. I explored how clinical interventions aimed at engaging – even encouraging – these dissociated aspects might be useful adjuncts to more traditional psychoanalytic interventions, particularly as regards bolstering a woman's ability to leave her batterer. That work propelled a larger research initiative aimed at investigating more thoroughly the emotional subtext of abusive relationships, the antecedent and contemporaneous contexts in which affects – particularly "negative" ones – are dissociated, and women's perceptions of the emotional shift that immediately prefigured decisions to leave the relationship.

Toward this end, I interviewed 12 women who had ended or escaped long-term violent relationships. Using a psychoanalytically oriented interview format, I collected over 24 hours of narrative about the women's experiences, thoughts, feelings, and fantasies. The narratives allowed me to examine relationships among victimization, the dissociation of aggressive affects, imperviousness to danger, and the paralysis that truncated women's ability to protect themselves from harm. In analyzing them, I was able to document powerful associations among experiences of child abuse, masochistic self-states that tolerate adult violence, the absence of negative emotions like indignation, outrage, and contempt, and the forfeiture of agency during intimate relationships.

Trauma, dissociation, and repetitive enactment

While much of the literature on domestic violence has called attention to the fact that women's material needs for shelter, daycare, employment, and legal protection often render them helpless to leave toxic relationships, it seems equally true that many women who are offered these services free of charge – or can afford them independently – remain nonetheless tightly wound in their abusers' embrace.

Trauma experts suggest that battering relationships may endure because of the physiological imprint that violence leaves, a condition which van der Kolk (1989) calls "traumatic bonding." Behavioral theorists note that traumatic bonding is reinforced through the intermittent schedule on which both abuse and love are doled out, a reward/punishment timetable that instills behavioral patterns "that are difficult to extinguish or terminate, and which develop the strongest experimentally produced emotional bonds" (Dutton and Painter, 1993, p. 107). Both of these processes likely contribute to the intractability of abusive relationships; however, the recognition of them offers no clinical pathway out of the abyss. I want to suggest that our attention to other aspects of the relational framework may be more useful in determining treatments that break the oft-cited "cycle of violence" (Walker, 1979).

My interviews and their analyses are based upon a body of work, done over many years and through different disciplinary lenses, that posits a connection between early traumatic experience and later re-victimization or perpetration, through the psychological mechanism of dissociated enactment. Simply stated, trauma – dissociation theories speculate that these are the most excruciating physical sensations, and the cognitions and affects they potentially trigger – are disowned by the self experiencing them and become perceptual orphans, unlinked to any organizing schema that would give them meaning. Although traumatic experiences invite what I like to call the Sullivan (1956b) trifecta of uncanny emotion: awe, dread, and horror, they remain largely unformulated (Stern, 1997; Bromberg, 1998). At best, these barely memorialized experiences – and their attendant affects – drift in and out of conscious awareness, although their power to shape the perception of present day experience remains intact. At worst, unformulated experiences remain submerged in a way that severs felt agency even as it flashes dangerously into active, often destructive, contact with other people. Sullivan (1956b) called this the "malevolent transformation" of what is endured into what is transmitted (p. 213). How does this relate to the seeming intractability of destructive, even violent, relationships?

New relationships built on the kindling of older abusive ones seem destined somehow to recapitulate their darkness and, indeed, all too often we discover that each party to a violent conflagration has a long history of similar interpersonal events. While the developmental histories of violent perpetrators are known to be rife with scenarios of maltreatment (Stein, 2007), a less frequently acknowledged fact is that childhood abuse is also considered one of the most significant factors in women's violent re-victimization as adults (Tjaden and Thoennes, 2000; National Institutc of Justicc, 2004; Curric and Tckin, 2006; Kimcrling ct al., 2007). Judith Herman (1992a) has written extensively of the sequelae of child abuse, in particular early maltreatment's transmogrifying effect on relational dynamics in adulthood, when "oscillations in attachment, with the formation of intense, unstable relationships are frequent" and interlocking dependencies without appropriate boundaries may become the norm (p. 365). Similarly, Allison and her colleagues (2008) identified distinct patterns of pursuit and distancing operations in violent dyads, often echoing behaviors that infants and children use to increase proximity to caretakers. According to attachment theorists, here the working model for connection internalized early on is fraught with threat and the anticipation of abandonment or even pain (Bowlby 1969). The child must suppress the normal reactions of sadness or rage both in order to attempt control over the response of the caregiver and to protect their relationship from dissolution (Fonagy et al., 2002). Safran (1993) describes how the adult then carries this interpersonal schema into maturity as a fail-safe way of retaining relatedness to the new primary love object.

> Because of the emotional deprivation the individual has experienced, and because of the ongoing experience of failure to establish real contact, he or she seeks desperate solutions to either maintain or establish some semblance of contact, and to avoid further rejection. The very solution which the individual attempts, however, ultimately impedes real relatedness.
>
> (p. 19)

It seems likely that antecedent trauma has rendered both players – the perpetrator of assaults and his victim – vulnerable in ways that undermine more self-protective functions of the self. Those who have been groomed to ignore, deny, or dissociate violence in childhood may be oblivious to imminent danger as adults, or unable to respond effectively when they encounter it.

Indeed, Taft and colleagues (2007), in a large study of coping behaviors among battered women, found that women with a history of childhood abuse and peritraumatic dissociation were more likely to use what they called "disengagement" strategies (avoidance, wishful thinking, withdrawal, self-criticism) in adult violent relationships than their non-abused counterparts. What Taft et al. call "escapist" thoughts and behaviors (p. 12) I see as strongly linked to the dissociation of negative affect, as the victim attempts to nullify an abysmal reality by simply not attending to it cognitively or emotionally. As Sullivan (1956b) said, the self system tries "to keep one safe from any possibility of passing into that extremely unpleasant state of living which can be called the uncanny emotions; and these aspects of the self system can only be inferred, except in case of disaster" (p. 316). For my subjects, all too often, it was the dissociation itself that invited disaster. In other words, *not only was dissociation a reaction to trauma, dissociation played a primary role in inducing and maintaining traumatic circumstances.*

Taking as a basic assumption that past relationships affect present ones, I examine the specific fault lines in early relationships that may have disabled the women's ability to leave current destructive ones. Conversely, I enumerate the ways in which the coming to consciousness of amputated states of anger, indignation, and contempt in the present may inaugurate a more realistic appraisal of the past. Ultimately, I argue that the integration of these formerly dissociated negative states may facilitate a turn toward greater agency and away from seriously damaging relationships.

Ileana's story

Ileana answered an ad for research subjects. She sailed into my office, more the arched masthead on a ship's prow than the brutalized woman I had expected. Ileana was handsome, with strongly defined features, impeccably dressed, sure of herself. Almost as soon as she lowered herself onto one of the available chairs, though, there was trouble. Panic creased her brow: she patted her face and neck, she darted her eyes. "You've lost something?" I said and she agreed, choking back tears. "Yes, an earring. My favorite. My. Favorite. Earrings." We looked for a while: shook out her coat, her scarf. I suggested going out to the hallway to search. "No," Ileana said, adamantly pulling her posture erect, "I'll live."

Sometimes the first 5 minutes tells the whole story.

Ileana spoke to me about a family she hadn't known was fractured until high school, when grown siblings from an earlier relationship of her mother's suddenly materialized. Their existence had been, well, previously undocumented. Despite some initial shock and awe when they appeared, with plenty of collateral damage, there was an eventual rapprochement and now, all the siblings "love each other to death." Minutes later she dwelled momentarily on the particularly hard time that one brother had at his father's abandonment. But now that's over: "my older brother loves us to death."

Ileana had almost a linguistic tic: every query about her feelings toward those who had hurt her (mother, sister, husband, father, children) would be met with an acknowledgment of the harm quickly followed with the disclaimer "but I love them to death" or "but they love me to death." The negation underlined her dissociation of the knowledge of other's malign intent and annihilating actions, even as the cliché exposed her anger toward them.

There was a "very decent childhood. Better than most; I was grateful for that." The parents stayed together or, it seemed, the father refused to leave and Ileana believed this to be because "I was daddy's little girl. My daddy was not leaving my sister and me." He taught them not to let anyone hurt them. There was no violence.

Only that one time, when she was 9 and her mother

> got behind me, got a belt and beat me . . . she left a mark between my fingers. That was the first time my father got into a complete rage: he punched my mother, gave her a black eye for leaving a mark on his baby girl. I realized then what my father's threshold was. On the street once, a man disrespected me and he flew into a rage. My father and I were very close, extremely close.

She grimaced, spoke in an aside: "My daughters, though, they love my mother to death. If we were all in a burning building, I don't know who they would choose." Ileana laughed, resigned to the disregard of all the females in her life: "I might be a goner." There was a very long pause. "Yes, my daughters love my mother to death." Another pause, some explicating text, more breathing space, and finally:

"I love my mother to death. But my mother is very hard on me." I bet, I thought, and asked: how so? Discipline, Ileana said, was by way of ironing cord. But not at her father's hands. He was "a quiet alcoholic. He was harmless."

Thus did Ileana traverse the Oedipal landscape, from dangerous mother to superficially passive father. It was not dissimilar to the Oedipal triangle in Phoebe's house: a crazy intrusive mom, a father who was absent most of the time, the ultimate redress through another man who could engage, and assuage the narcissistic injury of such rejections. As Goldner (2004) notes, women in abusive relationships have often been devalued by their mothers: their talents ignored, their strengths belittled, their needs disavowed. According to Goldner (p. 351), they seek out the father, not because – as Freudian theory would have it – they want a penis, but to avoid "the despair of negation and invisibility." In this context, the eventual bonding with an abuser is not so surprising. The abuser's incapacity to give must feel familiar, while their battery – emotional or physical – is a kind of twisted recognition of the abused person's power to arouse interest, even from a stone cold narcissist.

At 16, Ileana met Lester ice-skating. Her sister introduced them. Lester was 16 too. He was different, seemed like he had values, he was never disrespectful. Things had been good. Except that one time, in the park, sitting on the bench talking, she didn't remember what about.

> He hit me so hard he knocked my earring out of my ear. He said "When I tell you to do something, you do it. Now bend down and pick up your earring." I uppercut him on the way up, busted his lip. "Don't you ever hit me again," I told him, "I only have one father and he's never laid a hand on me." I didn't tell anyone. I hid the handprint he left on my face.

"His busted lip took longer to heal," she boasted.

There are moments in intimate violence where shame is strongly evoked; where personal pride feels so endangered that consciousness itself must be jettisoned, only to be replaced with pure rage (Hockenberry, 1995). On the way from shame to rage, pride will sometimes morph into arrogance (Bion, 1958), as it did when Ileana recounted the story of her response to Lester in the aftermath of his punch. Sullivan, speaking of the same defensive reaction, neatly counterposed pride with humiliation, the remedy to which becomes a kind of toxic conceit based on "a ficticious self-appraisal, set up to conceal something that is not adequate in the self-organization" (1956a, p. 120). This seems like such a moment to me in Ileana's nascent relationship with Lester: the pride before the fall. Her story would be studded with moments where the main dynamic seemed to be her need to prove that "nobody hits me," after she had been clearly, utterly hit. Reflecting on how Ileana had entered my office and promptly lost an earring, I wondered how far behind the uppercut might lurk.

Ileana said that there had been indicators of Lester's abusive nature but that she had been really naïve. She left her friends and family to join him on a military base far from home. The first night Ileana found a letter from another woman to whom Lester had apparently proposed. She saw the leasing agreement for the apartment and her name wasn't on it. She confronted Lester and they fought. Ileana told no one. When the first phone bill came Lester told her she was no longer allowed to call home; he checked the redial function to make sure. He took the car and left her alone with no way out. Lester brought home whatever they needed: the groceries and other supplies. *And* the venereal infections, which he perversely accused her of generating even though she had been held hostage in the house. (By the way, this is a typical accusatory scenario in abusive dyads, as if the woman could be gaslighted into imagining herself as pernicious and promiscuous, although this was rarely, in my experience, the case.)

On a trip back home, Lester punched her in public in front of her sister, who said nothing. "But," Ileana said, I still love her to death. She's still my sister." When she threatened to go to his commanding officer about the abuse, Lester said he would kill her. So she tried to kill herself instead.

> I didn't do anything. I didn't deserve to be hit, like his child. But he knew that I loved him to death. He was my first. Who else would want me? I was cooking, cleaning, everything a wife should do. My mother told me to turn the other cheek. She didn't know what it was like. I just wanted the pain to stop.

Reporting him wouldn't have mattered, she found out later. No one at headquarters believed her anyway. Lester told them she was crazy; her suicide attempt became the proof. He cast himself as a rescuer: "I saved your life, bitch."

In no time at all Ileana got pregnant thinking, as so many women do, that now the abuse would stop. Once the identity shift inherent in pregnancy and mothering kicks in, there is an attendant magical thinking about one's own power to renegotiate the abusive relationship on better terms. (This is why I so feared Phoebe's foregoing of birth control in her second abusive relationship.) One day Lester came home with a BB gun and started shooting up the house. Ileana was five months along and eating breakfast when he put the gun in her face. "What will happen if I pull the trigger right now?" he said. "You'll take my eye out," Ileana whispered, and turned away.

> He shot me, point blank, in the back. There was blood running down. He laughed. He thought it was funny. He put me in a headlock, pushed my face into the couch, got me on the floor, tried to choke me. I didn't go to the hospital.
>
> I couldn't believe it. I couldn't absorb it.
>
> Do I look like a dog you come home and kick?
>
> It was a lot that particular day.

She gave birth to a daughter. One day, when the baby was feverish and crying, "Lester grabbed himself and said 'I'll give her something to shut her up.' When he said that, I knew he wasn't just mean. There was really something wrong with him. I could not leave my daughter alone with him." After the baby's birth though, they needed money. Lester decided to let her work. She described how she would work until 9 p.m., just to be out of the house, pick up the baby from the sitter, go home and wait on Lester, cooking and cleaning while trying to avoid his eyes. Ileana started plotting her escape.

> I took ten dollars; five dollars to open up a savings account, five dollars to open up a checking account. And every penny that I could squirrel away in those accounts, is what I did. By then I was already pregnant again. By the time I went back for my six-week check-up I was pregnant again.
>
> So when I found out I was pregnant again, "Okay, fine I'm working. I'm gonna work as long as I can. I'm gonna work, and then I'm gonna start to plan, you know, how I wanna do this. Do I wanna . . . stay and continue to get beat on? Or, do I wanna take my chances, go back home . . . eat crow, be told, "I told you so," a hundred-million times. What's better for me? And that's . . . what I spent my time doing. Weighing my options.
>
> He used to always threaten that he knew where I was, and that he'd hurt me if I left him. So I always had that to consider as well. So it wasn't as easy as just picking up and leaving.

Ileana turned out to be pregnant with twins, which Lester wanted her to abort. Ileana was deeply religious and this, finally, earned her scorn: "Just go away. I'm not begging you to stay with me. Just go! You're doing all of us a favor by just *leaving*. Cause you're *pitiful*. I mean, I don't want my daughters to know somebody like you as their father, because, you know, you're really *pathetic*." Almost immediately, Ileana said, she felt better. She was "really letting it all hang out." Because the pregnancy was high risk, Ileana became more determined than ever to get to someplace that felt safe. Lester sensed the impending abandonment.

> I was going toward the closet to get some clothes and needed to go to the supermarket and he grabbed me from behind. And he had me in a chokehold. And my ex-husband was 6′1″ and I'm only 5′7″ and he had me in a chokehold till he pulled me off my feet. Pulled my . . . my back, bent my back. Pulled me off my feet and he was whispering in my ear, "You can't leave me." And I could not leave.
>
> And then . . . he grabbed me, while I was still, you know, I was tryin' to get my grip. He grabbed me and he pulled me into the light switch that was at the top of the stairs. He tried to throw me down the stairs, and I was fighting him. Um . . . next thing I know he went . . . he left to go to work. He took my car keys, he took my house keys, I couldn't go anywhere [until he came home].
>
> I sat . . . and waited for my husband to drive me to the hospital. He watched a basketball game, he ate a sandwich, and I sat there all that time, for the

game to be over, for him to take me to the hospital. He took me to the hospital, he dropped me off . . . me and the baby off, and he left. I was in full blown labor.

I told them that my husband had strangled me and cut off my air. The doctor said, "That's what sent [the babies] into distress, cutting off the air." And then, um, the bruises started showing. I had marks around my neck from where he had broken blood vessels from around my neck when he strangled me. I had bruises on my arms from when he had pulled me into the wall with the lightswitch.

They couldn't stop my labor, so they took me up to the emergency room. They were trying to find a vein, all my veins collapsed. It was kind of hectic there for a bit. After a while I started losin' track of time. I remember the doctors, they had put my legs up in the stirrups, and the doctor, he was standin' in front of me. He looked at somebody to say something to him, and I heard the doctor scream, "Oh *shit*!" and I saw him bend down. And I saw . . . he took the baby . . . he had the baby upside down like this, that was the first baby that was born. She came out on her own. She came out, was born feet first. [The first] was breach, so they were tryin' to hold her until the anesthesiologist came to give me an emergency C-section.

My husband did not come around [until the next day]. And that's when he told me that my daughter had died. The first baby had died.

The doctors, having seen Ileana's bruises, called the police but she refused to press charges. At the baby's funeral, Lester tried to put his arm around her but "I found it really repulsive, it made me nauseous." They had buried the baby while Ileana was still in the hospital. *Lester had put only his own name on the tombstone*. It was merely a matter of time after that, she said. When the other baby got out of ICU, she left.

Asked about how it felt to discuss her history with me, after what she implied were many years of silence, she said it was "okay to walk into the past, I can walk out of here and just go back into my life. I'm good. I'm here."

There seemed not an ounce of vitriol in her, although after hearing her story, *I* was ready to hit someone. But, right before I turned off the tape recorder, she shared some evidence that aggression, no matter how dissociated, will always run the risk of surfacing in an extreme enactment. After assuring me again that her life was now good, and that she, indeed, felt quite lucky, Ileana shared a recent incident.

But, um, something happened to me, a few months ago at my house, that caused me . . . this man had said something threatening. He had threatened my family, threatened my kids, and threatened my family. And I tried my best, to break every bone in his body. Right there in front of my house, I took a bat and I . . . whacked his ribs. I was goin' for his knees, and I was just swinging the bat . . . like some lunatic, for about . . . it took two seconds. And that's about all I remember.

> I haven't been the same since. I stayed agitated. I felt out of control, like I did 20 years ago. Just highly agitated. I've alienated myself from my family . . . my [second] husband. Very, just on-edge . . . about *everything*. You know, I can't sleep, the slightest thing would set me off . . . like into a rage. It wasn't even anger, it was more of a *rage*.

Twenty years after the fact, Ileana has been diagnosed with post traumatic stress disorder (PTSD) and is taking antidepressants. She had been in therapy for a while and found it helpful but her insurance will not cover further sessions. She says that the drugs no longer seem to help her contain her aggression.

Working with self-states

Ileana's story continues to raise important questions about how clinicians and other domestic violence service providers might work differently to reverse the usual trajectory of abusive relationships. How important is the exploration of past trauma in counseling women about current situations of abuse? How do rhetorical debates over victim versus survivor labels affect the assimilation of self-states? Might a broader, less pejorative understanding of masochistic self-states enhance our ability to appreciate the relational construction of battering relationships? Would techniques such as psychodrama enhance core dynamic and analytic work and better facilitate the integration of aggressive states? These are the psychological questions. But stepping back to view the wider landscape of gender relations – occluded by a focus on individual cases of abuse – forces us to ask social questions, too.

- Is not a fundamental piece of consciousness, of necessity, political? (The implication being that every individual analysis of a battered woman must be informed by knowledge of the collective historical and psychological position of women.)
- Might this more expansive conception suggest new ways of working with women around issues of gross inequality in their relationships, even when abuse has not been explicitly physical?
- Would the therapists treating women in such circumstances have to reckon more directly with their own participation in systems of oppression?
- Finally, would female clients so empowered be more likely to recognize and halt their participation in destructive intimacy?

While, in some ways, my suggestions expand the dialogue into the terrain of what has become fairly conventional feminist thinking on domestic violence, in other ways this work goes against the political tide. Questioning the displacement of words like "victim" with words like "survivor," reintroducing concepts like masochism, and insinuating in any way that women are complicit in their horrific situations, can put one on the feminist third rail. *Rightfully so*, because psychiatric and psychoanalytic constructions of victimhood, masochism, and perceived agency have more often than not been used to recapitulate in the consulting room the oppression of women in the wider society. Yet, I am convinced that, in our fervor to rewrite women's narratives in a more powerful and agentic light, we have deprived women of the sojourn with their own states of desperate attachment, shameful acquiescence, guilty fantasies of revenge, and dissociated contempt: states which must be acknowledged and incorporated before we can all get to a place of liberation. I say "all" here because implicit in the struggle of the client to substantiate a claim to full personhood is the labor of the clinician to recognize his or her own victimhood and perpetration in the dyad, particularly around issues of gender. Traditionally there has been great reluctance on the part of clinicians, I think, to acknowledge the subtle operations of gendered privilege and benefit as they assert themselves in the transference although, notably, writers like Jessica Benjamin, Nancy Chodorow, Muriel Dimen, Virginia Goldner, and Adrienne Harris have, over the last 20 years, opened the speculum, so to speak, on this deepest, darkest interiority.

The psychosocial subject

Psychosocial theory posits that what we have traditionally conceptualized as competing spheres of knowledge (psychology and sociology, for example, or psychoanalysis and political theory) are, in truth, quite complementary. The idea isn't new – it has been pressed over the last century by leading scholars coming from many different kinds of training. Anthropologist George Devereux (1978), writing in *Ethnopsychoanalysis*, argued that "it is not only possible but *mandatory* to explain a behavior, already explained in one way, also in another way, with another frame of reference."

In physics, complementarity refers to the fact that the world is realized in dual ways; everything has a visible and an invisible side. When we perceive red, we can't perceive green. They are color complements. This doesn't mean that one color stops existing when you see the other. The principle is most aptly illustrated in figure–ground illusions: here, you see a vase; there, two profiles meeting. It has been used to great effect in art, such as Dali's famous painting, *Abraham Lincoln*. If you view the painting from afar, you see only the face of the former president. If observed up close, the painting details the death of Christ. You can never see both images at once, although they exist simultaneously and, in fact, are mutually constituted. Literally, without the lines and shapes and colors that make Christ, there is no Lincoln. The painting demonstrates Dali's skillfulness in art because he can pull off this feat of mixed perspective on the canvas. But the same thing can be said of Dali's artful metaphor in the painting: *without the lines and shapes and colors that make Christ, there is no Lincoln.*

Similarly, the social and the psychological are not merely separate domains that interact and end up having an additive effect on subjects. For example, if you are both poor and seduced by a parent and happen to be gendered as female, you are more likely to grow up to be a prostitute than if you endure any of the three conditions alone. This is because the sexual self in this case is *simultaneously* constituted by anatomy, patriarchy, economic status, and personal trauma. A psychosocial subject is *simultaneously* a social construction and a psychic production, a psychosocial subject is, *simultaneously*, completely idiosyncratic and an embodiment of universal themes. In regard to work with battered women, this outlook leads to the conclusion that "relationships in which women are abused are not unique but, rather, exemplify in extremis the stereotypical gender arrangements that structure intimacy between men and women generally" (Goldner et al., 1990, p. 344). It is with this understanding of subjects and subjective accounts that I began speaking with women.

The absence of aggression, the presence of violence

The stories of women in my sample illustrate the extreme degree to which the suppression, repression, and/or dissociation of aggressive thoughts and feelings can auger bad endings. Every woman in my sample struggled with her own aggression, at times cutting anger off simply because it was safer to do so; at other times clinging to a self image of goodness, or silent suffering, that precluded assertion. Mostly, the dissociation of aggressive affects became second nature: a default to passivity that allowed women to maintain both a romanticized version of their situation and the illusion of choice, even as dissociation inhibited any true agency.

Many women at the time of the interview still felt extremely protective of their battering partners as if, even from this long remove, they feared the repercussions of their own harsh thoughts and words. Rarely, in fact, were there angry proclamations. Even when questioned specifically about aggressive feelings in response to their unjust treatment, most women denied having ever felt indignant, outraged, or contemptuous of their abusers at the time violence was occurring, although some (particularly those who had received some long term counseling) now said that, in retrospect, they could recognize that the absence of such emotion had contributed to their inability to muster the strength or energy to leave their relationships.

Extreme dissociation

Doris in many ways typified the dissociative trajectory of women in abusive relationships. She came from a background of severe maltreatment. Doris's father punished her with a knotted electrical cord in the bathtub: "One lash could remove your skin if he did it with enough force. Takes the skin right off your body." Her husband reminded her of that father, she said, the first time he hauled off and hit her for cursing at him in a fight. Yet she took the punch as a sign that the relationship was deepening. Threatened but strangely buoyed, she remembered "it frightened me but it made, in my own insanity, [me think], wow, he's really starting to care for me. Even though it should have been scary, it was welcome because now I know he cares." Even as his control of her reached alarming proportions, any negative feelings on Doris's part were suppressed or dissociated. Doris even told me that she considered the fact that her husband stayed in the room while she had sex with strange men for money as his way of protecting her. I realize that this may have been true on some level but was quite struck by Doris's reluctance to impute any other possible intention to him, or to acknowledge any even marginally mixed feelings within herself.

Even after her husband had been jailed a dozen times for beating her, she says, "I didn't think it was a problem. We just had a little spat. Oh, we're gonna make this work." They had been together many years and she tried to remember better times, before alcohol and drugs had twisted their love into Gordian knots. Doris dispassionately related that her husband anally raped her.

Interviewer: Did you tell anyone?
Doris: Who was there to tell, Doctor? My mother was a victim. Her mother was a victim. Our lives were predominantly taken over by the males in our households. *Who were we going to tell? Each other?*

Doris never admitted that she was angry at her husband, to herself, her family, or him. Then, one night, she severed her husband's jugular vein with a kitchen knife during a fight. Even when she killed him, she says, she was not aware of being angry. Interestingly, it was only in prison, serving time for his murder, that Doris began to acknowledge a broader range of emotion and to express anger in threatening circumstances.

> When I went to prison, I was very unique and tender. But after three years, I'm very angry. I'm quick to challenge and confront a person . . . Who do they think they are? I've already been down that road in my marriage.

Doris's dream is to open a domestic violence shelter. She does some outreach work to victims and batterers in her community. At a recent presentation, she overheard a male audience member say "Fuck a divorce. Just go home and kill the bitch" to another man complaining about his marriage. She says she knows the sentiment only too well, and wishes she had been mad enough to leave before finding herself in prison, guilty of a homicide she didn't intend to commit.

Mild dissociation

Bunny, on the other hand, experienced a slower build-up of violence in her relationship, was less dissociated, and was able to leave her batterer after the first episode of extreme violence. From a childhood home where her father beat her mother and her mother had beaten her while proclaiming "If not for you, I would not be in this relationship," Bunny was quick to recognize that her husband's possessiveness portended something worse. "I have no privacy. If I leave my bag and go to the ladies room, he will search this bag." He would drop her off at work at 8 a.m. but then "come back at 9, at 12. Not to talk to me, to show me that he can see me." She knew instinctively that something was very wrong.

Interviewer: What kinds of emotions were you having?
Bunny: I was angry at myself.
Interviewer: At yourself, not him?
Bunny: First, at myself.
Interviewer: How do you mean?
Bunny: Because I think that I didn't know. First I used to be mad at my mom. I said, okay, my mom should have told me about relationship and men. He didn't want me going to school, have a friend at school, talk to people . . . you have no privacy, no friend. Everybody leave you. The next time was the beating.
Interviewer: What did you do with your anger?
Bunny: I used to do painting with myself when I was angry. I used to do all this painting of one man with one side laughing and the other side is just like evil.

School and work kept Bunny alive. Then one day her husband surprised her in the shower and beat her very badly after she had announced that she had a job opportunity. She left the country shortly afterwards, leaving her children behind even though she knew that she could be charged with abandonment and lose custody of them. When asked what flipped for her that enabled her to leave, she answered, "What flipped for me was the truth." Asked to elaborate, Bunny said that she had learned to distinguish truth and lies. Her insight was a recognition of her husband's malign intent that, I would argue, was made possible by Bunny preserving her own anger, even if it was at the periphery of awareness. Bunny never disowned her own aggression, although it was often misdirected, and this allowed her to recognize similar states in her abuser.

> At first [when he followed me to work] all the employees would say "Oh, your husband loves you." or "Maybe he not trust you." But I know he's not holding my hand because he loves me so much. He's holding my hand because it's like "I arrest you." In my country there's no 911 to call in the middle of the night. I cried every day. I told myself, if I don't do that – *leave* – I will kill myself.

No dissociation

Hayal's father is a polygamist. She has ten siblings.

> My mom was very abusive to me and my sisters. She would bite us. Use hangers. She once closed the door on my foot and I had to get stitches. She

> was like a jungle woman. Her own mother died when [she] was eight. She was raised by village women who abused her.

In addition, Hayal's uncle and father often beat the women in the family: her aunts, nieces, sisters and mother were all victims.

> I remember my mom getting a miscarriage because of him. She was in a tub, it was full of blood, and just like a lot of violence. It was just really, very, very violent and the women were just terrified of the men.

In her teens, Hayal was taken to her father's home country and sold into an arranged marriage. "I was tricked. There's no 911. I didn't know how to get to the American Embassy." The groom had participated in the gang rape of a village girl and needed to get out of the country before he was forced to marry her. Hayal was married in a quick ceremony and the couple returned to the United States. They had two kids, nine months apart. Her husband stole the WIC checks meant to cover food for her babies. She remembered when he became enraged and hit her.

> My kids woke up in the middle of the night. I was trying to breastfeed one and I pushed the other away. He saw that I pushed my son and he slapped me. I talked back to him and cursed him. He grabbed me by my hair. The little one was on my chest. He pulled me to the floor. I mean he banged my head, punched me in the mouth. I was crying and sobbing and the little one was still on my chest. And I just kept telling him "The baby! The baby! The baby!"

The very next day, Hayal went to a domestic violence agency and began her safety planning. Then she signed up for college classes, against not only her husband's wishes, but those of her entire family.

> My mother was sorry she had helped me stay in school when I was younger, when the other female children were [illegally] taken out. She told me: "If I would have known, I would have left you in the house like a dog." My parents always stuck up for my husband because he's a man. My mother cursed me out "Oh, you don't want his dick? Do you want a bigger dick? Is his dick not big enough for you? You're a fucking slut."

Nonetheless. Hayal persevered.

> I got educated and started using terms like women and oppression. My husband was very intimidated. He didn't have a high school diploma. He would stalk me on the way to school. My mom would go tell him "She's still in love with you."

Hayal was terrorized, she said, the only time she admitted to a robotic interface with the facts of her life: "You do dissociate, you do"; yet she seemed to have employed the defensive tactic purposefully. Her husband would wake her up at night. He raped her and wouldn't let her use birth control. Amazingly, frightened as she was, she could not countenance the injustice of it. "I got pissed off and went to my DV worker," Hayal said. She got a diaphragm and an order of protection.

Interviewer: Sounds like you hated him.
Hayal: Of course. I wished he was dead. There was a part of me that wished he would die, like God, just kill him. I mean I definitely had a lot of resentment. Still do. I'm still afraid, also. That's okay. Yeah, there's still a lot of stuff I struggle with till now, but there's definitely been progress.

Hayal was by far the least dissociative of the women I interviewed, despite the intense level of abuse in her childhood home. (I wondered how the normative nature of abuse toward women and children in her country of origin affected the psychological processing of her experiences, perhaps rendering them less traumatic in some ironic way.) In hearing her story, I was impressed with her self-esteem, her realistic appraisal of her situation, and her agency in the face of extraordinary danger posed by not only her husband, but other members of her family who felt she had dishonored them.

By the end of the interview, it was late evening. I offered to walk Hayal out of the building to the street. She demurred, saying that there was a price on her head and she wouldn't want to put me in harm's way. Of course, I knew that on some level she must dissociate this, in order to go on living. Yet, Hayal seemed very aware and quite agentic, as she left my office for the dark streets below. I do not know how exactly she kept her aggression close enough to empower her throughout her ordeal, but she did. Her abusive relationship ended earlier than any other in my sample, although, owing to cultural conditions which supported her husband's "right" to beat her, she may have faced the greatest obstacles.

Victim self-states

The secondary self that rises in response to abuse can be quite circumscribed, arising on the scene unbidden in moments of stark fear and then retreating, or it can comprise a panoply of affects and cognitions that come to engender a parallel mode of living: "While the victim of a single acute trauma may say she is 'not herself' since the event, the victim of chronic trauma may lose the sense that she has a self" (Herman, 1992b, p. 385). Doris and Ileana are examples of how dissociation can get quite stark, in the sense that personality itself becomes built around unformulated experiences of trauma, and the identity that interfaces with the world is in total schism with itself. Such a strongly dissociated person, or a fragment of her, is skating on the edge of a donut hole. Others somehow escape this most dire dissociation and manage to skim the perimeter of attention with a less malignant splitting, one foot in enactment and the other not, aware that they behave in compartmentalized ways but clearly unable to stop themselves. The majority of women with whom I spoke demonstrated some mixture of this "strong" and "weak" dissociation (Stern, 1997).

While women committed to staying with abusive men abided their partner's tragic flaws, they had great trouble accepting the shadow versions of their own personalities, the avatars who walked, talked, and looked like them but housed few of the qualities that they could recognize as their own. For many women, the crux of bad love was not whether they could tolerate their tyrannical or impulsive mate but whether they could stomach who they themselves had become under his reign. For the women whose "benign split of the ego" (Stone, 1977) allowed them to consciously experience – at least partially – the actions of a second self, an overpowering wish to end such forced multiplicity drove them to end their relationships. A woman named Millie, whose story appears below, came to believe that it was the victim-self who obscured what she was and could be, much more than the man who stood sentry to her activities, and much more than the caregivers in whose image she had originally been cast.

Placing her addiction to a lover who abused her in perspective, Millie called her own child abuse "a gateway drug." Millie had been abandoned by her mother, and her father was in prison. While living with an abusive relative during her teen years, Millie got pregnant and left home to live with a man who ended up assaulting her both physically and sexually. She caught a break when he went to prison for shooting someone, she said, but then he returned, saying that he found God and pouring out "lots of sweet talk." Millie let him move back in but the "same stuff" happened again. It took six more years to get him out of the house: "You couldn't even imagine a worse movie." She waited for a particularly bad episode to have him taken away by the police.

Interviewer: How long has it been since he went away?

Millie: It's been a little over two years. Almost three years and I almost despise him.

Interviewer: Almost?

Millie: Almost.

Interviewer: What keeps you from despising him?

Millie: Because it's not worth it. For me to let him have that kind of emotion over my life. He's not that significant anymore.

Interviewer: Are you still frightened?

Millie: Somewhat. Somewhat. You know, because you just never know. Like, when's he gonna come out and [*inaudible*]. You know, try to disrupt my world. I don't think I'm frightened physically of what he'll do to me. That part's over. The only thing he can do to me is kill me. That's not my concern. And once I'm dead, I'm dead. That part doesn't even scare me. What scares me is that I'm so happy and I feel like he's like the only thing in the world that can take that away from me.

> I just didn't want to be that person anymore. I did not want to be that person anymore. I didn't like what I saw when I looked in the mirror. I wasn't happy. I lost so much weight. I just didn't like that person. I didn't like who she was. And I knew that he was the catalyst. That he had to go. That's the only way that I was going to get rid of *her*. The only way. Because as long as I was with *him*, I was going to be *her*. And I didn't want her raising my kids, and I didn't want her representing, you know, my family.

Stuart W. Twemlow (1995), writing of the dialectic between victim and victimizer, observed that "violence seems to bond people in a bizarre and perverse pathological intimacy" (p. 545). Such an attachment eschews the normal boundaries of interaction and pushes participants ever more deeply into the abyss of their acquired roles. Simply speaking, violent dyads trigger one another's worst selves. Self-states of power are dissociated by the victim just as states of vulnerability are disowned by the victimizer. Neither is a whole person; they come to desperately need one another just to feel complete.

It has been suggested that the woman in a situation of domestic violence is masochistic; after all, why does she stay in the face of escalating assaults, often marrying her abuser only after many years of dating violence, choosing to start a family with him just as abuse crests, or returning to him after finally getting up the nerve to walk out? A robust feminist literature has responded by outlining the many ways in which woman seek respite from their circumstances through both passive and active resistance (Waldrop and Resnick, 2004; Hyden, 1999). Andrea Westlund (1999) has even called attention to the punitive – albeit unconscious – tendency of clinicians in "helping" occupations (including psychiatry and psychoanalysis) to recapitulate the very master–slave dynamic that women are trying to escape by labeling the women "masochistic," thus blaming them for their own abuse. Indeed, the mantra at most victim advocacy organizations, that "domestic violence can happen to anyone," inveighs against the notion of any characterological propensity to become a target of spousal assault. But what then do we say about the way that childhood abuse predicts adult victimization, and the manner in which victims continue to engage their batterers long past any hope of ending the violence? If not trending toward dissociative defenses honed during early trauma, how do women ignore such blaring signals of danger? If not masochists, why are they behaving so masochistically? And given the particular cultural discourses that permeate the bonds between certain men and certain women, who could blame them?

Young and Gerson (1991) have persuasively argued that the ideas of "characterological development, survival strategies, and adaptations to trauma need not be viewed as being mutually exclusive, and are, in fact, inextricably intertwined." The authors move masochism away from its early Freudian roots, which defined masochism as a perverse pleasure in pain (Freud, 1924). In Young and Gerson's telling, "relational masochism" has nothing to do with pleasure. Masochism is reconfigured as the unavoidable cost of certain love arrangements; the price tag on attachment. We all know people who will bear almost any indignity to remain with a love object. But what would be the developmental pathway for such self-abasement?

Fonagy et al. (2002), utilizing attachment theory, have articulated ways in which abused children may internalize the perpetrator's state (withdrawal, rage, etc.) as part of their own self-structure, yet continue to experience it as alien, persecutory, and chaotic. Partnering with new abusers later in life could be seen as an attempt to externalize the source of danger in order to control it, much the same way that internalizing those same states once acted to titrate the sense of one's childhood caretaker as villainous. Such seesawing attachments have a kind of disorganized death grip on the strange homeostasis the relationship provides.

> Relational masochism is a defensive reaction to the sadism of another person, a reaction motivated by the need for love and attention. Such needs are basic for survival and therefore are apt to induce attempts at attachment even in the most paradoxical situations.
>
> (Young and Gerson, 1991, p. 33)

Goldner (1999) and others have repeatedly called attention to the way that the term masochism has been used to further bludgeon women by suggesting that they are somehow responsible for their own abuse (this theme is explored more fully in Chapter 3). Clearly, this *is* problematic. Indeed, even terms like battered woman's syndrome and diagnoses of post traumatic stress disorder, by focusing on the pathological aftermath of abuse for victims, shift the onus of abnormality to the woman's corner. On the other hand, in many quarters, it has become de rigueur to refer to women in situations of domestic violence as survivors rathers than victims, a designation that highlights their strengths but, by demanding that a particular kind of face be put on their experiences, may unintentionally deprive them of the full range of affect that accompanies trauma. Goldner's work at the Gender and Violence Project of the Ackerman Institute has in large part been devoted to articulating the emotional complexity of violent relationships, including couples' intransigent bonds, without forsaking the political and moral call to liberate victims from a second round of battering, in word or deed, this time by the institutions charged with helping them.

I agree that in its original sexualized meaning, "masochism" would not describe the character of any but a meager few female participants in violent relationships. (The term "sadism" in its original psychoanalytic conception would also not capture the character of many male abusers; with sadism however, we have accepted a more a generalized usage of the term.) However, I believe that in a broadened conceptual framework that considers the origins of entrenched self-states considered "not me" personifications of early developmental traumas, the terms masochism – and sadism – offer a useful way of understanding how a part of the self cranes towards relational darkness, repeatedly mistaking it for light. The idea of a victim self-state may also help to explain the paradox of battered women whose engagement with friends, colleagues, and acquaintances shows no hint of subservience, while their romantic encounters expose a consistent trend toward capitulation – in some cases studded with moments of unbridled aggression – whether or not they are threatened with explicit violence. Donnel Stern (2010) notes the conditional nature of dissociated enactments in that they are elicited only within specific interpersonal contexts; they are triggered by certain situations or in proximity to particular individuals.

> The more urgent the need to isolate one's own "not-me" in the other, the more hateful and intensely sadistic the enactments necessary to accomplish the task . . . it is much more likely in enactments that protect one from having to bear the unbearable, for the relatedness to degenerate into violence, physical or emotional.
>
> (p. 156)

Just as the child submits to the abuser in order to preserve the illusion of caretaking, so too does the battered woman indulge the fantasy of being loved through her surrender, an idea strongly reinforced within the social context of contemporary gender relations. As Socarides (1958) observed, the person in such a relationship develops a defensive, masochistic adaptation – to the demands of an overly harsh superego – that makes the punishment they have endured seem reasonable and perhaps even deserved. Add to this a cultural chorus of words and images that venerates female suffering as the prelude to rescue and romantic love. Indeed, in a 2008 study of "femininity" scripts, Boonzaier found that battered women's acceptance of cultural depictions of their sex as passive, loving caretakers often went hand in hand with their reluctance to leave abusive situations and to blame themselves for attacks. These women idealized romantic love even when their day-to-day reality was steeped in pain; dissociation allowed them to make that concession. In the poetic words of Deleuze (1989), "in masochism we find a progression from disavowal to suspense, from disavowal as a process of liberation from the pressures of the superego to suspense as incarnation of the ideal" (p. 127).

Whether the recipient of abuse is a child or an adult, what is demanded of the victim may be no less than a complete denial of her own aggression. Drained of self-righteous anger, child and adult victims alike are rendered impotent in the face of incursions into their physical and mental integrity: collapsed boundaries invite greater abuse, and masochistic entreaties maintain it. It is the premise of my research that, when an adult woman forfeits her aggression – often a defensive posture learned in childhood and maintained through cultural representations of gender – the main vehicle for her agency is gone. It becomes then nearly impossible for her to terminate the relationship; the batterer holds her outrage – and thus her ability to leave – hostage. As Judith Herman (1992a) has observed, the fear of retribution that inaugurates the dissociation of anger can persist past any actual threat from the perpetrator and may expand to encompass those perceived as bystanders to the abuse. The surfeit of energy used to keep this rage under control contributes to the likelihood that its ultimate expression will be volcanic. Indeed, the more dissociated the woman's aggression is, the more likely it becomes that the dénouement of the relationship will contain greatly increased levels of violence, with one or the other of the parties finally exploding the tension between them through a titanic enactment.

If this is true, then one implication for treatment with women in abusive relationships is that highly specific work on the integration and expression of dissociated aggression is a desirable adjunct to more general psychoanalytic methods. Despite its inherent dangers and difficulties, the reflective demonstration of negative emotions – such as anger and contempt – might be a necessary game-changer for women mired in violent relationships. Since social proscriptions surrounding women's expression of aggression may constrain even therapeutic endeavors, a particular attention to the operation of gender-related themes in the dyad is in order.

The idea of working specifically to integrate aggressive thoughts, feelings, and fantasies began for me during work with violent perpetrators (Stein, 2007). The idea expanded during my work with Phoebe, who had cycled through two abusive relationships, when I realized that her problems with dissociated aggression were not dissimilar to the problems of men I had interviewed in prison. For both abused women and violent perpetrators, the dissociation of negative feelings leads to troubling interpersonal enactments while the integration and expression of negative feelings fosters safety and survival.

I am persuaded that women who dissociate negative affect are likely to remain longer in their destructive relationships and that these relationships tend to be further along the continuum of violence. There is no way to know for sure whether chronic conditions of greater brutality lead to increased dissociation or whether dissociation itself provides the disabling context that enables men to increase their violence against women without fearing retribution or abandonment. When I unwound women's stories, both conditions seemed to hold: as I have averred elsewhere, it appears that "dissociation is both the harbinger of violence and its consequence" (Stein, 2007). However, it is not news that trauma causes dissociation. What has been less studied and discussed is the way that dissociation prolongs and even intensifies trauma by facilitating the relational dynamics of abuse. Increased violence, in turn, stokes dissociative rejoinders to threat, cementing the victim's failure to initiate action toward terminating the relationship or, at least, reducing the power differential, perhaps lessening the likelihood that abuse will occur.

Sometimes subjects' dissociative responses were rooted in their devaluation by their own mothers, a common childhood dynamic for adult women in abusive relationships. As mentioned above, according to Goldner (2004, p. 351), such women seek out the father not because they want a penis, but to avoid "the despair of negation and invisibility." In this context, the eventual bonding with an abuser is not so surprising. The abuser's incapacity to give must feel familiar, while their battery – emotional or physical – is a kind of twisted recognition of the abused person's power to wrest interest, even from the jaws of abandonment. Yet the implicit contract between the two lovers requires her to continually forget what is happening to her, just as she did in childhood.

Ileana, for example, had a childhood marked by the alternating conditions of abuse and neglect by parents to whom she remained loyal, despite their treatment of her. The cliché of being "loved to death" turned out to be a discerning and heartbreaking commentary about the final episode of her marriage. After all, what is trauma if not a massive linguistic failure, an end to the ability to use fantasy and metaphor in explaining one's world, a resort to hollow non-associative word strings lacking nuance and abstraction (Krystal, 1988)? In Ileana's case, the cliché was concretized when her husband pushed her down the stairs while she was pregnant with twins. One of them was, literally, loved to death.

Only retrospectively did Ileana recognize an early warning sign of her adult partner's emotional abandonment, when he cancelled their elaborate wedding plans at the last minute. Her automatic capitulation in the face of this emotional assault is stunning: "I didn't bother him anymore with it. What was I supposed to do? I'd spent all my money. Looking back, everything happens for a reason. Let sleeping dogs lie. Later he wanted to get married, so we eloped." The first night after this elopement, Ileana found a letter from another woman to whom her husband had apparently proposed. She saw the leasing agreement for the apartment they shared and her name wasn't on it. When the first phone bill came she was told that she was no longer allowed to call home. One time, he punched her in public in front of her sister, who said nothing. "But," Ileana said, I still love her to death. She's still my sister." Her loyalty knew no bounds. The more others betrayed her, the more she claimed to love them. Her anger even now, 20 years after the apocalyptic ending of her marriage, can only be glimpsed in the reckless enactments of her PTSD.

Another woman, Marta, demurred from expressing hostility toward the man who beat her, explaining that her anger was reserved for other women who thought it could not happen to them.

> [Mimicking] It wouldn't have been me. I don't care what happened. I would never accept that. You don't know that until you've been in that situation and if you haven't been educated as to, you know, not accepting abuse, or you've been abused as a child, the cycle continues and you just accept it because this is how you've been socialized. And people don't really believe that. But if you're an abused child, this is how you are – you are ingrained to believe that it's acceptable for someone to do this to you. And you have to know what it is to experience that for someone to say, "I love you but I hit you," or "I love you but I do these bad things to you." And if you learn this as a child, it's like learning the alphabet. And you learn that and it's right. And you go through your whole life reciting the alphabet. And you go through your whole life being abused and now as an adult, you're abused, it's OK because no one's

ever said to you, "The alphabet's wrong." And no one's ever said to you, "The abuse is wrong." So you accept it.

Bessel Van der Kolk and his colleagues (2005) have argued that the unique circumstances of ongoing interpersonal abuse bequeath a traumatic syndrome not reflected in current diagnostic criteria for post traumatic stress disorder (PTSD). They argue that victims are better described as suffering from Disorders of Extreme Stress Not Otherwise Specified (DESNOS), a designation that would capture the overwhelming loss of trust, safety, and coherent selfhood that endure, and that suggests a different treatment emphasis, particularly around issues of affect regulation and dissociation. Moreover, the behavioral adaptations to complex trauma – such as passivity, dependence, or hypervigilance – are often confused with characterological dispositions, leading clinicians toward misdiagnosis and badly formulated therapeutic interventions (Herman, 1992b).

The politics of passivity

Despite the powerful frame that childhood set, in speaking with women, it became clear to me that the facility with which they disowned aggressive parts of themselves was only partly born of the habituation to abuse in earlier relationships. Female passivity was as much a product of the cultural pressure to abide a set of gender regulations as was their partners' resort to the forceful show of power that masculinity demands. It is thus my strong belief that individual treatments working on intrapsychic and interpersonal levels to increase the consciousness of dissociated states must also work to raise political consciousness. Indeed, many of the women with whom I spoke had, in the wake of their own experiences, become involved in social action networks that educate others about domestic violence. Almost all who had done so found their awakening regarding gender inequality to be at least as important to their recovery – including staying away from abusive relationships – as the decision to enter individual therapy. Some recent empirical work suggests that battered women who can maintain the idea that ideal relationships are those in which partners have equivalent power ultimately perceive themselves as more agentic, with greater potential to assert themselves either in the relationship or by leaving (Baly, 2010). The analyzed and integrated psyche is less fragile than the blind and fragmented one, yes, but it is most robust in the context of this broader mindfulness. If work with abused women is to have a long lasting impact, they must be appreciated as psychological and social subjects, both. Indeed, my own work with Phoebe around her destructive romantic relationships taught me the importance of exploring with the client a world of collusive enactments around gender of which I, too, am a part.

Jessica Benjamin (1988) writes convincingly of the steep learning curve on which young girls become, by adulthood, the foil for men's desire to dominate. Women persevere in situations of chronic subjugation, in part, because they recognize the fragility underlying men's attitudes of supremacy and it falls to them to make the supposedly "moral" choice to maintain relations at any cost. If a prerequisite to the man's sadism is the shuttering of an empathic recognition of the woman he beats, then its counterpart is the victim's mirroring masochistic response of willingly forsaken subjectivity. A battered woman's identity and memory – especially their more contentious aspects – must be submerged to her partner's critique of her as unstable or provocative; her self-state of acquiescence emerges as the only viable contest to his violence, like some antique call-and-response slave chant. Although the call and the response to it hold many covert meanings, it is only from the safer distance that time without violence provides that a woman "can allow [herself] to remember . . . what emerges is often a deep anger and a great bitterness" (Goldner, 1998, p. 284).

Problematically, this dissociation of her aggression – which promotes an attitude of submission – rather than calming the perpetrator, serves to incite him further. As Benjamin's rendering of Winnicott's take on early dyadic interactions implies, the *lack* of embodied resistance to brutality is tantamount to her refusing to recognize his power, his presence, his very existence. Like Winnicott's infant, in the absence of boundaries, the attacker becomes enraged; he feels as "if the other caves in and withdraws under my act, my act drops off the edge of that emptiness, and I feel I will soon follow" (Benjamin, 1988, p. 165). As in war, increased aggression is the response to the provocation of retreat, making her dissociated withdrawal the cause, as well as the consequence, of his attack. Without indignation or anger as an organizing force, her capitulation to further attacks becomes a foregone conclusion, as does his advancing assault in search of a boundary.

These positions: male/female, dominant/submissive, passive/aggressive, batterer/victim are all binary and foreclose the possibility of a woman (and her partner, for that matter) embracing either a multiplicity of selves or a discourse not engineered along simple polarities. If, as Barvosa-Carter (2001) avers, agency is found in the odds that someone can at least choose a *variation* of the repetitive themes that constrain them, then therapists are honor bound to vary the cultural discourses they channel. This is particularly important in the area of gendered constructions of the emotions, where all that is aggressive may be labeled masculine and all that signals aggression having been turned inward, as in depression or self-destruction, is considered feminine (see Chodorow's patient "J.", 2002, p. 243).

Without a broader reflection on cultural scripts, male therapists may be unwittingly reproducing the dynamics of control and submission in abusive relationships. Merely by the selves they model in the consulting room, female therapists may unintentionally collude in the notion that attachment trumps the sovereignty of self, or that attunement is more valorous than differentiation. I myself, during the course of these interviews, and also in clinical work with abused women (Stein, 2011), have been forced to reflect upon my own compromises as a woman and mother living in a world that is not gender neutral when it comes to the assertion of control and the distribution of power. It was often difficult hearing about the various ways that my interviewees' egos had completely collapsed, knowing that they looked at me, because of my assigned role, as somehow less fragile. In truth, every woman – me included – can shamefully recall multiple measures of her own complicity in oppression.

Various kinds of therapy based on feminist theory have attempted to incorporate a greater sensitivity toward issues of gender by viewing individual problems in the context of the sociopolitical circumstances of men's and women's lives. Walker (1994) articulates a vision for incorporating the basic tenets of trauma therapy with this underlying holistic approach, one in which safety and empowerment are the two central goals of treatment. The treatment has a large educative component, aimed at helping women to identify the difference between abusive and normal encounters and to recognize their own aggressive behaviors. Walker's "survivor therapy" while acknowledging the dissociative array of adaptations to abuse, focuses primarily on "changing external situations rather than [. . .] internal intrapsychic problems" (p. 312). Therapists working with women still in situations of danger, indeed, may not have the luxury of exploring deeper levels of affect and motivation.

Psychoeducational models are very useful in work with battered women, whether or not they have left their abusers. As previously mentioned, some of the women in my study had become advocates and educators about domestic violence in their communities following membership in support groups that focused on the link between personal problems and cultural acceptance of violence against women. They found activism in itself to be a positive kind of therapy for their traumatic pasts.

Other women in my study had rejected support groups when they first came out of their relationships. They had been in therapy intermittently, depending mostly, they said, on their financial resources or insurance coverage. Two women had been in long-term therapy where they had worked on deeper issues of identity and affect in the wake of having suffered multiple types of abuse. As Judith Herman (1992a) says, "while patients with simple posttraumatic stress disorder fear they may be losing their minds, patients with the complex disorder often feel they have lost themselves" (p. 158).

Such patients may need intensive psychotherapy geared toward the reintegration of disparate self-states split off in a desperate attempt to maintain functionality in highly dysfunctional circumstances. The therapist must struggle with having the patient relive parts of the trauma in order to construct a meaningful narrative of events that incorporates affect yet does not retraumatize. The utmost concern is for creating a safe place for the retelling of trauma, the fantasies of suicide and homicide that may accompany them, and the profound sense of loss that follows having ceded parts of the self to the abuser.

This chapter has focused on just one element of what is often lost: the anger that is an appropriate response to threat or harm and which may fuel agency and self-protective action. Too often for the women I interviewed, anger became dislocated and consciously inaccessible. Anger was replaced by a self-state of shame and seemingly masochistic resolve that led women to, at best, endure and, at worst, provoke greater abuse from partners incited by their acquiescence. This, in turn, sometimes elicited even greater enactments of aggression from the women themselves, whose anger rose in unconscious and unstoppable waves of violence.

Chapter 4

Masochism as medium

You fit into me
Like a hook into an eye
A fish hook
An open eye
(Margaret Atwood, *Power Politics*)

Phoebe asked if I thought she was a masochist. "I don't know," I said, "what is a masochist?"

"Someone who does the same thing over and over and expects different results."

"I think that's the colloquial definition of insanity," I ventured.

Phoebe was undeterred: "Yeah. Same thing."

Visualizing Phoebe's self-states in relationship to men brought up images of haplessness and willful ignorance, a touch of *la belle indifférence*, but certainly not pain-seeking or exquisite suffering. She was no Réagian "O" (Réage, 1954). Phoebe's dissociative stations ran the gamut only from the naïve Justine, whose path to virtue ineluctably wound through a bramble of rape and torture (de Sade, 1791) to the loveless – but slightly more integrated – hedonist, Juliette (de Sade, 1797). We did not name her parts but this is how I thought of them, as the Marquis's complements, Juliette and Justine, a splintered self who artlessly caricatured both the "misfortunes of virtue" and the inevitable pitfalls of libertinage. Although de Sade repudiates the punitive conscience: "Nature has *not* got two voices, you know, one of them condemning all day what the other commands" (1795, p. 72, italics mine), Phoebe was proof of the conjoined twinship of such lived paradoxes. My office was the place that she condemned by day the siren song she answered on her darkest nights.

The nature of Phoebe's victimhood was somehow blundering and unintentional, in short: dissociated. Abusive interactions had an ethereal quality I would come to recognize in the stories of numerous women I interviewed, who seemed always to be getting sucker punched despite a well-worn history of similar engagements. Hearing their stories made me feel like the audience to a horror film where everyone knows what is coming well in advance of the unsuspecting female prey. One interviewee, for example, provided numerous anecdotes about having been ambushed and pummeled on entering the house, on leaving the bedroom, in the park, on the stairs, outside the movie theater. She finished each story with the menacing declaration, "Nobody punches me!", as if her tattered pride and split lip (and a sturdier self-state) could be conjured by such after-the-fact conceit.

Still, I was quick to protect Phoebe from the self-blame that the term "masochism" might invite. The term has been conflated in psychiatric nosology with sexual masochism, a condition where degradation, humiliation, and physical pain elicits sexual arousal and orgasm. In popular usage, the word can be a conversational shortcut to excuse a man's violence by shifting attention to a woman's supposed provocation. Even in certain psychoanalytic settings, where the dynamics of domestic violence may be poorly understood, "masochism" can be an imputation of female volition that shields the perpetrator from responsibility for his acts.

Honestly, it feels unsettling to even consider the role of masochism in abusive relationships, as if I am betraying my sex. However, when I think back on my own relationships, all the times I did not stand up for myself or draw a line to protect my autonomy, I wonder: Had I been trained, by virtue of my gender, into some Hegelian master–slave dialectic, as suggested by de Beauvoir (1952)? When I rush to tell Phoebe that she most certainly is *not* a masochist, is it a dry clinical assessment? Or a massive transference enactment?

In common parlance, a masochist is someone who likes to be hurt and I certainly detected no pleasure in Phoebe's abusive assignations. Even so, I was haunted by the specter of "Phoebe love," a kind of mutually parasitic arrangement I had come to expect in my patient's romances, an arrangement that each host dreaded yet consistently provoked, and one in which Phoebe ended up the paradigmatic loser. I told Phoebe that she was not a masochist, just someone for whom pain was remarkably familiar and thus habitually invoked. Like the majority of abused women I had interviewed, she came from a home in which all kinds of personal boundaries had been violated. For most of the women, pain was the order of the day; something simply to be borne without question or retaliation. They bonded to the pain as much as to the men who kept it in steady supply. After battering incidents, they pulled the pain over themselves like a scratchy woolen blanket. Accustomed to it, they endured. That is very different from saying that they "wanted" it. On the other hand, you can only parse so much.

Helplessness or hopefulness?

Some of the women I interviewed would not let go of their relationships even though there existed no obvious external reasons to remain, like financial dependency or child custody issues. Others repeatedly returned to men who hurt them terribly, or chose new men with similar behaviors. The literature has called this "learned helplessness" or even full blown PTSD, citing the destruction of felt agency in the face of constant blows to the ego. Others have cleverly called it "learned hopefulness," citing the enduring belief many women hold that their abusive partners will change despite abundant evidence to the contrary (LaViolette and Barnett, 2000). The women seem naïve at best and, at worst, gluttons for punishment. Yet, one of the most surprising things I found in talking to women victimized by men in long-term relationships is that the part of the self which is most prone to allowing such blatant trespass seems not to represent a general personality configuration at all.

Masochistic, self-defeating behaviors are rarely global and, although the focus of my thesis is not the sadistic partner, I have done enough work with violent men to testify that what appears as characterological heartlessness is usually fragmentary as well. I would describe most of the women in my sample as fairly potent with others, both at work and socially. However, a demarcated victim self seems to develop in response to particular environmental precursors and to become embedded as a security operation of the self-system. Rather than pursuing pleasure, or even satisfaction, a somewhat circumscribed piece of the person remains mired in developmental epochs where the avoidance of anxiety and the procurement of safety were paramount. This is especially true in the case of those who survived violence, or other chronic abuses, in their families of origin. As Sullivan (1956a) has articulated, where rage and the defenses against it have dominated the early picture, the longing for love, though intense, may be "gruesomely truncated and grimly caricatured in waking intimacy" (p. 104). Any attempted collaboration in love for such people evokes a primitive, dissociated terror and a resort to early modes of defense: fighting and fleeing. Sullivan could have been speaking of my female subjects and their partners when he recounted the ways in which anger at early caretakers, suppressed under strenuous social prohibition, is amalgamated unconsciously and lays in wait for the interpersonal key that will unlock its demons. In ways both wily and blatant – but dissociated too – the rageful self finds the perfect key in the hands of someone of similar flavor and design. Their mutual destructiveness is most often closeted, accruing to both the shame attached to losing control and the fact that closeness may be heightened by the secret deviance of their bond.

For some women, "victim" is a state of consciousness triggered by a particular partner while for others it is an attachment style, a deferential posture educed in reply to all men, or even all intimate relations. Personal agency for the women I interviewed seemed especially tenuous in response to interpersonal triggers around attachment and abandonment. Rather than feeling in horrific circumstances that they had nothing to lose, women counterintuitively clung to whatever shreds of dignity, identity, and love remained.

What I noticed in my sisters is an all too common pattern of affiliation for women, where attachment only grows stronger in response to Job-like tests of her fidelity. Such confederation is the romantic backbone of innumerable coupling scripts: "Here the betrayed forgives the betrayer, the battered forgives the batterer, and everyone lives happily ever after" (Weems, 1995, p. 89). Far from diminishing in intensity over repeated trials, the victim self in this scenario hardens over time. The more she lies down, the less interested she is in getting up. The servile register that has been characterized as learned helplessness syndrome is so much more than just answering a Pavlovian ringtone; it becomes a raison d'être, a feature of identity that defines the very way it feels to be alive. Life in the brutal lane, lived in existential crisis, brings a heightened sense of emotional engagement and immediacy. It can generate an impression of aliveness, even in the face of impending death. As the founders of an early refuge for battered women write, "The families have no permanent structures in their lives. Instead, their lives are dictated by violent events, and they organize their living around cataclysmic eruptions" (Pizzey and Shapiro, 1982, p. 41). Even in situations where terrible violence is not the organizing principle, the steady beat of betrayal, manipulation, and cruelty may signal to the receiver that someone is, at least, still on the line. To terminate that contact feels tantamount to being vaporized, or taking the risk of annihilating the other.

Accordingly, despite the various psychological tortures to which she had been subjected by men, Phoebe could not bear to lose touch with them. Rather than going through the expected process of mourning a love that was not reciprocated, Phoebe continually pursued both old and new love objects who did not love her back. I often found out, months or even years after an ill-fated romance had ended, that she was still engaged in sporadic communication with the men who had hurt her. She would explain to me that they were still "friends" although eventually, at my insistence, she might acknowledge that they had never been very friendly; in fact, that they had treated her quite cruelly. She blamed herself for this state of affairs, as if to appropriate the badness of her objects and, in doing so, to restore to them the exalted status that her idolization had all but guaranteed (Fairbairn, 1954). Eng (2000) puts it bluntly:

> The turning of the lost object into the ego not only marks a turning away from the external world of the social to the internal world of the psyche, it also simultaneously transforms all possible reproaches against the loved object into reproaches against the self.
>
> (p. 1276)

As Bollas (1987) observed, once a hated object is internalized, depression becomes the compromise between wanting to destroy the object and fearing that you will be punished for such a lethal wish. While complex factors drive the instigation of any mental disorder, the introjection may partly explain the high rates of depression, suicidality, and substance abuse among abused women (Golding, 1999).

At the same time, there was a marked guilt whenever Phoebe had thoughts of leaving men who mistreated her. These were echoed again and again by women who insisted that their batterers needed help and that to leave them would signal a betrayal greater than any physical assault. Guilt is triggered by the belief that to carve out a separate existence for themselves inevitably portends the psychic death of their partners (Modell, 1965). The partner can only be saved by the woman's continued masochism. This concept will be illustrated later in the chapter in the story of a research subject, Misty, who went to incredible – indeed death defying – lengths to rescue her assaultive partner, thereby assuaging her own guilt over wanting to leave him.

> They protect the object from their aggression by giving up the wish to separate and, instead, reunite or remain with the object and turn the aggression against the self.
>
> (Asch, 1976)

Phoebe had a visceral feel for her own deflation in this process but only partially grasped that it was the inevitable complement to her veneration of the men. She described an interaction with her ex-boyfriend, occurring at least a year after they had broken up, in which he obliterated any design she had on their past as a place of nostalgic reverie. When he described how he'd been "fucking" others all along, it literally caused her legs to buckle and she fell to the floor.

> I know I shouldn't have done this. I blame myself. I was asking for it. It's like someone was using me as a puppet. I was his favorite; he made me feel special. Others wanted my position. But then my fall from grace put me in the shit. I only wanted to numb myself because he didn't like me anymore. I bought some over the counter stuff and went home and put myself out.

Attachments such as these virtually require a diminution of self-esteem to keep functioning. Separation and mourning are avoided through the tenacious incorporation of the object in a compulsive fusion that fails to defuse its inherent sadomasochism (Steiner, 1990). Numbing, through substances or dissociation, preserves the fragile self against a tide of deprivation and injury, and the narcissistic rage they might stimulate if acknowledged (Menaker, 1953). One thing I have discovered about women who remain in abusive relationships is that they are even more terrified of their own anger than their companion's. This is expressed in twin mantras: *keep things friendly at all cost* and *stay unconscious*.

Indeed, the frequency of depression among women in general may be a product of such unacknowledged resentment. Freud (1917) imagined the conditions of mourning as inimical to men but part and parcel of the female repertoire, the foundation of a woman's inherent melancholy.

Freud argues in "Mourning and Melancholia" that melancholia is a pathological form of mourning: unable "properly" to grieve the loss of an object, a place, or an ideal, the melancholic, according to Freud, repudiates the finite process of mourning, languishing instead in the refusal to grieve. The melancholic is so militant in his or her denials that the lost object is finally incorporated into the self, turned into the shelter of the ego, and preserved as a form of ghostly identification. In this refusal to sever any attachments to the lost object, the melancholic becomes instead haunted by it. Loss denied is incorporated into the ego, and the ego thus becomes a remainder of unresolved grief (Eng, 2000, p. 1276).

Loss of the object must be averted, no matter what kind of denial of self its maintenance entails. Abandonment simply cannot be tolerated and thus, all anger that might trigger a separation must be suppressed. "Without the object, or the hope of an object, there is no possibility of maintaining an organized and coherent sense of self" writes David Celani (1994, p. 92) of battered women, underscoring the degree to which such women are reticent to give up the victimized identity that has become their organizing principle. Many women are profoundly, ironically, stabilized by intimate oppression, in the sense that it helps them subdue their own aggressive impulses and relieves them of the burden of agency (Stein, 2011). We do not confront because we are terrified of giving up not only the attachment to venerated objects but the veneration itself, even as it displaces our own value. The diminution of the self paradoxically buoys the self through acceptance by someone who is judged as worthy to gift it (Reik, 1972; Benjamin, 1988).

As awful and extreme as this may sound, this stance is not strictly within the purview of women fleeing violence; it is familiar to me and to my female colleagues and friends. Each of us has been able to recount ways in which a near-terror of confrontation drove our decisions to not challenge the men in our lives in a particular moment or, more troublingly, over the course of our lifespans. One woman I know spoke of being vaguely aware of making her body posture more subservient when delivering potentially inflammatory news to her husband, as if her voluntary diminution would ward off a physical blow that, in actuality, never came. This deliberately shrinking self became a compendium of repressed rage and shameful affect.

> How could I? I asked myself over and over. I wore a "kick me" sign. But I convinced myself I was outwitting him, defusing his temper. I thought I was being slick but I was always throwing in the towel before the fight even began. It only made him angrier anyway. He would accuse me of getting out of the way, of being too scared to fight. He was completely right about me. I was always afraid. Of being hurt, mostly. Of losing *to* him. But of losing him, too. I am ashamed to say that because another part of me is now invested in the idea of getting away, too. But for so long I have defined myself by this relationship . . . not just what I am but what I imagine I could have been if I *wasn't* in it . . . sometimes I think "what if I can't get anything going outside of this?" What if it's not true that [sotto voce] I coulda been a contender [laughs]. What if there is just nothing? Like a hollow shell.

Despite a fairly sharp third eye that understood the ways in which her obsequiousness incited further intimidation, she could not seem to control what appeared as a masochistic card played in response to her husband's aggression. Masochism is not a game of solitaire; it is a bid for love from someone incapable or unwilling to give it, at least in that sacrificial moment. It is a repetitive engagement that helps each partner avoid parts of themselves that feel like "not-me" – the most traumatized, vulnerable, or ugly parts – by projecting those parts into the other.

> How much more dependent must we be on our partners and spouses to maintain the enactments that protect us from an exposure to what we cannot bear to be, *must* not be? . . . The more urgent the need to isolate one's own "not-me" in the other, the more hateful and intensely sadistic the enactments necessary to accomplish the task.
>
> (Stern, 2010, p. 156)

"It takes two minds to think one's disturbing thoughts" is Bion's rethinking of Klein's projective identification, making it an interpersonal rather than an intrapsychic event (Ogden, 2008). The couple harboring disturbed thoughts is also embedded in a social context that both mirrors and elaborates the influence of gender on their pact. In a separate conversation, the woman above remembered how her initial attraction to her husband in their dating days was fueled by his ability to bend other men to his will, which functioned to make her feel safe from the usual hazards a girl might face on the streets of their town. "No one messed with me" she said, betraying a hint of pride before a grimace creased her face, "except, of course, him."

Breeding for masochism

Evolutionary biologists blame the female tendency to befriend those who would do us harm on the estrogen potentiated neuromodulator oxytocin, which rises in the bloodstream in response to stress. Where males might fight or flee from attack, females are more likely to estimate the danger of attacking, or the likelihood of escaping, and opt instead for the social benefit of enlisting the aggressor for future protection (Campbell, 2007). This seems true for certain voles and gerbils as well as a subset of women seen in clinical practice, forever seeking affection from intransigent and hostile, even violent, suitors. Like Bowlby's infants and Harlow's monkeys, the women engage in behaviors that reveal an anxious attachment, characterized by alternating techniques of avoidance and proximity-seeking. But we need not rely on biological determinism to explain the conundrum of choosing such unsympathetic mates.

Relational theories suggest that traumatizing attachments are bound up in the representational world of one's unavailable or abusive early objects, which then provide a template for contemporary affections (Renn, 2012). As if this double whammy of biological and developmental antecedents were not enough, women are socially groomed to live out their own aggressive fantasies through male surrogates and to experience sexual attraction as companionate to coercion. As Stephanie Coontz (2012) suggests, women "binge" on images that "associate intimidation with infatuation"; one need look no further than the modern romance novel to discover the supposed charms of submission. This is the commodification of masochism writ large on public consciousness.

Given that the political and policy implications of diagnoses for battered women may have grave consequences, I have, up until now, resisted calling this relational dynamic masochistic. Still, increasingly I wonder about the ways that masochism may be informing *all* relationships in which there is an unequal distribution of power. The word remains closeted because of the shame its name evokes. "But doctor," my patient pleads, "how can I do the same thing again and again and expect a different outcome? Tell me the truth, doctor, am I a masochist?"

Like Phoebe, women I interviewed for this project, surprisingly, did not reject the masochist label as I assumed they might. Even those who had worked their way out of an abyss of self-blame, and recognized all the ways in which they bore no responsibility for abuse, often understood their predicaments as collusive, especially early on in the escalation of violence. They put the lie to the simplistic nature of analyses that ignore the ways in which a woman's internal voices enhance her participation in patriarchal regimes, blaming her victimization solely on the gendered patterns of oppression that subsist in most cultures. Erich Fromm's observations (1929) are apt in this context. On the one hand, we should not truck in psychoanalytic explanations where political accounts are sufficient. On the other, we must also recognize that there is no abstract society divorced from individual thoughts and feelings; it is these idiosyncratic data that must be the subject of any sustained analysis of social phenomena.

Masochism: a primer

Originally, masochism was a guy thing and, like many guy things, it was only about sex. Although masochism had appeared in the medical literature as early as the sixteenth century (and in the writings of philosophers even before that), the term was only popularized in 1890, when Krafft-Ebing used it to describe a particular constellation of sexual fetish and perversion exhibited by the writer Leopold von Sacher-Masoch, whom Krafft-Ebing called "the poet of masochism." Sacher-Masoch's novel, *Venus in Furs* (1870), had elaborated the author's inclination toward being sexually enslaved and degraded, a predilection that Krafft-Ebing believed interfered with his legacy as a writer. (Ironically, although the majority of his works were never translated from their original German, Sacher-Masoch achieved global immortality by having a disorder named after him; more has probably been written about masochism than almost any other human condition except, perhaps, sadism.) Havelock Ellis (1940), the famed sexologist, wrote a brief biography of Sacher-Masoch. In it, Ellis claimed that the young Leopold had witnessed the savage beating of a man by his wife, who subsequently turned on the quivering ten-year-old Leopold and attacked him, arousing both intense pain and exquisite pleasure. The experience set a personal template for the primeval twinning of suffering and love that Krafft-Ebing would eventually codify and pathologize.

Throughout the early twentieth century, Freud took Krafft-Ebing's masochism and shaped it into a cornerstone of psychoanalytic theories of psychosexual development (Grossman, 1986). In the intervening decades, followers of Freud continued to expand and extend his ideas, which are discussed in a later section. One student of Freud's, the psychiatrist Wilhelm Reich, developed an influential social theory of masochism that countered Freud's instinctual one. According to Reich (1949), rather than evidencing a drive toward displeasure and death, masochistic character structure was the psychic armamentarium of the person who had in early life learned to experience love as painful and now chose it as a way of warding off even graver pain.

The medicalization of masochism reached apotheosis in the second *Diagnostic and Statistical Manual of Mental Disorders* (American Psychiatric Association, 1968) where sexual masochism was designated as a type of paraphilia. Following its inclusion in the DSM, owing in part to the continued interest of psychoanalysts, who at the time still held considerable sway in psychiatric circles, the term masochism began to be applied more broadly as a personality designation rather than a signature sexual preference. (I was surprised to learn that the idea of a purely mental masochism, characterized by submission to an object but without the physical pain, had actually begun with Krafft-Ebing, who called it *ideeler masochism*, and considered it the primary adaptation in masochistic behavior.) In 1979, the American Psychoanalytic Association hosted a panel discussion on evolving ideas of masochism. The panel reflected the growing influence of object relations theorists and concluded that masochistic behavior was both varied in presentation and multi-determined (Fuller, 1986). The diagnosis had moved from its origins as a sexual perversion to that of a general personality disorder.

Despite the concurrence among psychoanalysts, numerous attempts to classify a characterological strain of masochism as a mental disorder failed, although a version of the type, also known as self-defeating personality disorder, made it into the appendix of DSM III-R in 1987. Coterminous with this shift from a corporeal to a psychic location for masochism came a revival of the idea, originally proposed by Krafft-Ebing and later institutionalized by Freud, that the biological drive toward submissiveness was essentially female, whether it appeared in men or women. The diagnostic code 301.90, for Masochistic (Self-Defeating) Personality Disorder appeared with the following criteria:

1 Remains in relationship in which others exploit, abuse or take advantage of him or her, despite opportunities to alter the situation.
2 Believes that he or she almost always sacrifices own interests for those of others.
3 Rejects help, gifts, or favors so as not to be a burden on others.
4 Complains, directly or indirectly, about being unappreciated.
5 Responds to success or positive events by feeling undeserving or worrying about not being able to measure up to new responsibilities.
6 Always pessimistic about the future and preoccupied with the worst aspects of the past and present.

7 Thinks only about his or her worst features and ignores positive features.
8 Sabotages his or her own intended goals.
9 Repeatedly turns down opportunities for pleasure.

As the criteria almost laughably reflected the social role that most women were still being forced to play in 1987, the year that edition of the DSM hit the stands, the diagnosis of masochistic personality disorder, as it was now defined, inevitably augured the feminization of masochism. Despite the political implications of such naming in a world that had become increasingly sensitized to issues of gender bias, male psychiatrists remarkably proposed the diagnosis without guile, triggering a feminist groundswell that resulted in its exclusion from subsequent editions of the diagnostic manual. Paula Caplan (1984), a noted feminist clinician and research psychologist, whose book *The Myth of Masochism* blamed women's cultural subordination for their observed suffering and inability to act boldly on their own behalf, challenged the very use of the term to describe female behavior. A decade earlier, Clara Thompson (1974a, 1974b) had observed even more elegantly the imperative of a woman to submit to a man, as being loved was not only a desire on her part but a necessary condition of her security. "Masochism often proves to be a form of adaptation to an unsatisfactory and circumscribed life," averred Thompson (1964, p. 133), noting how the preordained slog toward domesticity and dependence shaped a woman's sense of her own negligible agency and mediated a preference for habitual capitulation.

A split developed in psychiatric circles, pitting those who, like Caplan, feared that the diagnosis – especially when applied to battered women – invited dire social, legal and political consequences (such as the idea that women somehow were to blame for their own abuse or that men had been provoked into beating them) against others who argued that even if the roots of masochism were developmental rather than instinctive, the diagnosis remained clinically useful (Cooper in Collins, 1985). Just because the term had been misapplied, said these clinicians, was no reason to eliminate it from the lexicon. For this group (mainly psychoanalysts; we will come to the genesis of their ideas in the next section) masochism consisted of a core fantasy, not necessarily confined to females, that propelled self-destructive behaviors.

> In the fantasies the subject is an innocent victim, who achieves through suffering reunion with the object, defense against aggressive destruction and loss of the object, avoidance of narcissistic pain, and instinctual gratification by fantasy participation in the oedipal situation. Suicidal pathology, masochistic perversions, certain forms of hypochondriasis and psychosomatic illness, and moral masochism have in common an *underlying fantasy structure*. In our view, this fantasy structure is [what Freud referred to as] the "essence of masochism."
>
> (Novick and Novick, 1987)

Indeed, despite the persistent controversy over its use, the concept of relational masochism continues to be used in the professional literature. Like other psychological nomenclatures, it has also become ubiquitous in popular usage, most often employed as an explanation for women's poor romantic choices. However, at the same time, postmodern analyses have demonstrated how cultural fantasies of sadomasochism act to maintain binary constructions of gender that then impose their logic on individual psyches, weaving a dynamic of power and powerlessness into all aspects of interpersonal relating (Uebel, 2002).

A reporter covering the American Psychiatric Association's attempt to revisit the masochism diagnosis in 2005 for the latest edition of the DSM commented that "hanging in the air was the belief that masochism existed but henceforth no woman will ever be diagnosed as suffering from it because the women's movement would be disappointed" (Leo, 2005). Antithetically, when an alternative diagnostic manual, the *Psychodynamic Diagnostic Manual* (PDM), was unveiled in 2006 to promote a more nuanced psychoanalytic understanding of individual personality types and patterns, both "moral masochistic" and "relational masochistic" appeared as clinical designations. Each describes ways of relating that are not *necessarily* disordered, reflecting Kernberg's observation that "because of the universality of masochistic behaviors and conflicts, it is not always easy to know when masochism belongs to the field of psychopathology" (1988, p. 1006). Still, in its more extreme manifestations, the PDM denotes relational forms of masochism as mental health disorders.

Courts, on the other hand, have rejected the use of the term in proceedings that involve domestic abuse victims, as well as in trials of women who kill their batterers. Because the belief that battered women are masochistic might prejudice jurors' deliberations, psychiatric experts may explicitly counter such ideas and offer testimony branding the idea of female masochism a widely held "myth." Indeed, Ewing and Aubrey (1987) have found that women, even more than men, endorse the statement that "the battered woman who stays is somewhat masochistic." They suggest that attorneys who assume women jurors will be sympathetic to female victims are making a serious error. I wonder if women jurors, themselves subject to the vagaries of the romantic marketplace, are not intimately familiar with the ways in which women facilitate their own oppression. Rejecting the masochistic label for themselves, they instead externalize the shame and handily affix it to their sisters.

Psychoanalytic ideas about masochism

Concomitant with the development of psychiatric thought about masochism, psychoanalysis developed its own hypotheses on the matter. Originally Freud had rejected the idea of primary masochism, instead seeing it as a derivative of sadism, an aggression turned inward. Troublingly however, masochism undermined Freud's theory of the pleasure principle, and he later revised his theory to allow for a death instinct that could accommodate a drive toward pain. In 1924, in "The

Economic Problem of Masochism," Freud described a biological erotogenic mechanism that accounted for arousal from painful stimuli. This allowed him to conceptualize two kinds of masochism – feminine and moral. *Feminine masochism* was considered an instinctive characteristic in women, thus warranting little investigation, but it was deemed pathological when exhibited by men, for whom infantile themes of impending castration signaled regressed sexuality. Women, it was assumed, were already symbolically castrated and thus naturally inclined toward submission. Clara Thompson, a proponent of the interpersonal psychoanalytic school of Harry Stack Sullivan, would later take great issue with all formulations based on Freud's notion of penis envy in women, saying simply that "Freud was very perceptive but he was a man. Penis envy is a male concept. It is the male who experiences the penis as a valuable organ and he assumes that women also must feel that way about it" (1974c, p. 65).

The second type of masochism hypothesized by Freud was more characterological than specifically sexual. *Moral masochism* referred to the introjection of a punitive parental imago, desexualized in normal superego development but resexualized in this competing masochistic narrative, as the person regresses to an Oedipal conflation of guilt and pleasure. Masud Khan (1981) referred to this kind of masochism as an "affect that the ego creates with characters, real or imaginary, in the space of fantasy . . . to create and sustain an atmosphere of pain, that stays under its control and can be libidinized" (p. 415). Such a relationship allows the masochist to externalize pain and rage, to have an angry experience without having to initiate it or take responsibility for its consequences (Ghent, 1990). In line with Ghent's comments, I observed how women in my sample often self-censored the expression of anger because it did not comport with their idealized visions of femininity, and instead attached themselves to men capable of extreme violence, in order to have a proxy for aggression. Some got a vicarious and conscious kick out of a man's demonstration of power, while for others it was a more subtle unburdening of the agentic self, whereby the man initiated and maintained all action in the real world while the woman could only exist in a reactive mode. Women abided such performances, even when the man's aggression turned against them, since it seemed merely a fleeting solo in a larger orchestration they had long ago accepted.

Over the years, other analysts took the idea of moral masochism in different directions. Reik (1941) renamed it "social masochism" and described self-destructive acts in which masochists manipulated others by provoking attacks, accepting martyrdom, and stimulating guilt, thereby attaining "victory in defeat." Many women are familiar with this ploy, having acted it out in stereotypically gendered relationships. I recall how many times as a young woman I had wished for bad behavior from a romantic object, to verify my own moral superiority, induce a guilty capitulation from the other, and hasten a détente in soured relations.

> This demonstration clearly shows that the woman complies with the ruling paradigm even in stressful situations, in a hope for positive sanctions

> like acceptance/approval from those in charge; an attempt to shape the distress in an acceptable way, to shape paranoia so it looks attractive to others.
>
> (Azundris, 2008, section 1.1.6)

The interpersonal sphere

The defensive organization around martyrdom was doubly realized for me in work with Phoebe, whose most persistent fantasy revolved around how sorry others would be for hurting her, not because she would avenge herself – that might require a straightforward expression of aggression – but because they would someday realize how perfect she had been and all they had lost by not recognizing this fact. A similar theme ran like a barbed wire through the accounts of women I interviewed about their relationships with batterers, some of whom considered their suffering a necessary way station on the road to some imaginary royal reckoning. Rigas (2008) has acknowledged the tenacity of the paranoid symbiosis that binds couples to one another in this ugly configuration. Only "upheaval, violence, and disorder" (p. 42) are recognized as contact, everything else is coded as abandonment and empty space.

Another way of looking at sadomasochistic arrangements is through the lens of what Mitrani (1994) called adhesive states, where there is little or no sense of an autonomous self or perceived agency. Mitrani and others used the concept to explicate autistic behaviors, and I have applied it elsewhere to the emotionless acts of some perpetrators (Stein, 2007). Meltzer (1975) notes the ease with which such people adapt themselves to the personalities of others, giving up their separate identity and easily "transform[ing] themselves into different personalities when they change their objects" (p. 308). Similarly, many women, caught in the grip of sadomasochistic relations, only feel potent through a symbiotic fusion with their attacker. They wish to completely lose themselves in love. Many become intensely involved very quickly and, once in, cannot extricate themselves. In true adhesive fashion, they are "stuck." The developmental picture underlying this form of defense is explained in regard to the infant's unbearable awareness of physical separation and the adult's subsequent search for an unbounded attachment that, paradoxically, provides a pathological containment of the splintered self (Ogden, 1989).

Although they come from a different set of premises, Jungian ideas about unity and transcendence of the self can draw on much the same clinical picture: a supplicant whose coherence is dependent on a totalizing host. Jung himself wrote nothing about masochism per se, although his analysand-cum-paramour, Sabina Spielrein, according to a popular adaptation of material about their love affair (Kerr, 1993), supposedly demanded that he whip her as a prelude to lovemaking. Jung (1916) seems ahead of his time when, in writing of the conflation of passion and self-destruction, he articulates a cultural argument for a female submissiveness bound up in the renunciation of erotic desire.

> A woman who, in today's society, abandons herself to passion soon leads herself to ruin. One need only contemplate the current bourgeois state of affairs to understand how a feeling of unbounded insecurity occurs in those who unconditionally surrender to Fate.
>
> (Jung in Spielrein, 1994, pp. 155–156)

Without saying so directly, Jung seems to imply that a woman who desires is contractually obligated to feel guilty and, hence, seeks punishment as a prerequisite to satisfaction. Rather than seeing this as problematic, Jung believed in deliverance through suffering and in a necessary incorporation of the "shadow" self who feeds on humiliation and powerlessness. Neo-Jungians have tentatively expanded on this notion and addressed the issue of masochism through the lens of divine existence, a common theme in analytical psychology. Rosemary Gordon, for example, has written of masochism as the shadow side of the archetypal need to idolize a superior being: "a longing for surrender, for dependence on others, for helplessness, for self-abnegation or for immersion or unity in and with an 'other'" (1987, p. 230). For Jungians, masochism is not a sexual perversion but an existential position, a place where symbiotic fusion with an erroneously exalted partner has miserably failed (Thibaudier, 2005). This imperative to surrender the self in order to be known is a recurring theme in theories of both masochism (Josephs, 1982) and the analysis of gendered patterns of love (Benjamin, 1988).

Despite its Christian themes, Jung's notion of the martyr seemed an analytic angle worth pursuing as I reviewed my notes on a heavyset blond woman who had converted to Orthodox Judaism after being beaten nearly to death by one of its adherents.

Misty's story

Misty grew up in the South, the product of what she described as an "Ozzie and Harriet" marriage, the oldest of four girls and decidedly the "most girly." She married young, had two children and divorced amicably. There was no violence in that marriage. She married again and another 15 years passed. This time there was again no violence but lying and cheating ruled the interaction almost from the start. As she described them to me, each relationship seemed a whim; days or weeks from meeting a man, things would become intensely serious. Misty insisted the feelings were always mutual and that she did not feel pressured to make a committment. Then she proceeded to tell me a story that contradicted her assertion.

Sometime after the break-up of the second marriage, she was waiting for a friend in a bar when a "nice" man sat down next to her and began a conversation. She wasn't certain that she was ready to date yet so, when he asked for her phone number she gave it but reversed the numbers so that he could not actually reach her. It seemed curiously juvenile, given her age and experience at the time. I asked why she had reversed the numbers instead of just refusing the request.

> Because I didn't know how to say no. I did not know how to say no. I'm a pleaser. I don't like confrontations. I don't like any conflict. It was just easier to make him go away with a bad phone number. And I thought he would just go away. Even though he had been very nice, he was just a little too nice and it made me feel very uncomfortable. He was completely like focusing on me throughout his entire dinner. He was sitting next to me. He was completely focused on me. And it just felt uncomfortable because he was a stranger. Looking back on it now, it was way too intense. Plus he was drinking. I mean, what do I expect from someone sitting at a bar? But I think he was drinking too much.

This initial piece of information regarding the inability, or refusal, to protect oneself from potential danger resonates with the risk-taking behaviors of many women in my sample. Many were hurt after failing to decline invitations from men who, they later admitted, had in some way covertly signaled their bad intentions. Upset that he had been given the wrong information, the man, Sam, tracked Misty down and demanded her correct number. Imagining how frightened I might be by such an adamant pursuit, I asked what she had felt about the insistence of Sam's chase. Rather than making her feel scared, she said, Sam's attention felt like a confirmation of her worth. This was a story that I heard many times during the course of my interviews.

> On one level, the more he was pursuing me, the more I felt wonderful about me. That somehow I was a desirable person again. And a man somehow throwing all of his attention and his desire on, all over me, made me feel like, well, maybe I'm not ugly and stupid and incompetent, and whatever. This person seems to think that I'm better than that. And that lifted me up.

I wondered about the source of Misty's fragile self-esteem. As she had first described her life, and particularly her adulthood, it seemed to me that she had worked hard and racked up an impressive set of accomplishments, even though the divorces had certainly been a blow to the sure footing of earlier years. It turned out that Misty never felt she was doing a good enough job. An imaginatively embodied alter ego, a dissociated companion, named "Naggy Maggie," sat on her shoulder and reminded her how much work was left to do and all the ways in which she did not measure up.

> I do really have a need to save the world. I learned that from my mother. She just saves people, one person at a time. When there was no foster care program for emergencies, for little children in the 1950s. And she found out that they were taking little children when their parents were in the hospital, or God forbid, there'd been a shooting or a horrible accident, or whatever, they had nowhere to take them. So they were putting them in some sort of an

> institution. She said, "That's not acceptable. You can't do that to small children. They're traumatized enough already. Bring them to my house."

And so it seemed that Misty found in her latest beau a perfect specimen for saving. He had drinking problems, substance problems, psychiatric symptoms, and anger issues. An "emotional illiterate," according to Misty, Sam chose estrangement from his family of origin over any relational compromise with them, yet this was topped off by a fear of abandonment so deeply cratered that he often could not pull himself to safety. Pulling Sam to safety became Misty's full-time occupation.

The violence started one night, in "this hazy, surrealistic blur that we were sitting there being lovey and cuddling on the sofa and the next thing, he's getting really, really rough and grabbing me by my hair and it doesn't even seem real." She did not sustain any injuries but "I was terrified. I was really afraid. Nobody had ever gotten, like, that kind of aggressive with me and that's what seemed very scary. And, compared to what he did in the future, subsequently, it's nothing. It's nothing."

Misty might run when he got drunk and nasty; if he used his hands or became sexually aggressive, she sometimes bolted the bedroom door. She even called the cops and had him removed from the premises a few times, although she did not press charges. I asked how she understood her own reluctance to cut Sam out of her life.

> So it was a bit of a disaster and I tried to get rid of him and he would come pounding on the doors and windows. You know, "I love you, I love you, I'm so sorry. Please open the door. I have to talk to you." And I would let him back in, over and over again. I had thought I was almost over him, but clearly when he showed up again, all filled with love, there I was. I was a complete sucker. So that's when the violence *really* started.

I mulled over Misty's statement: "I was a complete sucker. So that's when the violence *really* started." Only moments earlier in her tale, I had felt almost as if I was on the edge of a movie theater seat instead of a chair in my office. When Sam said "I have to talk to you," I was silently thinking "Oh no, oh no, don't let him in" and I had thought the word "sucker" almost simultaneous with Misty mouthing it. (The stories of my respondents often elicited such countertransferential reactions, as I matched their distancing techniques measure for measure. There was a tremendous pull to frame battered women's stories as movie scripts, for both the victim/survivor and the audience. It was a way of disregarding the reality of what had happened; screening it off, so to speak.)

I was struck by Misty's complete dissociation of both fear and anger in the face of Sam's entreaties; her complete surrender to love quickly became a one-way ticket to aggravated assault. By refusing to see Sam's ugliness and the force with which he was willing to impose it, she implicitly refused to see Sam who, one can assume, was quite desperate to be seen. Like Winnicott's infant, such an out-of-control man, unbounded and unmirrored, cannot experience his own existence and must provide ever greater demonstrations of potency. By refusing to acknowledge Sam's threat, by folding in the face of it, by failing to hold his excesses at bay, Misty unwittingly provoked even greater sadism, which engendered an even more marked capitulation on her part. Had this been a movie, I thought, it would end with a murder–suicide.

But Misty was still sitting with me, very much alive. The story speeded up, perhaps a product of my more rapid-fire questioning, as if we were both exhausted from imagining the repetitiveness of the remaining story and wanted to cut to the scene of Misty's resurrection as a single, and safe, woman. I wondered whether the pressing need to get her story over with at that juncture paralleled the sense that many battered women had shared with me that, at some point, they knew the beating was coming and they just wanted to get it over with. It is very hard for the researcher or clinician to sit with the pointlessness of someone's pain; easier to collude with their attempt to find meaning, one reason why tales of redemption are particularly popular narrative tropes for battered women (Haaken, 2010). The triumphal addendums to their stories of suffering imply that the great lesson learned made the violence somehow worth it but, as far as I could see, there was nothing ennobling in any of the women's ordeals. Misty had suffered more than most and learned less than many. I could not get her story over with fast enough.

> Sometimes he would hurt me and then lie on the floor, in a stupor, so drunk that he would piss all over himself. He would lie on the floor and scream for help. And if he wasn't doing that, then he was up and doing things like throwing knives at the wall behind my head or throwing furniture and beating me. I was totally terrified. I lived in an absolute terror every single minute of every single day.

Sam broke her collarbone. She fled and called the police. He spent six months in jail. When he got out and knocked on her door, she let him in once more. Sam cracked her jaw, broke the orbit of her eye, put a pillow over her face and tried to smother her. Misty managed to escape, running down the street almost naked at 1 a.m. She remembers the police and ambulance coming. Even with the seriousness of her injuries obvious, she tried to cover for him, telling the authorities "I walked into a wall," the almost clichéd report of an abused woman. The police knew, of course, that she had been beaten. Still, she tried to rescue him.

> I said, you know, "You can't arrest him. He's sick. He needs treatment. He doesn't need to be in jail. Jail will kill him." That was my mantra.

Sam was arrested though, not that night but eventually, and is now in jail awaiting sentencing on 13 felony and seven misdemeanor counts of assault. Misty has had a lot of therapy, lives alone, and walks with a limp. She granted that it was "a miracle" that she had survived ten years of such astronomical violence. I asked what had finally let her stop trying to rescue Sam.

> The level of patience that the advocates [at the domestic violence court] have is amazing. Because they listened to me say, "But he doesn't really mean to hurt me." And they'd say, "We know. And we're going to get him the help that he needs." They let me talk about it. The whole time, of course, going in the back room and probably just pummeling a pillow themselves so they could continue to say those things to my face. But taking away the responsibility. They were going to take care of him now. It wasn't my problem anymore. They were going to help. They didn't judge me. They didn't say, "We hear this stupid story from every woman who comes in here with a black eye, but you know they're all rotten to the core." They didn't say that. They gave me permission to turn him over to somebody else.

I was happy that Misty felt released from her obligation to care for Sam and her guilt over abandoning him to the prison system. Yet, given her history, Misty's final words felt less like a resolution than a new, albeit more productive, focus for sacrifice.

> It's just really, really important to me to understand how I got here and how I'm getting out so that I can help other women. And it's really my mission, to save at least one other person. And I don't know how that's going to come about, or where that person is going to appear in my life, but I'm really looking to do something to try to save and rescue someone else. I know I can't save the whole world, but if there's anything about me telling my story that helps . . .

End of interview.

Countertransference with patients and subjects

Most of the research on countertransference with victims of domestic assault has been performed in emergency venues or shelter settings. Because clinicians in those circumstances are seeing clients either in states of high arousal, when the abuse has just occurred, or in transitional sites where safety is the primary concern, the research is not necessarily sensitive to the more subtle transferential issues around dissociation and enactment that affect long-term therapeutic dyads. Still, the literature offers an outline of the kinds of issues that crop up in both short and long-term clinical situations with traumatized women, whether interventions are primarily supportive and psychoeducational, or more deeply psychoanalytic. To explore further issues of countertransference in the latter, I ran a focus group at a psychoanalytic institute in New York. Fourteen analysts joined me to discuss their work with patients in abusive relationships who they felt had presented with masochistic self-states and/or attachment styles.[1] Their observations are incorporated into my discussion of countertransference reactions below.

There is a laundry list of clinical responses familiar to people who work with victims of abuse, especially when the abuse is ongoing: disbelief in the seriousness of the patient's allegations of abuse, vicarious traumatization, complicity in suppressing clients' detailed memories of violent incidents, over-identification with the client's powerlessness, fear for one's personal safety and that of the client. Iliffe and Steed (2000) surveyed domestic violence counselors who said that what they found most challenging about the work was their loss of a sense of professional competence when clients remained in abusive relationships. Others cited the struggle to remain respectful of the abused woman despite the poor choices she might make, and the tendency to assume too much responsibility for women's safety. Clinicians working in crisis centers may also have complex transferential reactions to the larger institutions with which their clients must interface for both services and legal dispositions, reactions which complicate the primary relationship with the client.

Psychoanalysts I spoke with echoed these concerns and also noted the ways in which such patients aroused their contempt ("it feels sadistic to me when I take on the same language he [the abuser] might use. I think but don't say, 'how can you be so stupid?'"), seduced and provoked them ("I find myself holding back from asking a question because I am afraid that sadism is behind it"), and tested their skills ("I was wrestling with a professional wrestler and I was an intermediate weight"). Attempting to hold patients' inability to tolerate either togetherness or aloneness, clinicians described sometimes being pulled into manic cycles of attachment and abandonment. They expressed how often they were drawn away from pure analysis and into more directive forms of interaction ("I gave her the name of a lawyer. She needed to take it seriously" and "You need to let them know they have a choice. 'What do you mean he won't let you have a bank account? There's a bank on every corner.'"). Many felt that these were very necessary detours from analysis but still sometimes resented just how concrete interventions needed to be.

Some of the psychoanalysts in the focus group were discussing work with private full-fee patients while others were reporting about low-fee referrals that had been made through the courts or agencies for battered women. Thirteen of the psychoanalysts were Caucasian and one was a light-skinned Cuban; regretfully, I did not query them about the race or ethnicity of the patients they discussed. Although interracial dyads have traditionally been the rule rather than the exception in shelter and advocacy treatment programs, the special difficulties that arise for white clinicians and their multicultural patients have been largely ignored. Many treatment programs, in striving to be "colorblind," actually stoke destructive countertransferences around race that remain dissociated and, hence, unresolved (Williams and Becker, 1994). Bell and Mattis (2000), in discussing the impact of race and ethnicity on the creation of a therapeutic alliance, describe how white practitioners tend to downplay the significance of race in their relationships with clients. The clinician's diffidence – or outright dissociation – around such subject matter potentially leaves unspoken a cauldron of feelings about hierarchy and status. The silence is an open invitation to parallel processes where power struggles between patient and clinician mimic those that the client is facing with the institutionalized racism of the other systems with which she must interface in order to receive help. Moreover, clinicians may unconsciously hold stereotypes about the women they counsel, such as a belief that African American women are especially strong or even prone to violence; that Asian women are always compliant; or that Latinas are likely to stand by their men no matter what. Transference is further complicated by the fact that women themselves may internalize these beliefs and attempt unconsciously to live up to the characterizations. When difference is not articulated, the patient may harbor a range of expectations beyond the usual ones, both positive and negative, around her therapist's competence, intelligence, or power to effect change.

No matter the color of participants, the setting in which treatment takes place, the educational background or orientation of the treatment provider, the most poignant struggle for therapists and their clients is the intransigence of sadomasochistic patterns of coupling. The focus group discussed the feeling of pressure to help people end destructive relationships while being patient enough to let them define boundaries for themselves.

J: What is tricky for us is that it is easy to start to own the piece, any desire or sense of urgency for the patient to leave. We get into our own feeling states of "How is it possible? Doesn't she see?" Whether we say anything or not, the patient feels it and it really contributes to maintaining the dissociation of any aggression or any desire that they may have to leave. I had to do a lot of work on my own head. If I spoke my mind freely, I would be shaming her for staying. I had to let go of my own desires for her well-being and health. I had to make a space for her to start feeling her own distress instead of my getting distressed on her behalf.

S: It can work the other way, too. That's the delicacy of it. They have never had a role model.

E: It is like work with drug addicts. Some people, if you take on the righteous indignation, they have no other position than "but we have great sex . . ." It is so easy to fall into that.

A: By the time I meet someone they have been getting knocked around for years. I have to remember, to me it's an emergency but to her it's just another Thursday.

Many issues arise over the clinician's feelings about their patient's provocativeness. An analyst who had treated a violent couple got to hear, from both sides, the details of what inaugurated their explosions.

> He was harshly physically abusive at times, bashing her head against the wall. She has a textbook history of having been abused. I see them together

> and listen to the story of how this unfolds. While he is harsh, verbally and physically, she is very powerful in turning it into that. When it turns physical, she is almost always the first person to make it physical – she does something small, like scratch him – and then he goes postal; she has bruises, she's in very bad shape. She abuses him in other ways, too. He feels impotent until he does something like that.

An interesting point is that the patient's choice to remain in an abusive relationship can feel like a provocation aimed directly at the therapist. In a more classical vein, this might be thought of as part and parcel of resistance but Bromberg (1998) has refigured such repetitions as evidence of the incompatibility of a patient's self-states, some of which are transforming while others still hold tenaciously to the primitive defenses that barricade trauma. In terms of its dyadic dimension, resistance to getting better is a warning to the therapist that "I am my illness and I will not let you cure me of who I am" (p. 208). There may be a Herculean clash between a clinician's insistence that the victim of domestic abuse must relinquish her destructive romantic patterns (after all, isn't this why she came to the police, the shelter, counseling, or psychotherapy?) and the client's effort to avoid any knowledge of her own participation in what the therapist surely sees as an ongoing tragedy. Just as the therapist's investigation of the patient's masochism can become sadistic, the patient's resistance to surrendering her tried and true narrative of masochism can in itself be a sadistic reversal. What gets lost in the transferential soup is the sense of negotiation around how "me" (the one who must be beaten) might incrementally accommodate "not me" (in this case, the one who must repel a beating). In this regard, I relate a longer clinical vignette about Phoebe, whose story began this chapter.

Phoebe once walked into a session and announced that she was about to reveal something that "would make me very proud of her." A few weeks earlier she had broken off yet another relationship that was beginning to show signs of emotional abuse. Encouragingly, she had not fallen in love with the man and had even had a dramatic kiss-off scene, leaving him standing on a street corner, clearly the loser to her superior verbal acrobatics.

Although careful not to be too profuse in my admiration, I had to acknowledge the change in Phoebe. I remembered thinking how far she had come: the man was not as abusive as former lovers, she had left him sooner, she had expressed her anger and drawn a line regarding what she was willing to tolerate. I felt not only a spreading glee on Phoebe's behalf but that aggrandizing self-satisfaction familiar to clinicians who too soon conclude that the patient's health is a by-product of their own giftedness and perseverance. So, when Phoebe asserted that I would soon be proud of her, I felt something good was about to happen, put my watchfulness aside and, like a thousand naïve Justines before me, assumed the position. Paralleling Phoebe's dissociated performance, I was about to get screwed. Surprise, surprise.

Phoebe proceeded to tell me a tale about how she had been in contact with the man for weeks, not acknowledging that she had previously led me to believe that she had broken off all communications. She then recited (and sometimes read) to me reams of text messages in which he berated her, accused her of betrayal and abandonment in the harshest language, and spliced his vindictive sallies with requests that Phoebe "come over and blow me." At no point had she shown anger or discontinued the calls; she had even initiated some of them. With a preternatural effort of will, I tried to put myself in her mind, to imagine myself tethered to this textual torture in such a way. Would I have been too afraid to complain, too stunned to speak, aroused even in the thick of it, strangely content with any semblance of a connection? I finally spoke, asking in that curious clinical voice we adopt, the voice that strives to be non-judgmental even as it contains a semi-conscious appraisal, "What would he have needed to say for you to hang up on him?"

Phoebe turned that around in the unfazed way she had and said "Not sure." I began to imagine that she might have been similarly unfazed during the texting marathons. Texting itself was a preferred method of interaction for Phoebe and, although I admit there may be some cross-generational finger-wagging in my dismay over her default to this inherently less confrontational communicative mode, there seemed to be something that invited dissociation in the choice. How much easier to ignore "Blow me, slut" on the screen than in the ear.

During the session I pressed her somewhat relentlessly about how she had felt while he harangued her but she answered the queries with an assessment of his "assholeness," never really articulating how things had seemed to her in the moment. She said that she really had not felt anything because she knew he was a jerk; she said that she had continued the conversation because he was a sorry sap who needed nursing; she could not explain to me why she felt so obligated to care for someone with whom she, admittedly, was not even particularly impressed, much less in love. I felt furious at the fact that she had allowed herself to be trammeled once again and even angrier at the bait and switch she had performed with me. I wanted to scream "Why would you think I'd be *proud* of you? Are you trying to provoke me? Are you mad?" I said none of this, of course. The following week I wondered aloud with her if I had seemed sadistic in my press for details. Yes, she had perceived my anger. We discussed what had brought out the sadist and masochist in me, how my interrogation had had the same coldness as her ex-lover's uglier tract, and how her inability to tell me to back off in the moment mirrored the eerie dissociative calm of her interaction with his verbal abusiveness. Phoebe's abatement of agency in these situations and her strangely affectless response to my somewhat ruthless inquiry was described artfully by Masud Khan, writing of his own masochistic patient. While Khan (1979) was discussing a masochism that expressed itself in a more directly sexual way than Phoebe's, the analysis resonates.

> This mechanism of splitting plays a decisive role in sustaining that sense of innocence that characterizes the "victim" in the pervert-contract. It is the

> splitting that makes the patient impersonal to her fate in the pervert-contract and leads to an idolization of the active pervert's will and power.
>
> (p. 208)

Phoebe had made me the tyrant-pervert on this and other occasions as well as holding me masochistically enthralled in the grip of her traumatic repetition compulsions. A delight, in our lighter moments, was to examine our own repetition of these forms in light of our de-gendered roles (in my room, we could each equally play at being man, woman, sadist, masochistic, subject, object, agent, passive recipient); we could begin to put the lie to the idea that the woman had to be the supplicant.

If cure is somehow wrapped up in the ability to forsake dissociation, even when knowledge delivers a painful blow, then Phoebe had a healthy moment of recognition that revealed to me some of the "catastrophic disillusionment" that she was so strenuously guarded against (Khan, 1979, p. 136). Phoebe had been invested for many years in the belief that there was generally a time with her lovers, before the men became abusive, that had been wonderful and loving. Her staying in soured relationships was, to a great extent, about trying to recreate what she believed were reciprocal moments of love and closeness although she could not provide evidence of that mutuality having ever existed. One day, in going over accounts concerning a particular man (the one with whom she had felt the most powerful connection) she suddenly recognized how he had been sadistic and manipulative from the start. Rather than precipitating a moment of clarity and vision that would liberate her from the still present pull of her romantic fantasy, the recognition completely deflated her. I could almost hear the whoosh as Phoebe's faith in her own desirability left her body and she seemed to collapse inward on the couch. Twice she repeated "then it was for nothing," once as a fish-eyed observation of her history, the other as a wail that signaled the profound loss of any belief that she was loveable. It was very painful to hear, even as it announced some kind of breakthrough in consciousness.

From pain to poiesis

Both psychology and the law have struggled to ensure victim's rights by placing the onset of symptoms at the site of the violence itself. If women are "normal" until enduring adult trauma – and psychologically undone only afterwards – then developmental models become superfluous. Instead we have point of entry theories, meaning that any vulnerabilities that one brings to the dynamic endgame are discounted when searching for contributing causes. When it comes to explaining the abusive situations in which many women find themselves, such reductionism puts us on a fool's errand. When a girl looks for love, how does she imagine its messenger except from the internal models she developed in childhood? When a woman, under threat of extinction, must call into service every tool of survival she has, what does she draw from, other than her own earlier battles in similar arenas? The past and present are not mutually exclusive. Indeed, they form a sailor's knot.

The relational masochism I have discussed has nothing to do with Freudian drives, whips and chains or, least of all, hedonic pleasure. Instead it is a self-state where pain and suffering are simply part of the cost of a romantic attachment. The self-state is tightly tethered to a world view (and the world's denizens are complicit in manipulating the viewfinder) where people – and women in particular – are expected to gleefully succumb to both the treasures and humiliations wrought by love. Certainly, the automatic and reactive capitulation to another's demands has to be learned somewhere; otherwise we would flee the scene at the first sign of danger. Given this, it is no surprise that 72 percent of my overall sample grew up in physically abusive homes while about 40 percent had been sexually molested as children.

Conversely, the strength to *resist* such rampant social messages about masochistic ways of relating may be seeded in earlier loving experiences that somehow challenged the idea of desire as a zero sum game. The case of Misty was an outlier, in a way. She had not endured abuse at her parent's hands; more of a benign neglect because other children were deemed more deserving of parental ministrations. In her violent adult relationship, Misty took on her mother's role of savior to an emotional orphan while simultaneously being traumatized herself, like the foster children her mother had taken in. In this sacrificial role, perhaps she finally felt worthy of her mother's love.

Children who have come from homes where little is expected and much is endured normalize such relations. The malignity of the perpetrating or neglectful parent may become located in the child as a way to preserve the fantasy of a good caretaker; I have often seen this in violent adults (Stein, 2007). Alternately, children may externalize that internal chaos, projecting it onto innocent others or actively seeking out disorganized violent partners in an attempt to localize and control the danger. This is often the story of the victim of adult domestic violence.

These interpersonal arrangements can become intricate pas de deux between well matched Juliets and their Romeos. Masochism is a defensive bow to the other person's sadism, almost always inspired by a deep need to be desired and cared for; the violent thrust that should dislodge the lovers only tends to make them adhere more thoroughly. Many develop a "you and me against the world" intransigence. The harder the social worker, the police, the courts, and their friends try to separate them, the more they assert their magical connection. Their inseparableness is a dynamic enactment that protects each of them from the bogyman "not me," where a panicked unlovability resides. For the moment, abandonment is staved off, as is rage. The temporal dimension that collapses during the violence between them is restored to its rightful place as the gatekeeper of innumerable unmediated violations. For the moment at least, one's hopes and dreams obscure the fear and hatred, as these are projected instead onto those who want to save the couple from themselves, as many couple's therapists can testify.

> Family violence is often spoken of in terms of victims and perpetrators, evoking a kind of conceptual and emotional splitting, and compelling others, including professionals, to take sides. However, despite their experience of abuse, women and children often continue to feel a strong attachment to the person they have come to the shelter to escape. In order to hear clients' stories in all their complexity, it is necessary to listen for, and actively elicit, the full range of feelings associated with these relationships.
>
> (Madsen et al., 2003)

I have offered evidence in this chapter for the necessity of more dimensionalized work with women in abusive relationships, treatment that respects the nature of attachment in such relationships and the very fragmented defensive response it engenders. Lynn Chancer (1992) describes the sadomasochistic attachment quite accurately as having four basic and interrelated components: (1) an excessive and symbiotic attachment with a compulsive need for connection to the other; (2) contact that is repetitively structured, perhaps even ritualistic; (3) the consequences for challenging the status quo are severe; and (4) there is a "dialectical interaction" in that "each faces the possibility and perpetual risk of turning into the other" (pp. 3–4). While this was clearly not the set-up of all, or even most, of the relationships that I discussed with interviewees, there was a subset of subjects, *the ones who had the most difficulty leaving battering relationships*, where I felt this dynamic was clearly demonstrated. It is critical for practitioners to recognize that the last component offers a potential lever to spring women from destructive attachment, for it is the incorporation of her own aggression that defuses her dependence on him, and offers an escape hatch.

In less volatile relationships, over time, this may even open up space for a man to concede his own dependency needs, neutralizing their annihilatory power. It is those dependency needs, and the threat they entailed, that probably inaugurated violence in the first place (Benjamin, 1983). Although rhetoric has long held that there will be no surcease from intimate violence once it begins and, based on this, advocates for women have presumed that the only successful resolution is one in which the relationship is severed, the reality is that many women choose to soldier on, for a variety of reasons, and need a constructive rubric for setting limits and changing the power differential within their relationships. The idea of empowerment in clinical work specifically addresses the way that traditional interventions have undermined women's autonomy by simply providing a new cultural script by which she must abide, this one centering on how she must throw off her chains and rise Lazarus-like from the conjugal bed. In non-emergency situations – ones in which the woman's life or limb is not imminently endangered – a more realistic intervention might center on incremental changes within a particular relationship. In cases where the woman changes relationships but keeps her serial arrangements essentially sadomasochistic, greater attention should be focused on her own role in retaining an "inelastic ritual of dominance and subordination"

(Chancer, 1992, p. 1) even as she, often with great flourish, relinquishes a particular partner for his sadistic ways.

Women surrender their ego and agency in a Faustian bargain for love, a recurring motif in cultural representations of gender relations. For women it might be said, as Chuck Palahniuk (2002, p. 72) observed in another context, "masochism is a valuable job skill." Women often accept stereotypic gender assignments, particularly those that call upon them to nurture rather than rebel when faced with a man's aggression. This mindset inscribes blame on the woman for her lover's transgressions: if only she had been a better caretaker he would not have lost control; if only she had behaved herself and not challenged his authority, she would be adored instead of assaulted.

Underneath this easy acceptance of "femininity scripts" (Boonzaier, 2008) many of the women with whom I spoke revealed a naïve idealism about romantic love that countervailed the reality of broken bones and black eyes. This can only be accomplished through an adamant dissociative process, one that both disavows and distorts truth. As Deleuze (1989) observed, masochism can unchain one from the demands of a guilty conscience by elevating punishment to art form, a kind of ideal. Rather than the pity a victim receives, a masochist receives absolution. She has both chosen and been chosen and her faux agency becomes a prime defense against feeling victimized. In this aspect, masochism can be almost triumphal. Although it strips power, it can simultaneously convey superiority and, in doing so, protect the ego from narcissistic injury (Buie et al., 1996). If she *chooses* this, it is not an attack but a strategy to accept the proximal pain of a beating in lieu of the greater pain of abandonment. It is not unlike the decision of a cutter to end her anxiety via razorblade, or this enactment recounted in an unsolicited email from a woman who described her aggression as being sequestered in a "horrid blankness":

> I've taken to whacking myself in the face with a city yellow pages. It's heavy enough, when wielded with both hands, to simulate how hard I was slapped by both parents. It makes me feel . . . comforted. They used slaps as punctuations during tirades.

In attempting to salvage the self-esteem of women who have survived brutal relationships, advocates in the shelter system, as well as practitioners, play to the idea that women have resisted violence in paradoxical ways, sometimes through behaviors that seem to the observer to be masochistic but are really demonstrations of strength. Indeed, in many cases, this is true. Women do develop conscious strategies to protect themselves that may include multiple levels of submission to what they consider lesser evils (remember the woman who, as a matter of course, adopted an ingratiating posture around her unpredictable husband). Uebel (2002) goes so far as to describe masochism as "a tactic of power predicated upon power's disavowal" and even broadens this concept to include the social world's interpellation of the victim's predicament. He sees the contemporary embrace of victimhood/survivorship as a strategy of political resistance, where oppressed groups (including, one could assume, battered women en masse) participate in "politically idealized suffering in the name of future rewards" (p. 395). In fact, the efficaciousness of women's support groups in "healing" women may depend upon the adoption of this kind of communalizing narrative. I do not deny its power in that forum, only the limited utility it has for the psychoanalytic treatment of intimate violence.

The re-enactment of earlier trauma through masochism may indeed be a strategy of control, even mastery, over those abusive encounters. What seems equally central to address are women's dissociated attempts to control their own aggression through the motif of suffering. This speaks to the conflation of rage and pain; the suppression of the former having been effected only by a well policed capitulation to the latter. The aggression is externalized and turned back against the rageful self, making what might become agentic power into total impotence. One of the analysts in my focus group described his masochistic patient's "melding" of these forms.

> She cannot imagine potency that isn't overly aggressive; that is what potency is. She can get enraged, she gets hysterically angry but it is an impotent rage. She is identified *with* these guys' power. She is identified *by* these guys' power. But there is no real power in her yell. It is all bark and no bite.

Khan (1979) has written of the critical role played by the confluence of pain and anger in sexualized expressions of masochism, when a deadening kind of psychic pain (conveyed through apathy, depression or immobilizing anxiety) becomes enlivened by actual suffering. In one clinical vignette, what allows Khan's patient to leave her sadistic lover is recognizing his powerlessness or, rather, that the illusion of his power can be sustained only with her cooperation. This conundrum undoubtedly has parallels in the transference between therapist and patient, bringing Khan to question his own intentions in much the same way that members of my focus group questioned theirs. Where does the masochistic patient find will and power in the analyst? To what degree is the analyst–patient contract a simulacrum of the sadomasochistic gamesmanship in her romantic life?

> The crucial difference seemed to lay in the different use of the patient as a person, by her lover and by her analyst . . . her lover compelled her into the role of his subjective object. He had to devalue and disrupt all functions in her that gave her a separate identity and existence. She was merely a puppet that actualized his will and command, his intents and fantasies. In the analytic contract, per contrast, she sought help to be enabled to find her own will and power in her life situations. The empathy she required was in the service of the actualization of her own capacities and functions toward personal autonomy.
>
> (Khan, 1979, p. 208)

Khan suggests work around the exploration of alternate power structures in the therapeutic relationship, and I found this Winnicottian kind of playing successful in my work with Phoebe. In our haste to save a woman from the shame that so often accompanies her admission of complicity, we may be forestalling the integration of the very parts of herself that are likely to fall into repetitive enactments of violence. That Phoebe might explore the shame induced by others, as well as at my own hand, but also play at being the humiliator, the contemptress, even the savage murderer, became an integral part of our work, a therapeutic shapeshifting. If she sees herself as only a pawn in some masculine power game, a woman's agency can never be constructed in other than a reactive mode. She needs to see her part in the destructive dance.

In developmental terms, not until there is an apprehension of the self as separate from the caretaker can there be the opportunity for mutual recognition and impact (Winnicott, 1965). As Pollock and Slavin have articulated (1998), in the absence of true agency in the adult, there can be no real attachment, only a fantasied merger. The sense of fusion between the individuals in an abusive situation is undergirded by sadomasochistic maintenance systems, which protect each from taking responsibility for their anger or admitting their terror of loss. The romantic script upon which they rely is both excuse and justification for acting badly.

I am taken with the possibility of moving from this pain, which in its Latin form – poena – means not random injury but a kind of divine punishment, to poiesis, the Greek root of the word poetry. Heidigger expanded poiesis to encompass any threshold experience where one thing becomes another. A transformation is effected, like the one we desire for women trapped in sadomasochistic cycles of abuse: ice to water, object to subject, passivity to agency, caterpillar to butterfly.

Note

1 To protect patient privacy, I will not name the institute or the clinicians who shared their insights with me, although I am very grateful for their help in sifting through my own thoughts and feelings about working with women in abusive relationships.

Chapter 5

Theater of judicial absurdity

> Maternal femininity is the carrier for shame, and so the oppression of women provides the archetypal fuel, so to speak, for shame's annihilating capacity to create non-existence.
>
> (Mary Ayers, *Masculine Shame*)

> Absurdism, like methodical doubt, has wiped the slate clean. It leaves us in a blind alley. But, like methodical doubt, it can, by returning upon itself, open up a new field of investigation, and in the process of reasoning then pursues the same course. I proclaim that I believe in nothing and that everything is absurd, but I cannot doubt the validity of my proclamation and I must at least believe in my protest.
>
> (Albert Camus, *The Rebel*)

> And so I felt it was my responsibility to go out there and speak about the type of violence I'm suffering. And I was always, I'm always, I always dress really – it's graphic because I wear blood and rope. And the imagery that I project is of a woman who is dead because I feel dead without my daughter. I feel that it is a death and nobody sees it.
>
> (One of four interview subjects who lost custody of their children to their abuser)

I did not believe her. Although the interview had lasted over three hours, I thought there must be more to the story. Women did not lose custody of their children for no reason. Especially not to men who had assaulted them. In her story, Rosalie had lost custody, and then had supervised visitation imposed by the court, after her daughter had come home from a paternal visit with bruises and a vaginal discharge which Rosalie subsequently brought to the attention of a physician at Child Advocacy Services. The tale seemed Kafkaesque; the patient, I discerned, very split. The "bride's march" Rosalie described, where she donned rope and fake blood, had a gothic, hysterical taint. On the other hand, her delivery was preternaturally calm. The tape recorder off, she handed me a CD and asked that I please carry her message.

I put the CD aside and only popped it in the computer weeks later, after I started receiving unsolicited emails from an organization fighting for the rights of battered women who had lost their children to their ex-husbands. It was a video of testimonials from women like Rosalie. It was not the trauma porn I had expected, meant to rend the hearts of mothers everywhere. Like the subject I had interviewed, all the women seemed opaque in pain. Invisible piano wire held their gazes steady and their mouths open expansively, pleading another iteration of a case they had long ago lost. A woman in the video, who had not seen her children in six and a half years, explained, "If my children had died, I would be grieving and I would be thinking of them but I would have been able to go forward. But because my children live and I love them and I know they are in harm's way, I cannot go on with my life. I have to continue fighting" (Hannah and Waller, 2008). The non-custodial mother, in her revolt, imposed a kind of affective order on an illogical system, whispering "I proclaim that I believe in nothing and that everything is absurd, but I cannot doubt the validity of my proclamation and I must at least believe in my protest" (Camus, 1992). Her story, multiplied tenfold in the video, becomes a movement that attempts to catalyze anger toward the goal of political reformation as well as personal salvation.

Doing some homework, I learned that fathers who batter the mother are twice as likely to seek exclusive custody of the children as non-violent fathers (American Psychological Association, 1996). In one jurisdiction studied, offenders received sole custody in 37 percent of cases brought before the family court (VOW, 2008). During the course of my research project, I met the women who lived that statistic. Fully a third of the women in my small sample had lost their children to the men who had terrified and tortured them. As in Jericho, the wall of my denial began to crumble under the insistent blare of their trumpets.

The clinician in me struggled to understand my earlier disbelief and the more massive institutional dissociation that undergirds such stories of maternal loss, which I have learned, to my great shame, are fairly common. By the time that a psychoanalyst in my focus group questioned whether the fears of a patient that her husband would follow through on his threats to "take the kids and throw you out; you'll have nothing" were realistic ("What if she believes him? He doesn't really mean it," said the clinician), I was prepared with a cautionary soliloquy about mothers put on trial, for the crime of having been assaulted.

Disbelief is a common theme when it comes to spousal abuse. Denial persists, even in a public grown familiar with the spectra of private violence through voyeuristic media accounts; indeed, media saturation may increase viewer cynicism in the long run. To some degree, it has been the insistence on viewing domestic violence through a myopic and Manichean lens, one that replaces the idea of complex unconscious interpersonal interaction with cardboard cutouts of villains and victims, that drives the backlash of indifference. Desensitization inspires doubt and, in the way that any undue exposure eventually seeds a conspiracy theory, gives birth to psychological treatises that cover up the true nature of trauma. Thus, police see "couples prone to violence" rather than recognizing the relative abilities of gendered parties to inflict injury. Mediators in the court system urge women to "get over it," and view their inability to do so as an impediment to good faith negotiations. Emergency room physicians ask questions that depersonalize and de-historize events, unlinking the physical consequences of abuse from the actions of perpetrators. Psychologists resist detailed inquiries that might reveal even more catastrophic internal injuries than initially observed. The public, fed in recent years by a raft of sociological research purporting to find "gender symmetry" in domestic violence, may have embraced a more egalitarian – but far less accurate – portrait of intimate conflict (for a critique of these studies, see Kimmel, 2002). Younger people in particular often view couples' violence as reciprocal and rarely see its presence as grounds to end a relationship. The intertwining of violence and romance is seen as acceptable by a growing number of teens (James et al., 2000). There seems to be a strong backlash against the storied images of female victims that saturated public consciousness at the height of the women's movement.

Thus we have, as a growing response to women's battery in intimate relationships, the idea that women are feigning abuse to get large financial settlements, to deflect attention from their own negligence or bad behavior, or to deprive fathers of meaningful connections to their children. In the wish to attenuate trauma, the court system in particular has relocated its attention seamlessly from the sufferer of pain to its architect or, to use Benjamin's (2004) image, from those who are "done to" to the "doers" of malign acts. For victims, the reversal publicly undoes trauma while privately compounding it. For offenders, the switch confers a new victim status with all its attendant rights and privileges.

All these things constitute an attempt *at the macro level* to undo trauma. Undoing is a counterfactual narration of events with the unconscious intent of remaking what has happened into something other than what it was: a massive physical and/or psychological injury. Obviously, in reality this is an impossible feat; nothing that has happened can actually be undone. However, with appropriate mental acrobatics, one can mitigate painful memories by rewriting things with the victim in a more masterful position or by telescoping the ordeal itself to more manageable proportions. The defensive process of undoing occurs most often in situations where shame is a central traumatic affect. Clinicians since Freud have observed how this *ungeschehenmachen* functions in an individual psyche when it is overwhelmed by experience; here I argue that the institutions that moderate violence against women collectivize these defenses as a way of coping with the massive failure of systems designed to protect women.

Institutional dissociations

Dissociation is usually described as an alteration in consciousness that allows a person to disengage from his environment; the environment one needs to escape may be external or internal. Volumes have been devoted to personal dissociation as a defense mechanism, against both massive trauma and life's more minor vicissitudes whose accumulation, for some people, can be as lacerating as a trauma that is more singular. (Less has been said about dissociation at the cultural level, although the dissociative quality of certain mass hysterias has been remarked upon by social commentators.) Dissociation has been conceptualized as a kind of hypnotic state (Freud, 1896; Janet, 1889), and as a normal or pathological inattention whereby perceptual experience is not integrated in a cohered sense of selfhood (Sullivan, 1956b; Bucci, 2002). The diagnosis of dissociation usually occurs on an individual level, where symptoms are reported and signs are documented: flashbacks, amnesias, automatisms, fugues, and conversions are noted along with more subtle and common indicators, like denial of experience, disowning of agency, and detachment from the affective subtext of life. Dissociation, once thought of as an exotic symptom of severe illness, is now considered to be an unavoidable side effect of normal brain function, where data overload – for any variety of reasons – results in some percepts being excluded from the mental processes that usually schematize them.

Contemporary psychoanalytic theory posits that many experiences that have been split off from awareness, usually because they were traumatic, emerge in unconscious enactments. One goal of therapy is to facilitate the consciousness of fragmented mind-states and integrate them into a more unitary sense of self, even as we admit that such single mindedness is merely a useful illusion. Since Freud, psychoanalysts have believed that consciousness dispels the blind enactments which can be so destructive to the self and others.

The study of dissociation on the personal level has informed the bulk of work on child abuse and domestic violence. Highly traumatic, these violent experiences are dissociated so that people can survive them and remain somewhat functional. Part of recovery for victims entails remembering and coming to terms with what has happened to them. Of course, this does not happen in a vacuum. Women and children have long acknowledged the feelings of betrayal when their stories are disbelieved by family members or friends, and we know that such betrayal may be even more traumatic than abuse itself. Any blanket denial of the reality of abuse by outsiders constitutes a dissociative lapse coterminous with the victims' consciousness of the violation she has endured. Thus, at the very moment a victim has overcome her own inclination to deny abuse, someone else dissociates the trauma in her stead; trauma becomes a game of hot potato where a shared consciousness of events cannot exist. The same is true when information about violence is presented at the institutional level. Bloom (2005) has explored how dissociation arises in organizations in response to unmanageable affect.

> Organizations can also distort memories of the past as individuals can. Organizations may selectively omit disagreeable facts, may exaggerate or embellish positive deeds, may deny the truth. They may manipulate linkages by focusing on one cause of an event while ignoring or denying other causes. (p. 101)

In fact, the further one moves from the personal, the more abstracted – and meaningless – the story of violence against women becomes. Abused women become a blur of black and blue on a subway poster, indistinguishable from the adjacent advertisement for some new slasher film. In the institutional realm, dissociation is a pragmatic initiative that protects its inhabitants from traumatic knowledge. Labels like "the injured party" become arbitrary and interchangeable. And, because collective thinkers are particularly inept at inference and nuance, it is in institutional settings that we find the greatest harm being done to the already injured.

As the vignettes I will present suggest, when local denial becomes entrenched in mechanisms intended to provide support for victims, such as policing, law, the judiciary, medical services, psychiatry, and psychology, it compounds the trauma. Institutions can easily become perpetrators in this regard. Hospitals that ignore possible signs of domestic violence, policing policies that mandate dual arrests, civil and family courts that award custody not to the protective parent but the assaultive one, exemplify this transferential parallelism. The actions of the institutions that oversee domestic violence are both an embodiment of our cultural veneration/denigration of women, particularly mothers, and a traumatic response to the horrific violence they suffer.

Doctoring abuse

In one study, 71 percent of medical doctors surveyed felt that questioning patients about domestic violence was not a worthwhile pursuit; given the time constraints of managed care and their lack of training in protocols to help reticent patients open up about disturbing events, doctors' abdication of the caretaker role is not surprising (Gremillion and Kanof, 1996). This is doubly upsetting given that research has demonstrated that a very large number of women come into medical settings with symptoms consonant with intimate battering but are rarely queried about the issue (Warshaw, 1989; McCauley et al., 1995). Luckily, many hospitals now ask any injured woman showing up in the emergency room to fill out a form that asks, among more routine queries, whether her injuries were caused by her domestic partner. At least one woman in my sample was rescued from her violent marriage via this simple questionnaire.

Mental health practitioners may be no better at recognizing abuse or may be reluctant to intervene forcefully because they have been trained to allow patients to find answers at their own pace. In psychoanalysis, in particular, the rate of change may be glacial, with patients taking many years to identify a partner's actions as abusive even when conflicts are physical. Many therapists are reluctant to qualify abuse for the patient, believing that the potency of their authority in the therapeutic relationship argues for only the most judicious use of influence; after all, it is the patient's insight – not the therapist's – that augers lasting change. Arguably though, it is a task of therapy, if not a duty, to bring someone to the doorstep of objective reality and urge them to stick a toe over the saddle. While we can easily devolve into theoretical arguments over whether any "objective" reality exists, whether the therapist has enough information to extend an interpretation of events, and whether the unequal distribution of power in their relationship should foreclose the issuance of directives, more pressing should be the need of a therapist to tell a patient, seemingly held hostage by abuse, what they see and recommend, even if some moderating statement is in order. While a lack of discretion in self-revelations by the therapist may create a zone of danger and even re-traumatization, a trend toward integration is forestalled by too much clinician timidity. Bromberg (2006) argues that, in post-classical models, an analyst's ability to tunefully share her perceptions is not an injection of one subjectivity into another but an invitation to mutual processing that ultimately facilitates "intersubjective negotiation" (p. 132) even as it may – momentarily – derail it.

> If the analyst's commitment to attunement is honored, a transitional reality can begin to take shape between patient and analyst that has room for the subjective experience of each partner and space for relational negotiation that is affectively alive. This in turn enhances the patient's capacity for intersubjective functioning in areas of personality where the capacity to bear intersubjective conflict has been preempted by dissociation.
>
> (p. 134)

One woman, in a long-term psychoanalysis, told me that although she entered analysis in part because she was frightened of her husband, it was at least six years before she became aware that his pattern of control and intimidation constituted abuse, and that it was only *after* she began discussing this in sessions that her analyst shared how concerned he too had been many times over the years, worrying that the husband's threats were moving closer to physical substantiation. Retrospectively, this woman wished that her analyst had disclosed his thoughts earlier, perhaps precipitating a speedier rise to consciousness for the material. One supposes that the analyst might have felt that the patient had not been ready to hear that her husband was abusive and might have fled therapy if the view felt imposed. Perhaps this is true. Conversely, the analyst may have been unconsciously titrating his own fear by holding back an assessment that, once voiced, might precipitate an action on the patient's part that was rash or even dangerous. Another strong possibility is that the therapist was having a complementary dissociation around the husband's potential for violence.

For example, the woman remembered a particular dream she had related in therapy whose interpretation had engendered some conflict between the analytic pair. In the dream, she had been shot in the side and taken to a kind of safe house, the way that a criminal injured during a robbery attempt might be brought to a "mob doctor." She was deposited, bleeding, in the bathtub where she waited for a doctor to remove the bullet. What disturbed her about the dream was that the bullet hole in her side was puckered, like a sphincter muscle. She felt that this was a very important aspect of the dream but could not associate to it fruitfully. Her analyst offered no interpretation and, though the analysand pressed, the therapist insisted he had no idea what it meant and they moved away from exploring the material further. The patient had the vague feeling that her therapist just "could not be in this dream with me" and sensed that he was a little irritated with her focus on interpreting the appearance of the bullet hole. Many years later, well after termination, the patient suddenly knew what the image in the dream signified. Laughing, she told me:

> It was so concrete, how could we have missed it? I had an asshole at my side! And I wanted my doctor to get rid of it . . . um, him. I was trying so hard to get the message but, in this case, my analyst was just as unable to look at the truth as I. We got to this eventually in another way, and it was tremendously liberating and empowering for me, but I still fantasize how different things might have been if my analyst had been more confrontative about what was going on in my marriage. Maybe I would have rejected the interpretation, who knows? But maybe it would have freed me sooner.

Law and dissociation

Despite public health campaigns that urge women to report abuse, many marginalized women still face huge obstacles when it comes to picking up the phone. Those without legal immigration status may fear deportation, those dependent on partners for economic support may fear homelessness. Even Congress has acknowledged that housing authorities often evict victims from public housing because of the behavior of their spouses or because their own calls for help, even to the police, constitute a disturbance of the peace. Landlords often disbelieve women's claims that their partner's violence was beyond their control (US Department of Housing and Urban Development, 2011) and throw them out on the street at the very moment that they most need shelter. All women fear that violence may escalate once a man returns from jail or court. In the case of unemployed men and those with prior criminal records, the fear is especially well founded (Mills, 1998).

While the policing of domestic violence has changed in some positive ways over the years, with better training of officers to handle disputes and the inclusion of female officers on teams answering domestic violence calls, of late we seem to have descended into another circle of absurdity where political correctness has trumped sound policy. The illogical extension of mandatory arrest policies has been to remove discretion and democratize the process by arresting both parties when each is injured. This has resulted in the frequent lock-up of female victims prior to arraignment, particularly young, black, or strident women who do not fit the victim stereotype (Miller, 2001).

Once in court, women face another consequence of the move toward gender neutrality: the issuing of mutual orders of protection rather than the standard restraining order against perpetrators that once accompanied claims of intimate violence. In her comprehensive overview of the legal implications of this trend, Topliffe (1991–1992) suggests that many judges have moved in this direction because it is less time consuming, obviating the need for a legal hearing to show cause. Judges, rarely schooled in the psychological intricacies of battering relationships, have long struggled with the issue of women who request protection but make the enforcement of restraining orders impossible. One judge, who has since come to recognize the danger of his own denial, wrote the following reflection on his unenlightened 19 years on the circuit court in Illinois (Hornsby, 2010):

> I was upset when the victims, often visibly injured, came into my court and requested another order of protection. I was annoyed that the victims were wasting my time because I suspected they would not require the abusers to obey the protective orders and would allow them back into their homes while the orders were in effect, often resulting in other incidents of domestic violence and necessary protective orders.
>
> (p. 73)

In circumstances like the one above, judges can impose non-voluntary mutual orders of protection, which ostensibly make any actions on the part of the women, such as letting a man into her home, cause for her arrest and prosecution. However, not all mutual orders are involuntary. Women often readily agree to reciprocal emergency protective orders to expedite the process and get quickly home to children that have been taken into custodial care by children's services following police intervention. Once an emergency order is in place it is easier for men to counterclaim abuse and fight for permanent restraint of the women who have suffered at their hands. Topliffe notes that these court orders may be hard to fight for women who do not have the means to pay filing fees or hire attorneys to represent them, particularly if they have been economically dependent on their partners. After all, she observes, they cannot quite ask their husbands to lend them the money. Most damaging, women rarely recognize the implication of either their arrest record or the protective order against them when it comes to future court decisions regarding divorce, civil liability, custody, and criminal proceedings against the batterer. On an emotional level, having such legal injunctions in place may predispose women to taking on a greater share of the blame for abuse, while men may enthusiastically internalize the court's support for the idea that their wife was equally culpable for the violence between them.

Rosalie, who was quoted in the chapter epigraph, described what seemed like a calculated plan on the part of her partner to orchestrate a scenario, through the use of police intervention, that would favor him later on in custody arrangements. Although he was the physical aggressor, he would often call the cops when she expressed anger or defended herself. Being unmarried and in an interracial relationship (she was Hispanic, her partner was white) may have increased the odds that the police would believe the partner's version of events.

> He called again. This time, I saw, I knew he called because he shoved me. It was an argument about – it was almost going to be our four year anniversary

> and I asked him about marriage, you know. "What are we doing? It's going to be our anniversary and where's this all going?" And I don't know what he said, but I threw a cup. I didn't throw it at him, but I threw it out of rage and it broke. And then he came back and he grabbed me and he shoved me so hard across the kitchen floor, the kitchen table broke my fall. And I was like, wow, really? And I went to the living room. I went to the fire place and I took a poker and I told him, "Come. Come touch me again." [My daughter was] sleeping in the bedroom upstairs. She's already three. And he didn't come. He didn't come near me. We were a good distance away 'cause our living room was really, really big. And he was in his nice suit, wearing his expensive coat, with his briefcase. He was leaving for work. And he went downstairs and he called the cops.

He told the police that Rosalie had threatened him. By the time they arrived, Rosalie had retrieved her crying child, awakened by the arguing. She was crying herself, in disbelief that the cops were accusing *her* of potential violence.

Rosalie: And there was the poker. And I remember they were trying to speak to me, but I couldn't speak because I was crying. I was so emotional. I stopped crying when I heard the cop in the family room tell him something about an order of protection and custody. I want you to know I lived in white town. I was the only Hispanic on that street. I walked around with a birth certificate to prove that this little white child was mine. Because there was nobody else. So the cop – all the cops were white.

Interviewer: Did you tell them he shoved you?

Rosalie: I don't remember saying that. I don't remember being able to say anything in my defense. Remember, here I am, right? Maybe [inaudible], in my bathrobe, and here's this nice-smelling, very calm businessman saying that his live-in girlfriend – because he never failed to fuckin' mention that I was just his live-in girlfriend. Oh my god. That used to drive me nuts! I mean, I later found out in the paper, but that's how he treated me. The cops left and I knew I had to get out of there. I knew I had to get out because there was, I wasn't, I was gonna go to jail. I knew it.

Failure to protect

Recent family law journals have unmasked a subterranean shift in custody assignments in cases of domestic violence over the last quarter century, one that severely disadvantages female victims who find it impossible to defend themselves from escalating violence. The imputation of Battered Women's Syndrome (BWS), which once seemed like a salvaging narrative for abused women, is now used against them in legal adjudications, where any insinuation of mental illness may undermine credibility and competence. While, on the one hand, women may be encouraged to present themselves as traumatized and debilitated in order to add believability to abuse claims, the very same presentation may convince a divorce judge next door that they are not capable of caring for their children. With its central concept of "learned helplessness," BWS offered an explanatory framework for women's paralysis in violent relationships, using the example of Seligman's captive dog[1] to make the point. But, according to the courts, passivity on the part of mothers may lead to the neglect or endangerment of their children. Strict liability standards hold the mother responsible for harm to the child without identifying the cause of that harm or its true perpetrator; such a standard "requires the mother to do what society is incapable of doing" (Miccio, 1994–1995, p. 1094), in other words, restrain the abuser. In addition to losing custody, these victims may even be civilly prosecuted under the "failure to protect" statutes that are codified in most jurisdictions.

> In New York, parents can be found to have abused their children by "allowing" either physical or sexual abuse, or "allowing" an environment where such abuse can take place. Neglect findings can be made when the parent fails to exercise a minimum degree of care and that failure results or will result in physical, emotional, or psychological impairment to the child.
>
> (p. 1089)

Absurdly, while women can be charged with a failure to protect children when they remain in abusive relationships, they are often accused of making false accusations about fathers' violence if they try to protect children once the marriage has dissolved (Bancroft and Silverman, 2005). In fact, mothers, fearful of losing their children, are often forced into divorce mediation where part of settlement negotiations include their dropping restraining orders or agreeing to unsupervised visits by the battering partner, in order to demonstrate that they do not intend to "brainwash" the children against the father (Dragiewicz, 2010). A bogus psychological construct, "Parental Alienation Syndrome," has been used to great effect to wrest custody from women in high conflict divorces. Parental Alienation Syndrome (PAS) is a term coined by psychiatrist Richard Gardner (1992) to describe "children who have been programmed by their mothers to hate their father and subject him to a campaign of denigration" (p. 159). Although PAS has been discredited under scientific review (Walker et al., 2004), it continues to be used in the courts as a way of undermining women's allegations of abuse during custody disputes (Erickson, 2010). Judith Wallenstein, reviewing a book on the clinician's role in custody decisions by Gardner for an issue of the *Journal of the American Psychoanalytic Association*, wrote:

> Another troublesome note which occurs in Dr. Gardner's useful discussion of the role of the clinician in divorce-related court litigation is his effort to assess "strong maternal capacity" as part of a custody investigation at the behest of

> the court. Among the many questions Dr. Gardner asks the mother in his intensive custody evaluation is whether she is "a baby-carriage peeker," whether she has strong yearnings for another child, and whether she prefers "talking to men" or talking about her children to other women. "The woman who says 'I prefer talking to the men; I have enough of children all day long,' may be healthy, but may also be reflecting some deficiency in her maternal capacity." Surely, it is late in the day to assert that the answers to such simplistic, stereotyped, and prejudiced questions will shed meaningful light on the complexity of a mother's capacity to parent her own children.
>
> (Wallerstein, 1977, p. 738)

That was written in *1977*. A more recent critique notes the detrimental consequences of Gardner's influence.

> Most controversial are the radical recommendations that follow from Gardner's view that an alienating parent is the principal if not the sole cause of the problem. In severe cases of PAS, he recommends changing custody (placing the child with the "hated" parent) as well as other punitive measures that have resulted, for instance, in the child's detention in juvenile hall or inpatient psychiatric facility, and/or the jailing and fining of the offending parent.
>
> (Kelly and Johnston, 2005, p. 250)

Contemporary psychiatric experts testifying to the presence of the syndrome posit that women are attempting to turn their children against the father "and that often the particular lies a mother tries to brainwash a child into believing (and parroting back to other adults) are that the father has abused the mother and/or the children" (Erickson, 2010, ch. 20, p. 3). Because of the erroneous belief that stories of violence are apocryphal, as many as half of cases where allegations are made may not be thoroughly investigated (Johnston et al., 2005), even though a number of studies indicate that false allegations of abuse in custody disputes are rare (see Erickson, 2010, fn. 9). A common problem women face in substantiating child abuse is that there may, indeed, have been no abuse prior to the couple's separation, making it seem as if the charges have been suddenly fabricated. But abuse of the children often does not begin until after a woman leaves, as a way to punish her by proxy (Liss and Stahly, 1993). Rosalie explained how, despite her strongest efforts to provide documentation to the court, any evidence that her partner's abuse had spilled over to their child during her absence was minimized or ignored.

> I walked in thinking, oh my god, [my baby] has bruises, I have pictures, I have the police report, he's been physically abusive to her, he's done. He's fried meat 'cause he's not going to be able to get away with this now.
>
> I walk out without custody. That day, I walked out without custody.

Men often claim that women are poisoning the children's minds. Indeed, it would be hard to imagine a battered woman who joyfully anticipated a close co-parenting relationship with her ex-spouse and kept her comments to the kids totally free of bias, but this does not constitute brainwashing. On the other hand, research has shown that it is often the case that, during visitation, batterers themselves exploit children in an effort to intimidate or control the mother.

> They manipulated, harassed, and interrogated children in order to obtain information about the protective parent. Visitation was often used to send threats or violent messages. In our study, a perpetrator who was denied access to weapons by the court, returned the children from visitation with a full set of toy weapons in an effort to terrorize the protective parent. He accompanied his threat by making comments to the protective parent's family and friends that he could do whatever he wanted to her.
>
> (Araji and Bosek, 2010, ch. 6, p. 29)

Some women in such circumstances, terrorized, flee with their children. This virtually guarantees that, if found, sole custody will be awarded to the batterer. State courts may prosecute women under kidnapping statutes for running away from their abuser (Zorza, 2010). Of almost 204,000 parental abductions yearly, about half involve couples where there is history of violence (National Clearinghouse for the Defense of Battered Women, 2005).

> When parents take their children in domestic violence cases, the abductions generally occur in one of two distinct contexts. In one set of circumstances, batterers take the children in order to harm victims further. In another, victims flee with their children in an effort to protect themselves and their children from the batterers' violence. Despite the dramatic difference between these two acts – one vindictive and the other protective – the criminal justice system rarely considers the context of abductions. Typically, the response to perpetrators and to victims of domestic violence is the same regardless of the reasons why the parents left with the children.
>
> (pp. 2–3)

In a related scenario, mothers who flee alone from their batterers can be charged with abandoning their children and also lose custody. Although some state statutes consider domestic violence a justification for fleeing the home on an emergency basis, abandonment will still be charged if the escaping parent does not either reunite with child, provide care from afar, or make certain that the child is safe from violence within a relatively short time frame. In many states, abandonment is considered a subcategory of child abuse and women who run from batterers may be charged under abuse statutes. One of my subjects, Bunny, who had tried for years to develop an escape plan for herself and her children, was suddenly offered an opportunity to travel abroad through her job. Desperate to get away, she seized the opportunity, believing that she would be in a better position to figure out a solution when she was free. She never thought that she would lose her children if she left. After eight months, despite her attempts at contact, her husband did receive permanent custody of them. As far as Bunny is concerned, she had no choice:

> And one of the things that they give me is a scholarship to go [overseas]. That's where, you know, he wanted to kill me. And he tell me, "Ok." I thought it was an "OK," but it was not an "OK" because what he did – and then I go and I have all the papers from the government, I sign everything, and the passport, the visa to go, everything. First thing that he did was take the passport. And he put the passport somewhere that I wouldn't get it. And then, for me, when I ask him for the passport, he beat me. And he tell me that, "You will never go [away]." For me, really, going [there] was my last chance. Really last one. Last, last one.
>
> No matter what people can say, "You should not do it – leave your children," I know that this escape plot, I am the owner of it.
>
> So I – even when people can blame me because I leave the children behind. That was the only way. The only escape way of surviving. Only. For me, it was not, because many nights, I told myself, if I don't do that, I will kill myself. That was my true option. Because telling people what is happening, people don't believe me. If I die, I will leave a note and people will read the note to my children. That was my only option. I say, OK, if I died, people will read the note to my children.

Earlier in their relationship, when Bunny had tried to leave her husband, he had kidnapped the children and secreted them with his brother. In her small town, she had been unable to get any help from family or friends.

> No, it's like, OK, you are the bad one, let's – so it's not like they didn't accept it. Or maybe they think it's normal because modern-day man, they can beat, they can – so it's, it's not something that if you go and say your husband's beating you, that people will be so, like, it's the first time that this happened. It's not that it's the first time that you need assistance or nothing. Go back to your husband. Maybe you did something wrong. So that's how I feel.

Needless to say, doubting her own perception of events, Bunny did return to him. Of course, he was never punished for taking the children and concealing their whereabouts from Bunny. After he gained custody, he kept the children away from their mother until they were grown. Other men, conversely, once they win the children, want nothing more to do with them. Paula choked back tears as she described her ex-husband's indifference. Sometimes she spoke in the present tense as if this were all happening now, even though it had happened at least a decade earlier.

> I talk to them on the phone. I spoke to the little one this morning. But I mean, he was bent on destroying them because how dare I leave? And I couldn't get the court to hear all of that. I have them very organized and they're very organized children so he decides he's going to destroy all that. And within less than a month of having custody of them, he put them on the streets, like, "Go. Bye." They were in . . . I think like middle school. Is it middle school? I can't remember.

Courts seem to be enamored of dads asserting their wish to be involved with their children, even after extended periods of neglect. It is rare that custody is reversed, even in these instances. Paula failed in repeated attempts to regain custody of her children.

> And when I tell the courts that I found out they're on the streets and every time I try to get them, he takes them back, and you know, when he gets them back, within 24 hours, they're on the streets again, but you know, the court wouldn't listen. They told the judge I was a liar. And his lawyer was saying the same thing and so they didn't listen. They didn't investigate or anything. And my kids now, they're 26, 27, they're still trying to work their way off the streets.

Evaluating the evaluators

The most recent technical report on custody evaluations where abuse is alleged, submitted to the US Department of Justice in late 2011 (Saunders et al., 2011),[2] concluded that surprisingly high numbers of custody evaluators still are ignorant about the psychological effects of domestic violence on mothers and children, still believe that false allegations of abuse are common although there is no empirical evidence to support that claim, and are willing to grant either unsupervised visitation or, 15 to 20 percent of the time, sole physical custody to the perpetrators of abuse. Joint custody arrangements and unsupervised visitations are equally common in cases where abuse has occurred as in cases where it has not (Kernic et al., 2005). Saunders and his colleagues found that awarding custody to offenders rather than victims was significantly related to several background beliefs held by the evaluators: that victimized mothers alienate children from their fathers, that abuse allegations are typically false, that children are hurt if mothers resist co-parenting and, most alarming, that domestic violence is not an important consideration in custody decisions. Unsurprisingly, evaluators who endorsed those statements also strongly supported what the authors termed "patriarchal norms": that women have achieved equality with men, that the world is a just place, and that social hierarchies are good. In the researchers' interviews with women who had been on the losing end of custody decisions, a numbers of grievances emerged: that evaluations were rushed, that abuse was minimized or ignored, that mothers were reprimanded for reporting child abuse, and that the mental health consequences of victimization were prejudicially weighted in determining mothers' ability to care for their children. A mother who participated in the Department of Justice study (Saunders et al., 2011) related how seeking treatment for the sequela of her husband's violence redounded to her husband's benefit.

> One of the things that the custody evaluator said to me that I've never gotten over on that day . . . was that it does not look good for me because I was hospitalized for depression and that it did not look good for him, because he was a registered sex offender. . . . How you can compare the two? And how you can hold [it] against somebody for getting help for themselves? . . . Somehow they compared that and they chose him over me. . . . It makes no sense to me.
>
> (p. 105)

"Batterers win custody of their children with greater frequency than is generally realized," says Lundy Bancroft, a writer and advocate for battered women, "although it is widely believed that family courts have a bias in favor of mothers, custody studies have demonstrated that, since the 1970s, fathers have been at a marked advantage in custody suits" (Bancroft and Silverman, 2005, p. 157). The reasons seem not so surprising when considered in the context of the patriarchal institutions that oversee custody: law and psychology.

First, men are more likely to work outside the home than are women; if both partners work, men will usually be the higher earners. In addition to having the resources to mount compelling legal cases, evaluators may feel that children are better off in homes that are financially secure. Rosalie told me how twisted things became on paper, where her husband's financial edge haloed him and marked her as a loser.

> What went on the record was that he was a fabulous father, he was engaged to a woman who was a preschool teacher, he had a house on a traffic-free, beautiful community in [the suburbs], and that he could provide a better life for [our daughter]. And that this woman [meaning herself], she's unstable. She's unstable. She works a part-time job in a church. She hits herself on the wall. She calls the cops and makes false allegations. She's not fit to be a mother. And I wish I could tell you that that was the worst.
>
> Do you know what that bastard did after I left him? He went to the court, he filed for custody and child support. How am I gonna pay him child support? I was a stay-at-home mom. No money, no job. He filed for child support.

Second, psychological testing used by evaluators may disadvantage victims whose experiences have left them angry, depressed, paranoid, confused, and fearful. Conversely, batterers may emerge from their relationships comparatively unscathed. When the clinical picture veers toward psychopathy, men may be particularly adroit at winning over court personnel. Another woman I interviewed, Janice, described how her husband would provoke her and then use her subsequent loss of control against her in court proceedings.

> So the point is, you're not – they're labeling it "high conflict," but the fact is I was afraid for my life. There's no arguing with someone who's unreasonable. You know? And the irony is that they find, they, there's these projections that are really their condition and their problem and their issue and they succeed in convincing people, it's you.
>
> And so I sought help, I sought protection. And not only was I ultimately not believed, or the court was manipulated by the classic good-looking charmer, who did the exact same thing to me to get me to do whatever he wanted me to do, was exercising it on every party to the court, with the exception of his attorney who also appeared to be very enamored of him, and he used that as well. Not to say that, well, he – but he charmed everyone.

The revictimization of women and children in the custody context has only recently been exposed through legal research. It has been essentially ignored by psychologists who, let's not forget, are often employed as evaluators by the courts or by private parties. A search for "domestic violence and child custody" on the largest digital database in psychoanalysis yielded zero results. The few researchers who do write about the issue argue that the courts have provided a stunning means for violent men to continue their abuse post-separation (Chesler, 1986; Dohrn, 1995; Silverman et al., 2004; Hannah and Goldstein, 2010). As Bernadine Dohrn (1995) points out, this is not surprising: the courts have had a long history of punishing women for "bad" mothering, condemning maternal practices that mainly reflect women's poverty or, in some cases, their tendency to challenge patriarchal arrangements. At every turn, unfortunately, courts have relied on psychological theories to prop up assertions that women are failing to adequately mother their children. Battered women, often wracked with shame and guilt over the situations to which they have exposed their children, find it almost impossible to counter the narratives of their incompetence and/or venality.

Losing moms

Of the four women who lost custody of their children to the abusers, one had witnessed her mother being beaten while she was growing up, two had been abused by their mothers and, in two cases, women's mothers had not protected them from abuse by their fathers. All had conflicted relationships with their own mothers which, in turn, impacted their mothering and dramatically intensified their despair when losing custody. New Age guru Deepak Chopra once quipped that what we most fear has already happened to us and, for these women, the court-imposed slashing of the mother–child bond – overwhelming for any woman – represented a nightmarish repetition of past trauma.

Many women in my sample came from homes where wife battering was an honored tradition. They had witnessed horrific violence and been unable to save their own mothers. Some children in these awful circumstances teach themselves to dissociate the cacophony of events. Staying out of harm's way, both physically and psychologically, may mean "not knowing" what is happening two feet away. Peled (1993) captured one child's dissociative reaction as her mother was being battered.

> I wouldn't say anything. I would just sit there. Watch it . . . I was just, felt like I was just sitting there, listening to a TV show or something . . . It's like you just sit there to watch it, like a tapestry, you sit there.
>
> (p. 122)

A woman who participated in my research, Bunny, seemed to know what was happening to her mother as she was growing up but obeyed the unspoken rule that it not be openly discussed. In telling me about her recollections, she both remembers abuse and supplies a stream of reasons why she could not possibly know about abuse, including the size of her house, the children's exclusion from events, and not being allowed to question the things she saw. In an odd way, Bunny may have been internalizing her mother's own wish to shield her from abuse. By "not knowing" the full extent of abuse, Bunny performed for herself the protective function that her mother was incapable of providing and, with this tactic, also shielded her mother from evidence of the detrimental effects that her violent marriage was having on Bunny and her brothers. The first quotation below describes this state of knowing/not knowing about abuse in her family of origin. Compare her words to those in the second quotation, from a later point in the interview, when she discussed how her own violent marriage impacted her children. The quotes are eerily similar.

> *Bunny (quote 1, speaking of her mother)*: I do remember when I was, you know, young, she used to have – she is light-skinned. And because of the beating, her face got dark. All – she had different spots. And she used to go to – I didn't know that it was for the beating, but that's what I was seeing. That, you know, after seven days, the face became, you know. Maybe things happened that I really didn't know because it's not all the time that children get involved. The way that, because the house was big and you know. I can see my mother crying, but it's not like you can even go and ask. It was not that you can ask the same way like my brother can ask me what's going on. It's not like you can go and ask.

> *Bunny (quote 2, speaking of her children)*: The kids – I didn't realize that they saw until recently. When they tell me – my son told me, "Yeah, when my dad

did da da da da da, and I do remember that you were crying in the bedroom." I didn't realize that they saw the beating. I know that they knew about the name-calling, but beside that, the beating, I didn't, never knew that they saw that because it was always in the middle of the night when things escalated. But they did.

In another interesting juxtaposition of narratives, Bunny, rather than remembering her own impotence as eyewitness to such a personal crime, blamed her mother for the problems in the marriage. This was not atypical; many of the women I interviewed were more furious at the mothers who had endured beatings than the fathers who had meted them out. They often minimized or reframed what happened in a way that allows them to forgive the offending father. Ironically, children embrace the same constellation of inverted cognitions that will one day be used against them, when they suffer abuse. Still, at the time, shifting culpability for violence to their mothers walled off troubling feelings of disloyalty to their fathers, with whom they may have had otherwise loving relationships. Bunny, for example, had idolized the father who beat her mother, but hated her mother for her indifference toward Bunny. Only as an adult did she come to understand her mother through the lens of her own victimization. Again, note the strange echo between Bunny's construction of the relationship with her father in quote 1 and her ex-husband's relationship with her own children in the second quote.

Bunny (quote 1, speaking of her father): Like, you know, beating my mom was one thing that, even though I could not – for me, it was two adults fighting, but when I grow up, I realize, no, it's not two adults fighting. It's a man beating a woman. It was scary because as a child, you feel like if I don't escape myself, I can get beaten, too. But, on the contrary. I never get beaten by my father. Never even once. He never yell at me, he never did anything to me. But with my mom, it was like the evil, evil. It was like two different faces.

So usually when he came home, he always pretend to be the good dad and we used to see him as the good dad until I get married myself. Then I understand my mother was, you know, acting this way because she was abused by my father.

Bunny (quote 2, speaking of her ex-husband): But what he said was, after the separation, was to tell them, you know, "Your mom was this, your mom was that, your mom was this." And it'd take time and it will still take me time to try to explain. But I don't go into detail because I say, let time do the work for me because he told them so many bad stories. "Your mom didn't like you, that's why she leave." Not the real story.

Conversely, another subject, Paula, seemed to recognize her mother's tenuous position within a family of powerful and abusive men. Although she paid a grave price, enduring sexual abuse by her father and uncle when she was only seven, she understood why her mother was powerless to intervene.

> This is the 60s – nobody's going to stand up for my mom because who does she think she is anyway? You know, trying to take care of children when children belong with women and things like that. And my mother came from a dreadfully poor family. But my mom was very smart intellectually, so it's like she got along just fine in the school that she was in that she got a scholarship and things like that. So my mom did not have anybody that she could say, "Help me so these people don't take my kids from me."

Even in non-violent homes, daughters must process the split consciousness that their mothers' domestic autocracy does not extend to the broader world, where women are so often accorded second class status. In cases where the mother's fury is unleashed on the daughter, it is even more complicated. To contemplate the radical divide between a mother who tyrannizes you but is, in her turn, physically battered by your father, triggers such contradictory emotions that pity and hatred may be the only possible rejoinders.

> The conjunction of maternal power and powerlessness is difficult for children to comprehend. They confront and rely on a powerful maternal presence whom they inevitably resent as well as love. This powerful presence becomes powerless in front of their father, a teacher, welfare worker, doctor, judge, landlord – the world. Disappointed in their powerful mother, children can feel wildly "unmothered," forced to separate themselves from such a powerless power – indeed, forced to treat her with contempt.
>
> (Ruddick, 1989, p. 36)

Bunny described a particularly contemptible narcissism in her mother. She had "no memory of my mom being caring. I don't have even one picture with my mom." Yet, her mother went every single Monday to have a "professional" picture taken of herself at the local five and dime. Again, only after processing her own experiences did Bunny hazard a guess about her mother's motivation.

Interviewer: Well, that's an odd thing. Why was she taking a picture of herself every Monday?

Bunny: She likes to see herself, that's it. She will take the picture. Before she go to work every Monday, she will dress up really nice, she will go to a place to get this picture. If she likes it, she keeps it; if she doesn't like it, she will destroy it. I don't know why. I don't know why she – maybe, now being involved in advocacy and understand women issue, I can say maybe it was the only way to see herself as beautiful. That is only my understanding of why she was doing that, but I don't really know.

Other women who lost custody had endured abuse at the hands of their fathers as their mothers turned away, leaving a residue of abandonment that would later haunt their own consciousness regarding the children they lost. Janice described her treatment by a domineering father and absent mother:

Janice:	He used a paddle. He got very angry and yelled and screamed and called us names. Used us as servants. You know, he, you know, we had to ask permission to cross in front of him and the football game on the TV. [sighs] It was like we were – it was very clear early on that I was either a pet or an inconvenience.
Interviewer:	And where was your mother during all of that?
Janice:	She was working. She was at church. She did not intervene very much.

Two women had been the direct recipients of their mother's own displaced rage. Rosalie described being sat naked from the waist down at the table and "belted" (hit with a belt) for not eating, being intentionally burned with a heated spoon, and having her head split open with a sandal for lying. She was always waiting for a sign that her mother's rage was subsiding. In one of the saddest examples of Skinnerian conditioning I have heard, Rosalie described the bell that signaled her torture had ended:

> And I still remember that my mother was a chain smoker, and so when my mother was done beating me, being abusive, she would light up in the kitchen. So she was done. And I remember I hated cigarettes. I don't – I still, to this day, detest the smell of cigarettes. But when I was little, that was a sign of, you know, I was conditioned to know that it was over. That, for the time being, it was done.

Christopher Bollas (1987), in his evocative work on mother–child attachment, describes how a disturbed mother displaces her child's thoughts and feelings, depositing instead her own self-states of isolation, anguish, and fury. She projects something bad into the child, using her as a storage container for her own negative feelings. Even more disabling of the child's quest for agency, Bollas believes that a troubled mother also robs the child of her capacity to combat the ensuing emotional tsunami by ignoring or invalidating what the child says she feels. In denying her daughter's natural response to what she is experiencing, any reparative affects the girl might use to build her own reservoir of outrage or sorrow over abuse are incapacitated, replaced with her mother's internalized aggression. Thinking becomes an effortful wasteland, filled with confusion or blankness. As a consequence, says Bollas, the child can only know an object through "loving hate" (p. 127), a blackened relational template that may adhere for life, coloring all interpersonal contact. Paradoxically, though they often hover at the edge of annihilation, such relationships end up safeguarding attachment because meaning and connection can be powerfully construed through these oppositional forces. We can see how this works in adult repetitions of early fateful bonding practices. A perfect example was Ileana (Chapter 3), who described the emotional tether of every single one of her relationships with the cliché "I loved them [or they loved me] to death." She intoned this gaily 11 times during our interview, apparently missing the irony that she had only narrowly escaped death herself at the hands of her abuser and had lost a baby as the result of a beating during pregnancy. I will not reiterate the more metaphoric annihilations Ileana experienced at her mother's knee. The "loving hatred" Bollas articulated fueled every attachment Ileana had ever experienced.

The four women whose custody stories are told in this chapter have had ample time to reflect on the transgenerational repetition of severed maternal care. Whatever their early domestic experience, each woman had sworn that, when she grew up, this would never happen to her again. Each promised herself that she would be the best mother in the world and protect her child from the evils of the world.

> My mother was abusive to me. She was physically abusive, she was psychologically abusive. And I was determined that, as a mother, I would be different and I would be better. So it's inherent for a mother to want to protect her child, but when you've been abused, it becomes much more so. You know, to protect your child from anything that can hurt her. And I tried.
>
> (Rosalie)

It was truly breathtaking, the degree to which the women were emotionally orphaned. For little girls so forcefully isolated, obliged to be self-reliant too early, the search for a caretaker became relentless, often culminating only at the altar or in its vicinity. Ideas of romantic rescue perfused imagination and governed their choices in less than ideal ways. At the same time, women's mothers got taken up as negative role models and each sought to divine a path that veered in an opposite direction. Rosalie's story was typical. Narrative themes revealed a magical omnipotence in exact proportion to her actual vulnerability. Like many abused children, she likely had spent a lot of time in her head, willing away her scourges and prophesizing miracles.

As an adult, Rosalie was looking for someone "soulful" with whom she could have a "spiritual" tie. She met John online, and they wrote letters to one another for two months before meeting. Rosalie took care to tell me that these were not email communications but "real" letters. When they finally rendezvoused, it felt providential.

> It was like a freakin' movie. It really was. I was living out this fantasy. Yeah, it was a fantasy. And then we were together after spending, I think we were snowed in for about three days. The blizzard of '96. And then we were never apart again. And he took all his stuff, threw it in a bag, and came to my apartment.

> I found my soul mate. I was reading Thomas Moore, *Care of the Soul*. Oh, he's my soul mate. There was even a chapter there on letter writing.

The problems started almost immediately. John was angry, possessive, obsessively jealous. He "regulated" Rosalie's friends. But she was determined to learn from her mother's mistakes and make something better for herself. Unfortunately, she drew the wrong lesson: to avoid friction, be more compliant not less.

> I was like his ragdoll and he did whatever he wanted with me. And I was like, we went wherever he wanted and if there was ever a change in what he wanted, there would be trouble. He just controlled everything. What I wore, how I wore it, but I used to think, oh, I'm just pleasing him, right? He's asking for something and I'm pleasing him as any partner would. And what carries over about my mother and my father that they were full of pride and that nobody was ever wrong, nobody apologized for doing anything wrong, and so I kept saying, I'm going to do it different. I'm going to do it better. I'm going to learn from what my parents did and I'm going to be a better partner, better wife. So I found myself apologizing for stuff that, you know what? I had no business apologizing for, but I did it in the name of peace, right? I just lost myself. I just began, you know, do away with people, I moved from my home, I left my car, my sister, my career.

John eventually became physically abusive. Although Rosalie was able to leave her relationship before the onset of any extraordinary violence, she feels that by taking away her daughter, John exacted a price beyond blood. Whatever cruelty she endured in her relationship was just a prelude to what would happen after they split up.

> He was just – I had not seen this level of rage in this man. And I remember he pinned me to a corner right in front of the computer. There was nowhere I could move. And he had his head like that, up against mine and he was clenching his teeth and he was like, I don't know what he was saying, like, "Don't treat me like that. Don't treat me like that." And I remember thinking, whoa, I better be quiet. I better be calm. And I was saying, "Get off of me. Jay, get off of me. I don't do that to you, Jay. Get off of me." And he wouldn't get off of me. He was pushing up against me. I had a bruise when he was done.
>
> I was so proud when I left there. He is such a monster. But it's nothing what he did to me in the house and the way he ignored me and the way he dehumanized me is nothing, *nothing* compared to what he did to me in court.

In loco parentis

The expectation of every woman that I interviewed, even if they had witnessed the failure of institutional rescue as they were growing up, was that the police, the courts, and mental health care providers would protect them and aid them in bringing their abusers to justice. For many, this did indeed happen eventually, although they all described a bureaucratic mechanism Byzantine in design and sloppy in execution. For the four women who lost custody of their children, institutional betrayal replicated earlier experiences of neglect, abandonment, and abuse. They felt as brutalized by "the system" as they had been by mothers, fathers, uncles, husbands and boyfriends.

When we think of organizations, agencies, and institutions, we rarely characterize them as we might individuals, with unconscious as well as conscientious agendas. If we imagine institutional "brutality," we think of factory layoffs or, perhaps, environmental disasters prompted by corporate greed. Seldom do we think about the minute interpersonal dynamics that constitute the larger whole. Yet it is here that brutality is most likely parceled out to staff and clients, particularly in work environments that are overwhelming, threatening, and dysfunctional. The criminal and family justice systems fit this description. As the German philosopher Max Stirner said in 1845, "The State's behavior is violence, and it calls its violence 'law'" (Stirner and Byington, 1845/2010, p. 172). Stirner was referring to the power of state institutions to sanction behavior, often with the kinds of unjust consequences we have been discussing. I am referring to the human apparati who collectively put those unjust processes into play.

Bion (1961/1991) believed that, while the conscious activity of any work collective is to successfully complete its day-to-day work and fulfill the larger ideological mission to which it is pledged, the more important job of the group takes place unconsciously. Here, defense mechanisms work to moderate anxiety, to ensure the group's continued existence and, ultimately, to guarantee that the group will reproduce itself. With these survival goals foremost, institutions create systems that protect them in much the same way that individuals develop psychic armor to ward off threats. Organizations, like people, become rigid and impersonal. Agencies create hierarchal structures that leave little room for individual initiative not specifically geared toward rising through the ranks. The dominant relational schema in organizations is usually authority-compliance. The missions of institutions, although encoded in poetry, are customarily evinced in a more combative realm. This can leave broken bodies on the field, metaphorically or even literally, depending on the institution.

The criminal justice system, for example, has particularly lofty goals: the pursuit of truth; the provision of safety; the delivery of justice. Conversely, the day-to-day activities of criminal justice agents are much more humble, sometimes even base. On a regular basis, agents confront people in great pain, high foolishness, massive confusion, those who are dangerous, and those in the gravest of danger. For frontline personnel and their supervisors to continue doing what they do in such a high burnout field, a great deal of dissociation must come into play. With neither the time nor the training to customize more nuanced interventions, staff in criminal justice and ancillary family and civil agents (e.g. police, judges, forensic clinicians, etc.) come to rely on categorical judgments, often made on the basis of a defensive splitting that demonizes some players and glorifies others.

In examining the systemic impact of splitting defenses on organizational culture, Diamond and Allcorn (2004) argue that such unconscious mechanisms shape people's attachment to their institutions and institutional leaders, playing on their "desire to affiliate and form identifications with the organizational ideal" (p. 25). In the case of law and forensic psychology, the archetypal paradigms have to do with both identifying/remediating wrongs (justice) and figurative blindness (neutrality). In actions around domestic violence, this may be played out through arrest, custody, visitation, and support arrangements that strive for even-handedness regardless of specific mitigating or aggravating circumstances that should mandate the differential treatment of participants.

People are perceived as Good Guys and Bad Guys with no asterisks to signal exception. Defensive splitting superficially reinforces the stated missions of the criminal and family justice systems but in reality undermines the administration of justice. Once a black and white moralism dominates the institutional picture, reflective activity is discouraged, experiential learning becomes tautological, and not only do interpersonal acts of moral violence no longer produce outrage, they may be ignored, denied, or even subtly fostered (Diamond and Allcorn, 2004).

If the supposed über ethic in American law has been to protect vulnerable groups, the law *in vivo* often destabilizes their position; nowhere has this been truer than in relationship to women and children. At various times, women have been "protected" from work, travel, and voting. Now, it seems, the police are protecting them by arresting them along with their battering partners and the court is protecting their children from them under the pretense that they are somehow more injurious to those children than assaultive fathers. The system has thus "psychically imprisoned" women, to borrow Gilles Amado's (2009, p. 1) term for an interpersonal dynamic that proliferates in modern organizations. Psychic imprisonment enables mastery over other people, who are denoted as uncontrollable and even unknowable, in an attempt to neutralize their power, thereby reducing them to objects that can be assimilated (Dorey, 1986). This is accomplished by destroying reality and eradicating individual differences. It leaves the court a perverse and sadomasochist landscape. As Chasseguet-Smirgel (1991) observed, "the Sadian universe is one of confusion, chaos, mixture, inverted and abolished values" (p. 403), hardly what one is hoping to find at the bar of justice, but the surreal environment that greets many domestic violence victims.

To some extent, all organizations have the tendency to macerate and disempower their human contents; the criminal and family justice systems even more so because they interfere at the most personal level of human function and feeling. The way in which participants in such systems survive is to avoid critical thinking, conflict, and internal dialogue (Amado, 2009). The psychic dynamics of these institutions may even mimic Klein's paranoid–schizoid position (Sievers, 2009), where suspicion, hypervigilance, solipsism, and magical thinking preclude or worse, pervade, interpersonal attachment.

In the case of domestic violence, external and internal pressures to adapt to ever shifting landscapes of gender, law, and psychology force the hand of decision makers. Principal players may find it easier to decontextualize cases than scrutinize them, especially when their finer points are complicated, contradictory, or elude institutional attempts at control. Under threat to their own credibility regarding potential outcomes for couples and children in coercive or violent relationships, police, judges, and psychologists working with domestic abuse cases may come to rely on a host of primitive defenses that inspire caustic enactments. As Bion (1961/1991) observed, the more disturbed the organization, the more likely it is to rely on archaic fantasies and defenses to protect itself from extinction. In the case of institutions wedded by domestic violence, disturbance accrues from the constant exposure to disturbing material and the possibility that individual and institutional responses may do little to contravene intolerable outcomes. One collective defensive response is that criminal justice and allied institutions come to esteem knowledge (in law, this would be "evidence"; in psychology, "signs and symptoms") over truth but also distort and destroy knowledge through a rigid and narrow interpretation of its meaning. An example would be the granular interpretation of "best interest of the child" standards[3] that weigh a father's capacity for violence against his capacity to provide financially for his children, as if these two things can morally be judged as inverse equivalents.

Although institutions end up creating cultures that psychologically come to dominate individual actions, systems are still made up of people whose private experience, past and present, helps construct that public space. In addition to their personal histories, childhood encounters with maltreatment, or individual propensities for sadism and masochism, personnel working with victims and perpetrators are exposed to the second hand effects of trauma on a daily basis. Moreover, they are tasked with containing that trauma on behalf of a culture reluctant to acknowledge the eviscerating impact of domestic violence, not just on families, but on society at large. Our expectation that police, lawyers, clinicians, and judges manage "in the public domain private anguish and pain that has proved uncontainable in the family and community" (Laughlin and Sher, 2010, p. 3) is likely to induce defensive responses that (1) shut down emotion, and (2) unlink cognitions whose logical extension would force a greater toleration of ambiguity than is suitable for the speedy resolution of conflicting claims. The women I interviewed surmised that lawyers in family courts sometimes sold their souls to quickly rack up a win or, conversely, abandoned clients they imagined would lose.

Janice:

> Because the kind of attorney that gives attorneys bad names – the ones that represent batterers – they let them know very quickly that custody is cheaper than child support and it's the best way you can hurt her, to take her child away.

Rosalie:

> I had had like four different attorneys. I had taken out cash advances, I had borrowed from all my family members, I even had a fundraiser at a church to raise money for legal fees because they were trying to take my daughter away. I couldn't have fought any harder to be [my daughter's] mom. And then the trial comes. I don't have an attorney. [My lawyer] didn't want to subsidize the trial. I already owed her $4,000. She told me, "Give her up. You're going to lose. You're going to lose," she said. So I proceeded to trial alone. You see these movies and these shows and I'm like, that's not what really happens in court. That's not what really happens. And they ate me alive. They ate me alive.

Morgan-Jones (2006) has written that "the risks of poor judgment and decision making are great" in forensic situations (p. 29). Although he is speaking specifically of forensic hospital units, the same can be said of criminal and family justice institutions as a whole. When agencies monitoring domestic violence fail, the failure is often registered in human tragedies: physical and sexual assaults, kidnapping, homicides. Sometimes the human toll includes actual violence toward workers in the organization; mostly, though, the price of a forensic institutional affiliation is counted in sleepless nights, forfeited reputations, or the corrosion of one's sense of competence.

> This means that the [institution] functions as a container for multiple traumatized and traumatizing systems. Within these systems the specific [victims and perpetrators] are nodal points where the truths about the undigestible feelings surrounding those experiences recycle traumata.
>
> (p. 29)

Working in the domestic violence trenches may trigger a host of regressive transferences and countertransferences where the enacted refrains are paranoid and retaliatory. After all, the stakes could not be higher. If you arrest (or fail to): someone might die. If you recommend couples' counseling (or do not): someone might die. If you give custody to the "wrong" parent: someone might die. Someone might die and you might be held accountable by your peers and superiors, if not your conscience. Unavoidably, shame and guilt are central organizing principles, not only in violent intimate relationships but in the systems that are charged with managing them. Although management needs to be more scrupulous here than almost anywhere, under the guise of efficiency neglect can become an institutional imperative. This provokes even greater shame when it leads to the (psychological or physical) injury or death of an innocent party, like a battered woman or her child. Splitting and vilification are ways to deflect blame and get rid of unbearable shame and guilt.

To work in the shadow of such annihilation anxiety, one must call upon a range of dissociative defenses, including making victims and perpetrators alien or interchangeable (depersonalization), minimizing or denying interpersonal brutality and its consequences (derealization), defusing the emotional content of events (psychic numbing), intolerance of ambiguity (splitting) and not learning from past experience (institutional amnesia). Seen through this intellectual and affective stupor, an "object may be acted upon safely and without moral conscience" (Diamond and Allcorn, 2004, p. 35). I believe that this well describes the situation in which female victims of domestic violence find themselves as they attempt to traverse multiple institutional terrains nestled in the broader patriarchal culture.

Women's concerns, particularly regarding their children, are often dematerialized within a network of institutionalized dissociation that turns a thing (such as concern about children) into its Orwellian opposite (sadism, alienation, brainwashing) or simply refuses to acknowledge the authenticity of her claims. Institutional defenses prop up "the illusion that what is unconsciously excluded from the perception and meaning of 'reality' is not worth acknowledging, because it does not exist" (Sievers, 2009, p. 34). In a very real sense, many battered women simply cease to exist in the halls of justice.

Anger and agency: too little, too late

> And I was very calm. I was not emotional. And I just knew what I was saying and I knew what I was going to do. And I said, "I'm going to leave you." And he used to say – this isn't the first time he'd heard me say that, but I think with the demeanor that I said, I had never said it like that before. He used to say, "If you leave me, people are gonna say you're crazy. People are gonna think you're crazy. If you leave me, you're going to hurt the baby." He used to say, "If you leave me, you're going to regret it for the rest of your life."
>
> (Rosalie)

Though she felt that she had no choice but to leave her partner, Rosalie did come to regret everything that followed. She lost her daughter, the person who meant more to her than anything else in the world. Bunny, Janice, and Paula similarly had, at the time, seen no other way to handle things. They were not able to be sufficiently combative in the course of their relationships or the aftermath, for reasons ranging from a "natural" proclivity for niceness (e.g. "I didn't serve him with my custody papers because it was Father's Day weekend and I didn't want to ruin his weekend with custody.") to terror ("'Cause he had a gun. And I didn't want him to hurt us. Didn't want him to hurt me or the kids, so I just go along with whatever.").

Even now, the women's rage seemed remarkably controlled considering what they had been through. Dissociated serenity was a trick perfected in the shadow of parental abuses best ignored. Paula discussed how she had playacted during her father's middle-of-the-night sexual assaults ("I pretended I was sleeping because I was frightened. It went on a long time, but the issue of why I didn't scream or anything is no more than I didn't want to wake my sisters up."). Bunny explained that she had just "accepted" the reason for her mother's loss of control ("Yeah, she, she used to say, when she was beating us, she used to say, 'If it was not for you, I would not stay in this relationship.' For me, it was, OK, I am the subject of all this trouble."). When Rosalie spoke of suppressed rage against her mother, it prompted the following exchange.

Interviewer: I never saw such a big smile when somebody said, "rage."

Rosalie: I tell you that I know that I have felt rage and I know that I feel that it was terribly unjust of my mother to be so abusive to me, but I've forgiven her.

Interviewer: Well, that's now. But when it was going on, did you go in your room and punch a hole in the wall? Did you burst into tears?

Rosalie: I used to hit myself.

Interviewer: How? What did that look like?

Rosalie: You know what? I've never told anybody this. It just, I could, I used to go and hit myself and hit my arms and just, I wanted to, I did to myself what I wanted to do to my mother. Yeah. It was never productive. And I used to also chew the inside of my bottom lip. And when my mother found out, guess what she used to do? She used to put lemon in my mouth. She thought it was going to stop me, but it was really a nervous mechanism, you know. [pause] But I was hurtful to myself because I couldn't be hurtful to her.

These women struggled mightily to regain custody of their children, but even more so to maintain their composure. As I said at the beginning of this chapter, watching Hannah and Waller's (2008) CD of conference participants who had lost custody of their children to their abusive partners was an exercise in countertransferential horror, fury, and revulsion. Their uncanny emotions were cocooned within a dissociative stance that Sullivan (1956b) described as "a chilled turning away from things, quite different than chronic detestations" (p. 320). Their laments, recycled many times over through the years, now had the ring of a Janetian (Janet, 1889/1973) automatism. And so the uncanny became vested in me. I wanted to scream because the women could not. Finally having come to terms with their own anger, after years of denying it, they were now obliged to suppress it once again, lest anyone find them too loud, too mad, too hysterical, too unhinged, too potentially aggressive to have custody of their own children.

The women walk in cities across the nation in an event called the "Gladys Ricart Memorial March" which memorializes a woman who was shot and killed by her ex-boyfriend in 1999, only a few hours before she was to marry someone else. Troops in this strange parade don bridal gowns or black waistcoats. Rosalie wears blood and rope to signify that what happened to her was not a loss; it was a gutting.

Notes

1 In the learned helplessness experiment, a dog is exposed to electric shocks from which it cannot escape. Although the dog fights at first, eventually it stops trying to avoid the pain. Later, even when presented with an opportunity to escape, the dog lays inert on the floor of the cage. It has given up (Seligman and Meier, 1967).

2 The authors surveyed 465 custody evaluators, many of them psychologists and social workers, about the custody recommendations they had made in actual cases and would make in hypothetical vignettes. The authors also did in-depth interviews with domestic abuse victims who experienced negative custody or visitation outcomes.

3 Many states' custody laws list factors for courts to help them determine what is in the "best interest of the child." The factors are not ranked and the decision of how to weight various factors in custody decisions is determined by individual judges (Erickson, 2010).

Chapter 6

Venus with arms

No Rack can torture me
My Soul – at Liberty
Behind this mortal Bone
There knits a bolder One

You cannot prick with saw
Nor pierce with Scimitar
Two Bodies – therefore be
Bind One – The Other fly

The Eagle of his Nest
No easier divest
And gain the Sky
Than mayest Thou

Except Thyself may be
Thine Enemy
Captivity is Consciousness
So's Liberty.

(Emily Dickinson)

There is nothing easy about working with women in abusive relationships. It is scary. It often seems impossible to distinguish danger that is imminent from vague and distant threat. The work ignites every primitive need for security and safety in both client and therapist. Frustration is rampant. The client has experienced the tyranny and cruelty of loved ones in ways that make the clinician's offer of help highly suspect. Rage is pervasive but disowned by both members of the dyad, as the psychoanalyst fears becoming a shadow perpetrator and the patient's default setting is stuck at compliance. The work pulls at the threads of our moral fiber in ways we never thought possible. Accustomed to a non-judgmental stance, we find ourselves pulled into enactments of condemnation. Usually proselytizers of ambiguity, we find ourselves articulating a Manichean view of the world. The search for meaning, so central to psychoanalytic dialogue, becomes a dead end instead of the open vista we naïvely imagined.

Constructivism, a core organizing principle of contemporary psychoanalytic thinking, postulates that experience has little intrinsic connotation but, rather, is given meaning through various shaping mechanisms that influence how we perceive and interpret them. Interpersonal psychoanalytic theorists see experience as emergent – a product of continual discovery, refinement, and recontextualization – within the constraints imposed by certain objective facts and the relative flexibility or rigidity of one's temperamental endowments (Stern, 2010). In a perfect universe, the psychoanalyst rejects reductionism and a binary view of the world. Yet, phenomenologically and morally, these mark the very crossroads where domestic violence deposits us.

The feminist framing of domestic violence that has dominated scholarly discourse over the last two decades arose in direct response to the sense that psychoanalytic psychology had abdicated its moral responsibilities toward women by working too relativistically, in ways that drew scant distinction between the acts of batterer and battered. Let's not be ridiculous, feminist therapists insisted, how many ways are there to "interpret" a broken jaw, a single-signer bank account, or coerced sex? And if a patient understands it differently, are we not professionally bound to educate her otherwise? Few would disagree. However, problematically, in the rush to save women from destructive relationships, any sense of couples' lives as dynamically intertwined got lost. Nuance, usually the sine qua non of treatment was, perhaps understandably, sacrificed to a "defensive idealization of victims" that may have simplified therapeutic goals but denied a woman access to the "full range of her humanity" (Haaken, 2010, p. 58).

The tensions inherent in work with ongoing rather than past trauma, and the political overtones of gendered violence, create special conditions for the pace and rhythm of psychoanalysis and should push us toward reflective – rather than reflexive – activism around issues of intimate violence. They force us to look for ways of working that expand our repertoire, engaging both personal and political selves, without losing our focus on helping women to "represent, mentalize, and organize [the] feeling states of fear, shame, hate and rage" (Renn, 2012, p. 136) that are corrupted during conditions of ongoing threat. We are tasked with valuing the client's (or in the case of research, the subject's) agency even when, perhaps *especially* when, it rides roughshod over our own beliefs about what constitutes a healthy relationship.

A multiple-self theory, like the one seeded by Sullivan and nurtured by other interpersonal and relational theorists, presents the opportunity to "wrestle with, rather than submit to, moral discourses" around domestic violence (Goldner, 1999). Engaging the contradictions of multiplicity means accepting that each self presents its own fathomable reality, even when it exists only as an affective state defensively resisting articulation. Respect for multiplicity encourages us to refrain from either "analyzing away" surface assertions or, on the other hand, accepting them at face value. Instead of working along a single apocryphal gradient from darkness to truth, clinical and research techniques can be organized around the recognition and remediation of conflict between various selves by enabling "internal communication among them as a non-linear, repetitive process" (Bromberg, 2006a, p. 26). Interpersonal practice creates a space for the victim self to meet the perpetrator and the survivor self, the masochist to meet the sadistic self (as well as their matchmaker), the child to meet the adult, and for these configurations to forge a new reality independent of the constraints that tethered all the selves to violence.

Eliciting dissociated material

In most abusive relationships, physical violence is simply the exclamation point that adds emphasis to a more quietly repressive relational structure. A woman's emotional existence within that context can be hollow and autonomic. She is a dead woman walking, and dissociation is part of what makes it difficult for her to define experiences as having been abusive, particularly in the absence of physical injury. While there is generally a part of the self that knows that what is happening is wrong in an objective sense, other parts defensively conspire to unmake that meaning. And, though much attention has been paid to the physical violence that truncates memory, feeling, and identity, more subtle triggers may do even greater damage. Perhaps it seems counterintuitive that something non-physical could have such catastrophic consequences. However, as Foucault (1995) has pointed out, it is the very invisibility of psychological violence that grants it a uniquely damaging power to supplant, even obliterate, alternate narratives.

> A real subjection is born mechanically from a fictitious relation . . . By this very fact, the external power may throw off its physical weight; it tends to the non-corporal; and, the more it approaches this limit, the more constant, profound and permanent are its effects: it is a perpetual victory that avoids any physical confrontation and which is always decided in advance.
>
> (p. 202)

Foucault was speaking of the panopticon, a nineteenth-century architectural design for prisons that increased surveillance while keeping the observing source out of sight, like a nineteenth-century version of the two-way mirror. He argued that in modern systems of discipline, control comes not so much from the lash as the policing function internalized by the prisoner, who never knows when he is being watched and, so, behaves as if he is being watched at all times. A similar imprisoning mentality marks the actions of women who live with abusive men. Like the Quindlen protagonist mentioned in Chapter 1, who refrained from changing the television channel in case that was the one thing that would trigger a beating from her husband, many women told me about how they changed their behaviors, *even when their partners were nowhere to be seen*, because they had become convinced that somehow he would "know" they were contravening his wishes. One woman made no phone calls, another did not dare open the window or put on the air-conditioning, even in sweltering heat, because she had been instructed not to do so; still another left the TV tuned to "his" channel, although he was gone to work for the day.

Many women followed imaginary scripts for behavior made all the more indelible in the absence of explicit instruction. "No, he never told me I shouldn't" said one woman, discussing her decision to return to school in the evenings, "I was just sensitive to inconveniencing him in any way or giving him an excuse to stop me from going. It wasn't that big a deal except I had to worry more about getting home on time." She was caught up short when asked if she had a curfew, since she had referred to getting home at a specific time. "No, I don't think so. I just thought it was better if I was." In the vacuum created by what she imagined was her husband's silent disapproval, this woman built her own jail.

While battered women were conceivably sensitized to the cost of a partner's potential disapproval through the variable ratio schedule on which beatings occurred, I found that even women in relationships that were "only" psychologically abusive tended to almost instinctively behave in ways crafted to avoid potential conflicts or de-escalate them once they ensued. This was, of course, not so much instinct as a dissociative process so smoothly ingrained that it felt overwhelmingly natural to heed its call.

Interpersonal psychoanalysis is, among other things, an attempt to help people decode and respond to just these kinds of relational messages and the blind spots in consciousness they produce. The goal is to facilitate interpersonal learning, within a secure environment, through a combination of detailed inquiry and feedback (Evans, 1996). The idea of the detailed inquiry is to move patient's stories toward ever more finely grained iterations by asking follow-up questions, gently calling attention to inconsistencies, and responding authentically with alternate interpretations of events and suggestions for action. Although the interaction is primarily dynamic, with conversation following organically from the discovery of information, I doubt that Sullivan would have endorsed a line of questioning that was completely agenda-free. In this way, Sullivan shared a great deal of sympathy with social science researchers who set out to confirm or disconfirm particular hypotheses through a well thought out series of questions. In both research and clinical work with parties to domestic violence, it is crucial to know what types of questions to ask. Although the method of inquiry in clinical work may feel less interrogatory than its research counterpart, it should be no less thoughtful or thought provoking.

Clinicians would do well to familiarize themselves with domestic violence research that has teased apart effective lines of inquiry, while researchers could learn a great deal about the benefits of using one's native curiosity and creativity to open up associative pathways rather than foreclosing opportunities for elaboration, as the typical close-ended research question does. Closely deconstructing a discrete incident unleashes a torrent of new questions that spikes transference, animates further analysis, and puts the lie to simplistic formulations. Moreover, the very act of interruption may force a reordering of narrative alignment and give birth to new understandings of old, or previously dissociated, material (Levenson,

1988). Rather than acting as some stale intercession in which the asker seeks only to confirm an a priori interpretation (this is notoriously prevalent in both bad research and bad therapy), detailed inquiry in the analytic spirit succeeds precisely "because the question is clear and the answer is not" (Stern, 1990, p. 457).

Detailed inquiry is not a search for veridical truth but, as comic Steven Colbert might say, an investigation into the relevance of "truthiness," one's intuited version of narrative meaning as it exists independent of close inspection, unburdened by either evidence or logic. Truthiness is Sullivan's parataxic distortion, the organization of experience into private mythological constructs based on the defensive interpretations of earlier experiences. There is some truth there but it has been twisted into a fraudulent copy of the original event.

The power of abuse sometimes lies in the shock and awe it inspires, but other times in the very mask of benignity it wears. Without a detailed inquiry, we may never unmask it. I want to suggest some directions for the detailed inquiry in cases of suspected or disclosed abuse. By far the most important of these is a close investigation of the development and nature of self-states that have arisen defensively in response to psychological attacks. Yet many researchers and clinicians, like proverbial moths to the flame, are so drawn to the magnetic pull of manifest violence that they allow the subtler indices of abuse to escape notice. Their inattention virtually guarantees that material which is already dissociated will remain dissociated.

Physical abuse in adult intimate relationships tends to be episodic, and is usually remembered by victims even if defenses conspire to distort its various meanings. On the other hand, psychological and emotional mistreatment is ubiquitous and ongoing. It can blend into the background and thus be more easily dissociated than abuse that leaves visible scars. "A physically violent episode has a beginning and an end" and therefore provides a respite, however brief, from assault (Arais and Pape, 1999, p. 63). On the other hand, constant incitement, tests of loyalty, gaslighting, intimidation, and the threat of violence are inescapable. Hour by hour, they corrode a woman's self-esteem and agency. Battered women often report fearing and resenting psychological abuse more than physical abuse; its effects are staggering even when controlling for physical assault (Arias and Pape, 1999). Psychological abuse contributes to chronic illness, increased use of psychotropic medicines, and low levels of perceived control (Marshall, 1996). It has been shown to lead to depression, heavy drinking, and poor, even abusive, parenting (Arias et al., 1996; Arias and Street, 1996). The depletion from psychological abuse may render a woman incapable of leaving her mate or negotiating limits for her partner's behavior. Gwynne's domestic violence counselor cautioned her that, with a depression so debilitating, she was just not strong enough to undertake divorce proceedings, despite her husband's violent threats.

> I remember her telling me – this is before [I was on] anti-depressants – that I wasn't in a state to go through a divorce. If I wanted to go forward with a

> divorce, I had to be a lot stronger . . . it just required a lot of inner strength and she didn't think I was in a position. That was helpful to me [reciting the mantra]: "I'm not allowed to divorce right now. I need to get strong first."

Psychological trauma has no pivot point. While a number of physically abused women in my sample were able to tag a particular assault as having crossed the line and credited the moment with motivating them to leave or to draw a line in the sand, women living with abuse that is primarily emotional have much more difficulty with boundary making and with recognizing the lethality of a partner's intent or the intensification of his hostility. The ambiguity of his actions exploits whatever underlying ambivalence is already inside her, making it doubly hard to seek consensual validation in the eyes of a third party.

Can a woman tell the police that she is scared because a man sends too many flowers? Can she tell the court that her partner doesn't allow her to see friends, if that rule is not enforced through physical violence? Can she identify, even to a therapist, how she feels threatened when the threat is conveyed by sights much subtler than a shaking fist? Most pressingly, is it possible for a woman to conclude in her own mind that the situation is dire when she does not bear the physical marks that grant membership in the battered women's sorority?

For example, Gwynne could only attribute her queasy feelings about her husband's intense possessiveness to his being "too pursue-y." Try that on a jury! Like other psychologically abused women, she began the interview by qualifying that her husband had never hit her. In the interview, she compared a particularly bad time in her marriage to a play whose review she has just read.

> On the surface, everything seems reasonably normal but then this darkness comes over it. All this tension builds; our relationship is kind of distorted. There is this continuum between being passionate and being obsessive and stalking that is in our relationship. We had a dance. Sometimes he comes on too strong and I find it off-putting. I push him away. He comes back hyper, you know, intense.

Pushed to elaborate her husband's "pursue-y-ness," Gwynne explained that, at one point, he had become very territorial, and obsessed about her having an affair (which she did eventually have, but not at the peak of his fixation with her fidelity).

> He wasn't physically violent just very pushy with sex. He wanted sex all the time. He didn't care at all if I was there. He was just determined to have what he wants. I remember thinking at the time that if I had sex with him maybe he could just leave me alone.
>
> Before I even had the affair he had already started worrying about me having an affair. It was almost as if it became a self-fulfilling prophecy. I never thought of myself as a person who would have an affair. But, prior to me having an affair, he started to obsess when I was going on business trips.

> He had a colleague at work who would say "Oh, you're letting Gwynne go on business trips and she's going to have an affair" and he started hassling me about what I was doing on business trips. (It ended up being a guy that I was working with – not going on business trips with – anyway.) He just started getting sort of hyper-focused on whether I was having an affair and then I did, in fact, start having a relationship with this guy. I was very conflicted about it.
>
> [My husband] told me that if he ever found out that I was having an affair that he would kill me. He said it a couple of different times and in a couple of different contexts. I told my friend and that's when she suggested that I call the domestic violence hotline. It was like the review of that play . . . it was kind of spiraling into some distorted, negative state where I could envision something happening. Because he was so mad and I was so depressed and withdrawn. He was so manic about claiming me that I felt, at that time, it could potentially be violent . . . his intensity and the sword of his obsession with me.

Departing substantially from the script so many women I spoke with had adopted, Gwynne was able to define her husband's behavior as abusive. She even called a domestic violence hotline and sought counseling through victim services. I was struck by Gwynne's ability to distinguish that what was happening to her was not just objectionable, but abusive in ways that warranted outside intervention, when so many women in situations more imminently perilous could not.

Women are often scared but also perplexed by what to do about a partner's behavior. Penny, who also did not consider herself physically abused, spoke about an incident that she found frightening.

> Yeah, he shoved me a time or two, not very hard. Just a little bit. I remember one time in particular. One of the guys that worked for him and his wife was there [in our house] because there was some type of, I don't know, sales meeting going on. They were staying with us, and we all got up that morning and had breakfast. The two guys were going off to the meeting, and I walked over to him and said "Aren't you gonna kiss me goodbye?" And he put his arms around me and hugged me so hard I thought my ribs were going to break. It was so hard and so painful I couldn't breathe. I was just like "uh" [gasp] and then he stopped. I think [the guests] realized that it was not a hug of affection. [Lapsing into the present tense] You must really want to kill me. Why would that make you so angry that I say "Aren't you gonna kiss me goodbye?"
>
> I mean what was it? It was extreme anger on his part. What's so crazy about it . . . a lot of it didn't even make any sense of it all. But I have to tell you, maybe I'm the crazy one because, after we were divorced, he would find any excuse. When I finally gave him my new phone number, he'd find any excuse to call me.

Penny described her ex-husband to me as a heavy drinker with a tendency towards baseless jealousy who happened to keep a gun in the nightstand. She was not certain how to define the contours of her marriage, despite the husband's emotional manipulations and the fear they evoked in her.

> I never considered myself an abused wife. That term never entered my mind that it would apply to me. After I was divorced from this man, a friend of mine was talking to me and she used the term abuse and I said "Well, I can't really say that I was really abused. He never hit me." And she said, "He didn't need to. He controlled you quite nicely with all the verbal abuse and all the threats and all the temper tantrums . . ." [My friend] was right.

When asked to describe the verbal assaults she had endured, Penny lapsed mid-way into a dissociated elocution, as if the articulation of the experience had ruptured her ability to distinguish past from present. I have italicized the shifts in tense in Penny's narrative: "Like bitch, whore, slut, cocksucker. I mean really ugly, *ugly and stupid, what an idiot you are.*" Temporal shifts like this were common in the narratives of women I interviewed; indeed they are common in trauma survivors of all types because states of absolute distress resist complete integration even after years of safety and reflection. Past, present, and future congeal in an insoluble arc of despair.

> What takes the place of the memory is a "time condensation," a reliving of the past as a frozen replica that structures the person's image of the future and of the present. Instead of being able to deal with "what happened to me," the person enters therapy in order to deal with what he is sure *will* happen to him and what is happening to him now.
>
> (Bromberg, 1994, p. 537)

Bromberg urges the clinician to focus on the process of communication rather than strictly on content. Statements that appear temporally uninhabited in this way should be objects of curiosity just like affective shifts or lapses in memory. In fact, I would liken the job of a therapist or researcher hearing such an absence to that of a lifeguard at the beach scanning the horizon for a swimmer who is no longer visible. *There* is the location of the emergency; dive in. Detailed queries about the exact words that Penny's husband used (bitch, whore, slut, cocksucker) solidified the evocativeness of particular descriptive phrases in cementing her self-doubt, demonstrating that themes of sexual denigration remain potent back-drops for the instigation of more terroristic regimes of surveillance.

> He met me at the back door just having a screaming tantrum, because he thought I had been out with some other man, and I said why didn't you call me if you were worried that I wasn't where I said I was; why didn't you call? I gave you the number, and he didn't have any answer for that.

> There were a couple of times. One time he was really drunk and he, um, we had a gun. I mean he was a big hunter and all that, this was a pistol that was in the night stand drawer, and he got it out and was waving it around: "I'm just so miserable. I'm just gonna kill myself." I thought, you know, there's a fine line between I'm gonna kill myself and I'm gonna kill you. I was very frightened. I called a friend of his and said I think you need to come over. This friend came over and, you know, defused the situation.

Note that neither Gwynne nor Penny called the police when they found themselves in threatening situations; they endured. Follow-up in both cases revealed things about the women's sense of themselves even prior to any ill-treatment. Penny told me, "Well, I didn't really love him for one thing, but I just sorta had low self-esteem. [Then in the present tense] What am I going to do? You know I'll never meet anybody else." Penny had the sense that no one would want to marry her; that she was quickly reaching her expiration date. Gwynne said that she "was very unhappy at that point in my life . . . I mean I was really attracted to someone who was attracted to me. That met a need at that point in my life." Although Gwynne did speak of truly loving her partner at many junctures in their relationship, at least two other women I interviewed said explicitly that they did not love the men who abused them and yet found the benefits of a relationship – status in the eyes of family and peers, the ability to have children within a legal arrangement – so compelling that they could not leave. In both cases I wondered to what degree the absence of love for their male partners constituted the core threat that triggered the men's possessiveness, control, jealousy, or tyrannical rule enforcement.

There are numerous areas that present themselves for investigation in cases of physical abuse: the type and frequency of assault, precipitating incidents, degree of injury. Even when dealing with purely psychological coercion, indices can be oblique but queries do not have to be. "What does you partner call you?" may elicit anything from "baby" to "stinky," each of which triggers its own additional lines of questioning. (The most interesting response I ever got was "little shit," which the client only reluctantly entertained as being a less than complimentary diminutive.) The questions "Does he blame you for his problems?", "Does he make you feel crazy?", "Does he monitor your time and whereabouts?", "Does he restrict your use of the telephone?" are included in validated research protocols for the detection of psychological abuse (Tolman, 1999). A clinician can have versions of them in the back of her mind and introduce them in appropriate contexts as the situation dictates. One woman, for instance, when asked whether there were any particular rules her husband had set that now, upon further reflection, seemed strange or unfair, suddenly thought about how she "was not allowed" to have keys to the apartment's mailbox. The rule had no rhyme or reason yet she reflected disconcertedly that, at the time of its imposition, it had never occurred to her to question the command.

Indeed, one of the most important lines of questioning involves the unwritten rules and rituals of the household, which may seem on the surface to advance the smooth functioning of the couple or family, but instead become a strong-arming technique on the part of a single family member (Hart, 1996; Fischer et al., 1992–1993). Inquiring closely about the nature and quality of rules provides an expanded sense of a relationship's operational underbelly. Such an examination also presents an opportunity for connecting a client's history of compliance and violation with her susceptibility to similar enactments in the analytic dyad.

If you look back at the story of Phoebe earlier in the book, you can trace the impact of rule-making and rule-following as they present in a single case history. From their origins in Phoebe's mother's religiosity (no make-up, no parties, no dancing) to the arbitrary and capricious rules of Phoebe's lovers (don't ask questions, don't acknowledge our relationship publically, accept my infidelity but do not sleep with other men, walk behind me in the street), there is a static internalized narrative that constricts Phoebe's perception of agency and presages transferential enactments of both obedience and defiance with me over issues of absence, punctuality, payment, and verbal dominance in sessions.

In an equal relationship, rules are limited, generally reached by consensus, and appear reasonably flexible. In an abusive set up, there are consequences associated with the breaking of a rule that puts the person trying to abide it in a state of dread (Waits, 1998). Rules are abundant, rigid, and provoke violation insofar as they demand contradictory outcomes. For example, one man was adamant that his wife not challenge him about his drinking or gambling but then, following a drunk driving arrest or bad night at the casino, he would berate her mercilessly for not having spoken up to dissuade him. This is a classic double bind (Bateson, 1972) situation where compliance with one directive simultaneously produces failure to comply with the other. No matter which communication the woman chooses to follow, she is blamed for a grievous error in judgment.

A deconstruction of the rules in a romantic relationship may reveal distressing patterns including everything from one partner deciding unilaterally what, when, and where family members eat, which television shows they watch, and which household tasks they are expected to perform. Most disturbing are situations in which only one partner has the right to decide when the relationship will end. A deconstruction of the rules of the analytic relationship may reveal surprisingly similar patterns of fracture and mending as each partner attempts to negotiate relational power and status. This is true of any analytic partnership but it may assume a darker connotation with patients who have a recent history of domestic violence. These patients may need greater flexibility on the part of the clinician as they learn to inhabit agency. At the same time, clinicians need to be wary of becoming the object of sadistic reprisals that escape conscious analysis.

Another important area for inquiry has to do with the cultural milieu in which a woman's relationships are embedded. Abuse often involves the complicity of family, friends, and neighbors who are themselves embedded in institutional cultures with particular gender biases. Their involvement in a woman's decision-making process can be subtle or very direct, as in the case of the many women I interviewed who were told by their families to return to abusers, to "turn the other cheek," or to examine their own behavior in inviting abuse. More often, the people close to an abused woman are simply dissociative; perhaps encouraged by a victim's own denial, they create a blind space into which suspicious information disappears as if kiting over the Bermuda Triangle. Bunny (see Chapter 3) discussed how her liberation involved not just leaving a man but breaking the spell of a coterie of trusted others whose special interest was in preserving the woman's marriage despite its poisonous turn.

> What I think about me is that I am strong, but in that capacity, I let myself be used. That's my sentence. It's like, OK, well you are strong, make your own decision. No matter what people can say or do, whatever. So now, I can do whatever I need; it's an "I" statement now. I mean, I listen to people's advice, of course, but until I give my own answer, whatever people are saying, that's not my answer.
>
> Because for me, it's like people, no matter who they are, put my life in jeopardy once in my life. People, friends, priests, you know, coworkers, whatever. So now, it's like everything that I'm doing, it's me doing it. Everything, you know, I can chose to do whatever I . . . you know, I will not break the law, I will not do something that is painful for somebody else. But everything that I want to do that is good for me. I will ask myself if it's good for me. If it's not good for me, no matter what people are telling me, I will not do it.
>
> These people, people, people put me in one box and guess what? They put me in that box and left me. It's like I felt that not only one person abuses me. It was a collection of people abusing me.

Layton, observing the multilayered, conflicted, and subliminal nature of cultural impacts, echoes Sullivan's (1964) refrain that we are caught in the crosshairs of others' appraisals which, once internalized, contour our sense of self and agency through the anxiety they inevitably induce. Sullivan speaks of a host of invisible inner critics who proctor our lives, helping us fold ourselves into the intricate origamic shapes demanded by our particular culture. One of Sullivan's most famous lines came in his paper "The Illusion of Personal Individuality": "for all I know, every human being has as many personalities as he has interpersonal relations" (p. 221). In Bunny's case, unfortunately, a multitude of interpersonal relations yielded only a single directive: "Stay put."

Bunny described to me how her choice of mate was influenced by her need for approval from other community members ("I didn't have time to think . . . I didn't want people to think of me as the bad one. I didn't have this feeling of 'I love' you. Not really"), even though the man early on had become frighteningly possessive.

> Oh, [he was] more than abusive. Because when I first met him, for me, he was the picture of someone from the church, well-behaved, and then people from

> the church always tell me, "You are lucky to have such a man." And this was kind of motivation to push me to be with him because, "Oh, yeah, he's a nice guy. You can be married. You are lucky to have him." But in fact, I was not that lucky . . .

The moral of the story is clear. Absent a strong sense of the role of social regulatory practices like the ones that influenced Penny, Bunny, and others to marry men whose behaviors worried them, psychoanalysts' "tendency to not wonder [about cultural influences] produces the individual who reproduces the cultural status quo" (Layton, 2002, p. 297). Thus we must assume nothing and ask everything. Sadly, Layton explains, without attending to the special role of gendered expectations in the conception of agency that infuses psychoanalysis, we truly miss half the possibility for delivering an empowering and lasting treatment.

An empowering partnership

In Sullivan's model, the analyst is a participant-observer, dynamically involved in the process of re-contextualizing the confusions, mystifications, and dissociated data at whose mercy the analysand operates. Sullivan was not interested in the dispassionate countenance that characterized the classical psychoanalyst; he thought it an error to respond to patients' sordid, painful, or morbid experiences with anything other than authentic (though not overly dramatic) human emotion. Yet he was offering more than just the "corrective emotional experience" that Alexander and French (1946) would postulate as the core of psychic change. Sullivan did offer empathic support but also actively sought opportunities to disrupt patients' assumptions and expectations about human interaction. I imagine patients upset his beliefs on occasion, too.

Sullivan tried to help people use language (verbal and non-verbal) purposefully, to communicate, instead of as a way to avoid anxiety through the obfuscatory practices they had internalized in childhood. Moreover, he alleged that "resistance" in analysis was not simply a matter of Freudian repression but had to do with an elaborate evaluation of the social costs involved in coming clean with the therapist (this pressure within the dyad has been increasingly acknowledged by contemporary psychoanalysts). Finally, Sullivan was very much an advocate of action toward the end of solving one's problems in living. While insight was considered a necessary component of change, it was not by itself a convincing rationale for psychotherapy.

Interpersonal psychoanalysis and psychotherapy align with contemporary approaches to female empowerment which are similarly constructivist in nature. Again, constructivism postulates that experience has little intrinsic meaning but, rather, is given meaning through various shaping mechanisms that influence how we perceive and interpret them. Empowerment theories (Peled et al., 2000) emphasize the social hierarchy through which power relations assert a particularly strong shaping power. In work with abused women, attention is paid to aspects of the social surround that may inculcate attitudes that support or repudiate gender-based violence.

Empowerment strategies in psychotherapy are concerned with "the extent to which "needs" are translated into "rights" (p. 10). For example, a woman does not just *need* respect, security, safety, access to funds, etc. "Needing" puts delivery at the discretion of the abuser. On the other hand, if these conditions are her entitlement, her *right*, she has a different frame from which to pursue wholeness. For women in abusive relationships, this means constructing relational meaning in ways that emphasize freedom of choice, personal responsibility, and human agency. Although contemporary relational models have a different focus, highlighting traumatic attachment, dissociated enactment, and personality fragmentation, the methods are not at all contradictory. While interpersonal work privileges the incorporation of disparate self-states into an evolving identity, empowerment work creates a cognitive structure for problem solving that can turn incorporative insights into actualities. Ideally, work within a dual rubric encourages the integration of multiple and contradictory states, thoughts, affects, and personas while simultaneously facilitating the vision of a proprietary entity empowered to reappraise reality in ways that augment felt agency and enhance decision making.

Note that "freedom of choice" here does not imply that women necessarily choose to leave their abusive relationships. Perhaps the most difficult cognitive realignment for therapists incorporating an empowerment model will be the acceptance of a woman's decision to stay in what the therapist considers a bad, or even dangerous, situation. Of course therapists are forced to accept this state of affairs all the time anyway; what an empowerment model offers is a way to change practitioners' assumptions about what constitutes an ideal outcome for clients.

History demonstrates that we tend to like our victims a certain way, particularly our female victims. Battered women who choose to stay violate our assumptions about innocence, entrapment, and even self-interest (Dunn, 2005). One might argue that, given the psychological constraints imposed by a history of violence, the very notion of "choice" is false. Yet, the reality is that many women will elect to stay with men who have previously injured them and/or will continue to seek out new attachments whose dynamic is still abusive. Mental health practitioners are often too focused on the single goal of a woman leaving her relationship. Empowerment models offer useful ways of expanding the range of desirable outcomes, so that ending abuse remains primary but divergent paths to reaching that goal can be entertained.

Play, drama, and the creation of a new self

"In the aesthetic space one can be without being. Dead people are alive, the past becomes present, the future is today, duration is dissociated from time, everything is possible in the here and now, fiction is pure reality, and reality is fiction," wrote Augusto Boal (1996) about the theater in *The Rainbow of Desire* (p. 20). If this also sounds like a good description of analytic space, it is. Boal believed that memory and imagination could be projected onto the aesthetic space of a theater stage in especially therapeutic ways because a person's memory, desire, affect, motivation, and fantasy are concretized there: they are turned "into an object which is observable, by herself and by others" and thus "can better be studied, analyzed, and (who knows?) transformed" (p. 24).

The analysand, like the actor, gets to see herself as both subject and object, as a sentient being and as one who performs sentience, ever reflected in pairs of witnessing eyes that both spectate and perform in the improvised scene. The psychoanalytic drama unfolds in ways similar to a theatrical one. At its best, there is an inspired and original collaboration. Instantaneous improvisations move the story forward: ripening details, collateralizing movement and imbuing both silence and words with specialized meaning (Kindler and Gray, 2010). As in play techniques with children, an injection of theater zeitgeist into psychoanalytic work can help patients to deploy states of mind that normally resist exposure and analysis.

Therapeutic theater, or drama therapy, tries to replace the inertia of dissociated modes of interaction with more agentic forms. An example would be an exercise Boal used in a psychiatric hospital where patients, greeting the invitation to participate in a theater game with the response that they would rather "do nothing," are enticed into acting out "doing nothing." It becomes apparent that doing nothing is far from an empty state of mind and matter. Doing nothing, in fact, requires huge reserves of energy and inventiveness to pull off. The exercise offers multiple opportunities to examine the interstitial spaces between conscious and unconscious (doing nothing is different from being comatose, catatonic, asleep or knocked out), the power dynamics of inner protagonist and antagonist as they struggle to prevent or facilitate activity, and the multi-directional influences of various group members on one another's intentions to "do nothing."

A forerunner to Boal's work on the uses of theater for both personal and political transformation was J. L. Moreno's classical psychodrama, sometimes called the "Theater of Spontaneity." Psychodrama troupes, organized in Vienna in the early 1920s, grew out of Moreno's work with various disempowered groups: war refugees, juvenile delinquents, prostitutes, prisoners, and children. He later developed an approach to interpersonal relations (Moreno actually used the term before Sullivan) based on "sociometry," the study of the relationship between social forces and psychological health or pathology.

Like Sullivan, Moreno was very interested Kurt Lewin's theories (1935), which painted the social milieu as a dynamic field that greatly impacted personal consciousness. Moreno used dramatic role playing to frame personal dilemmas with the goal of having clients move away from pre-scripted, rigid, atonal life performances into what he called the "metarole": an integrated self, spontaneous and improvisational, directed by an inner manager rather than by the dictates of social position (Blatner, 2007). The process of creating a new self was completely experiential (as the creation of the old, stymied selves had been) which gave it more depth and permanency; it was not simply imagined or discussed, the new self was *enacted* (Moreno, 1987).

> The psychodrama presents a new method for studying roles. It provides an experimental milieu, free of boundaries of any particular community or culture. Here there is no need for an ultimate definition of roles . . . They are studied *statu nascendi* – they are not given, they emerge in the flesh, before our very eyes.
>
> (p. 93)

Drama therapies have been used in the treatment of psychiatric patients since the 1600s, often to counter delusions through symbolic enactment and to channel more productively energies that contributed to states of rage, panic, and despair. The development of psycho-dramatic technique was contemporaneous with the psychoanalytic study of groups. Techniques depended heavily on the notion that individual behavior was a product of social processes and could best be observed and transformed within a context that mimicked the one that produced it. Although the techniques are still most often used in group settings, they have been adapted for work with individuals and couples and may be modified in ways that avoid the natural self-consciousness that arises when one is asked to "perform" on cue.

Phil Ringstrom (2001) has been an exceptionally articulate proponent of the subtle incorporation of theatrical modalities into psychoanalytic work. His meditation on the curative properties of good psychotherapy uses improvisational theater as a working metaphor for the way in which going off script can enhance treatment.

> These improvisational moments ineluctably communicate to the patient a special instance of authenticity, which may well be antidotal to the crushing reality of the patient's life of pervasive inauthenticity. They also enable analysts to more readily engage disparate, often dissociatively disconnected parts of the patient through imaginative intersubjective engagement with each. This may take the form of reverie within the analyst – from which his own mental state of play informs his interpretation. Still, at other times, it may involve a form of spontaneous engagement that conveys not only a moment of deep recognition but also the purest state of authentic engagement – that is, one that cannot arise with comparable impact when reflection precedes the analyst's action.
>
> (p. 727)

Improvisation allows analysts and patients to step out of character in ways that would feel forbidden within a stricter frame but that acknowledges the shadow selves of each participant. Concern with safety (sometimes over attended with traumatized patients; more on that later) gives way to trust in the client's capacity to weather mild aggression and to give as good as she takes. An important point made by Ringstrom (2007) is that the spontaneity involved in improvisational engagements weeds out the premeditation entailed in "performing" the roles of patient and analyst, thereby allowing other actors/selves their close-ups in real time. Improv cuts right to the chase, where the two players co-create an artifact whose analysis is implicit in the interaction rather than staged through verbal acrobatics. Bringing disparate self-states into explicit view, as Davies (1998) points out, also employing a theater metaphor, exposes the "endless" round of "auditions and rehearsals" that defensive structure usually dictates (p. 65).

Most importantly for work with domestic violence, the therapist's office can become a place where spontaneity is occasionally privileged over safety, a situation that is unimaginable for battered women in their own homes. Clinicians working with victims of domestic violence understand that the creation of a safe space is paramount but they also should be careful about erring too much on the pacific side, effectively colluding with patients to sacrifice growth in order to maintain security. Paradoxically, the most secure moments in analysis may arise following those interactions that feel most threatening, precisely because the participants realize suddenly that their fear has a source other than the reality of the current face-off with the analyst. As the patient becomes accustomed to the idea that the water is not shark-infested, old projections can be fished out and discarded.

If traumatic reactions are in a more acute phase, theater practices may be transposed to playful forms through non-verbal techniques. Interpretations by the analyst, which can be experienced as coercive by women used to living under the regulatory regime of an abusive partner, are put aside in favor of silent partnering. For example, in work with Phoebe, for a long time I was intransigent in my reliance on a script where the patient started the conversation despite the fact that it clearly pained Phoebe to begin. When I became open to mirroring, even sometimes mimicking, her facial expression, or miming my own frustration, we were able to enter a less calculated space of exchange where forbidden thoughts could find expression without becoming "extremely loud and incredibly close," to borrow the title of a popular novel about a young boy's mastery of personal trauma (Foer, 2005). I had a similar interaction with a very paranoid woman who, parenthetically, grew up in a very disciplined and rule-laden environment. Upon entering my office, she handed me a note, inspiring an entire session comprised of back and forth writing, which I believe allowed us to "speak" in ways that seemed less threatening. (Although, upon leaving, she stealthily turned back from the door to filch the written pages from the desk where I had left them. Paranoia dies hard.) Like art therapy with traumatized children, non-verbal techniques may titrate painful affect enough so that silences can be broken without defenses being shattered.

Dreams of freedom

Penny was able to plot an escape with the help of her friends and a local lawyer who advised her how to open a bank account on the sly. She described the deliciousness of liberation, even as it was tagged with a residual fear:

> I felt this sense of jubilation; I mean just joy. Yes. I'm out of there. I didn't really believe until that moment that I would be able to get away from him. I just thought somehow he's going to find out. Somehow he's going to stop me from getting away from him and I'm going to be trapped. For weeks and months I had dreams that I was still married to him or that I had remarried him and I would just wake up in a cold sweat.

Sullivan himself said we can never deal with dreams directly, as they presented an impassable barrier; with characteristic wit, he implied that the psychiatrist who thought he could follow a patient's dream lucidly was laboring under a "very pleasant delusion" (1956b, p. 332). Still, he pressed for a meticulous accounting of all material, including dreams, as the patient's very need to report them constituted a plea to the psychiatrist to recognize something critical about, around, or inside, her. Sullivan felt that we shouldn't interpret dreams at all but work with them as we would any other material in a session. The therapist's job was to remove extraneous and insignificant details, zeroing in on what appeared most important, and provide feedback to the patient. In a somewhat snarky aside following the recitation of a patient's dream and his successful therapeutic intervention, which consisted of noting only the most obvious things about the manifest content of the dream, Sullivan points out that in his clinical notes he "has not discussed the latent content of the dream; but in psychotherapy, as I have come to consider it, one is occupied chiefly in benefitting the patient" (p. 339). Sullivan might have seen Penny's nightmare as self-explanatory: she was scared witless that her escape was only temporary – or even imaginary – and that she would be pulled backwards into a familiar, terrifying ordeal.

Moreno (1987), on the other hand, would have turned Penny's dream into a production. The dream as an isolated experience in which all parts are played by Penny, staged in her mind, without an audience, for Moreno becomes subordinate to a lived action in which Penny embodies and articulates her dreamt state. Moreno believed that the more one is asked to live the dream rather than recollect it, the more likely it is that the submerged will emerge. Others in a group, or the therapist alone, can intervene, change the scene, ask questions, impede or promote action, almost like a personification of free association. Penny would be encouraged to dream her dream again, extending it beyond her waking moment, ending it in a new way, or even choosing multiple contradictory conclusions. Moreno saw this technique as a way of inaugurating someone as their own "dream therapist" (p. 199). It is a very generative way of working with dreams that not only opens up dream analysis but stresses the dreamer's agency, even over unconscious material. It both promotes reverie and interpersonalizes the dream, rendering it accessible in ways that verbal analysis does not.

As Gentile (2010) has observed, the difficulty of bearing witness to someone's trauma is that the therapist is always "witnessing" something she cannot see. Dramatic techniques like Moreno's invite collaboration, potentially making possible what Gentile envisioned as essential in treatment: "altering the process of objectification by bringing someone back there with you; time traveling with a witness who can bear whatever it is" (p. 5).

Injecting oneself into the analysand's unconscious world is a Moreno-like intervention. A somewhat different approach to the interpersonalization of dream material is "social dreaming" techniques (Lawrence, 2005). I was first introduced to the idea of social dreaming while collecting background scholarship for a course I was teaching on dreaming. The materials of the course later inspired an article on the relationship between historical events and dreaming (Stein, 2010). I became particularly taken with the work of Charlotte Berandt (1966), a journalist who had smuggled out of Germany hundreds of recordings of dreams of ordinary Germans between 1933 and 1939. Her book examines the impact of cultural time and place on the individual psyche.

As both Berandt and Bruno Bettleheim, who authored the foreword, note, the anxiety, sense of persecution, and robotic interface with authority that suffuse the dreams auger the formation of a political unconscious which crafts its defenses in the anticipation of totalitarianism, and yet already, in 1933, finds those defenses insufficient to override Hitler's insidious psychic challenge (p. 126).

After reading Berandt, and combing through other published sources of dream material, as well as my own dream journal, I started to think about dreaming as a repository of socio-cultural, as well as idiosyncratic personal meaning. Eventually I attended a seminar at the White Institute in New York, taught by Mark Blechner, which utilized Lawrence's "social matrix" techniques to explore dream content. Simply stated, Dr. Blechner read us a dream that had been told to him by a patient and asked us to associate to it *as if it were our own dream* instead of the patient's. While the directive seemed at first ineffectual – how could something so deeply personal as someone's dream be tried on like a pair of store-bought shoes? – within seconds you could not have pried that dream from my psychic grasp. I was amazed at how the images in the dream acquired profound significance for me and seemed to expose deep desires crouching in the corners of my own unconscious.

Others in the class also quickly came to see the dream as their own. In sharing our associations, we were able to discover many universal themes that demonstrated the impact of social systems and broad cultural commandments on inner recesses and resources. The dream landscape became incredibly available in a way I had not experienced when investigating dreams with more traditional interpretative schemas. Not only did I experience the material as filled with collective associations and shared meanings, I could now hypothesize differently about the nature of repression and censorship in the dream, since it was no longer solely the domain of an individual's psychology but a broad exposé and critique of cultural norms. Suddenly, the problem to which I have alluded again and again in this book – how to work at both personal and political levels simultaneously, without forsaking meaning in one sphere for meaning in the other – became infinitely more manageable.

> The focus of the work in [social dreaming] is on the dream, not the dreamer. The dream is not a personal possession for it captures the social, political,

> institutional, and spiritual aspects of the dreamer's social environment. This is the difference with conventional psychotherapy since the shared dreams are not being interpreted. According to Lawrence, the interpretation is the death of new knowledge, for it is always grounded in old understandings. What makes this method unique is that [social dreaming] helps people to transform thinking through sharing dreams and using the methods of free association, amplification and systemic thinking, of analytical and synthetic thinking.
>
> (Laitinen, 2006)

Interestingly, the idea of social dreaming comports with Sullivan's (1956a) notion of dreams as both impetus and remedy for cultural mythologies.

> Some of us can remember dreams which are, in fact, a great improvement on any existing mythology for the current era. That type of process is primarily related to our sleeping state, for in the course of assimilating culture and learning how to live, we have specifically eliminated, in our conversation with our compeers, free access to that type of thinking. Thus it is of a different order of reality and implication from the type of process picked up from demonstrations in the home.
>
> (p. 349)

If you approach the following dream as your own, like Lawrence would, or even as Moreno might have, as a production in which you could take part, the possibilities for cross-pollination become endless. The dream was reported by a woman in a long marriage with no physical brutality but fluctuating levels of psychological maltreatment. I will start with some background.

Leidy's husband had never hit her. His youthful brush with the law, similar to her own delinquencies, was not taken as an indication of primary psychopathy by the couple but instead as a useful narrative trope that summarized the unpredictability of human development: they had both turned out intact, highly functional, and fairly successful. He had overcome earlier capitulations to his most damaged self and had settled into a self-absorbed, but mostly benign, character. He worked hard, supported the family, and loved the children. He trafficked in occasional intimidation; sometimes he even seemed menacing. He was given intermittently to provocative, belittling rhetoric. There were only a few overt threats, mostly about how he would take the children from Leidy if she left. This was very early in their marriage; way before the report of the dream.

There was no physical violence although, when they were younger, her husband's use of alcohol and over-the-counter stimulants had made Leidy fear more consciously the possibility, even imminence, of actual violence. At that time, he had been pounding people's car hoods if they didn't yield to his right of way when he crossed the street, and getting into constant fights with anyone he considered below him on the food chain. After the widely reported homicide of

Nicole Brown Simpson, Leidy left a note in a desk drawer, similar in content to the pre-mortem one left by Nicole that identified Orenthal James Simpson as her murderer. Leidy herself could not understand what drove her to leave the note, considering that there was no "real" indication he might become violent.

For most of her marriage, Leidy had lived quietly but determinedly, with little sense of her own agency despite a number of external successes. Within the marriage, she had grown a bit more forthright as the children grew and became alternate targets for her husband's anger. Age and many years of therapy had made her increasingly impatient with her own tentativeness and, although she was still determined "not to look for trouble," she was more apt to speak up than she had once been. In the intervening years, her husband had stopped drinking and her periodic excursions into bolder, more confrontational stances had "proven" sufficiently, if still not conclusively, that he was not about to devolve into a frenzy of domestic violence when she stood up to him. In fact, like many bullies, he often backed off or changed course when challenged. Having no scars to call into evidence, she sometimes wondered if she had only dreamt his more aggressive behaviors.

As much as any woman with whom I have spoken in the course of this project, Leidy embodies the magnificent dissociation of aggression that characterizes the abusive relationship. She shared that years earlier she had gone through times when she was convinced that her husband might kill her and the children; during one difficult period, she recurrently dreamed of calling 911 but, to add insult to impending injury, in the dream only a psychotherapist picked up the phone. More often she feared the reverse: that herself or one of her kids would one day, in the midst of a conflagration, lose control and kill him.

Leidy described the tortured circularity of her rage-filled thoughts as they blossomed into "as if" theatricals where she killed her husband but, because there was no concrete evidence of her partner's assaults, she had no forensic defense for her deadly crimes. She wondered obsessively if she had exaggerated his attacks, as well as her own and the children's emotional injuries. Had she made the whole thing up? Was it all a product of some massive paranoid projection on her part, where she had turned a run of the mill jerk into a demon predator? Leidy often stated that her express purpose in entering psychoanalysis was to see her husband as "just a regular asshole." She had borrowed the term from her best friend, who had befriended a woman whose outwardly "normal" partner ending up killing their daughter. Leidy remembered her friend saying that, when she had once briefly met the man, he had seemed like "just a regular asshole" but the woman had turned him into a powerful Svengali who ultimately twisted her into an accomplice. Leidy wondered whether she herself was an angry person looking for an excuse to actualize her own Leviathan. She said sometimes that she had learned to bear her husband's rage but could no longer bear her own.

The personal experience that had dominated the day of the night of the dream was a confrontation Leidy had with her husband following the husband's provocation of their son in an argument that had escalated to the point where Leidy had to step in, fearing where things might go. Leidy told the husband for the zillionth time how frightening and destructive his aggression toward her and the children felt and he had responded, like Captain Renault in *Casablanca*, she paraphrased, that he was "shocked, shocked" to hear such a thing and, now that he was aware of it, he would certainly change. That, too, had the risible ring to Leidy of Renault's sardonic promise to round up the usual suspects.

Leidy described her dream as powerful, perhaps even premonitory, although she had felt no strong emotions either in the dream or in its aftermath. In the dream, during the course of a routine ob-gyn exam, a middle-aged female doctor had performed an MRI on Leidy's shoulder and found an aggressive cancer. (In real life, Leidy had suffered for at least a dozen years with adhesive capsulitis in her right shoulder, a condition more commonly referred to as "frozen shoulder." The disorder limited the range of motion in her shoulder joint and produced a chronic but tolerable pain that would intermittently flare into a neuropathy quite dramatic and disabling, before again receding.) The room where the bad news was delivered in the dream was recalled as having been white and clean but not aggressively antiseptic; the doctor professional and kind, neither alarmist nor negligent.

Leidy remembered thinking in the dream that she had lived with the shooting pain down her arm for so long that it seemed queer that someone would suddenly interrogate it at all or, stranger still, come up with a serious diagnosis that warranted a drastic treatment, maybe chemotherapy and radiation or even amputation. Shoulders were not the business of gynecologists anyway, and Leidy wondered why this doctor had strayed so far from her catchment area. Not *that* queer, though, in the sense that the doctor, in the course of an annual examination, had simply inquired about general health and well-being issues in addition to matters more germane to her specialty. The doctor had just decided to be careful and get a closer reading of the radiculopathy. (When Leidy first used the word "radiculopathy" I mis-anticipated that she was about to say "a closer reading of the *ridiculous*." I wondered later what her situation, and my reaction to it, might be saying about ridicule, particularly the ridicule of patient by doctor.)

Associations to the dream demonstrated daytime residue: Leidy had recently watched a TV program about a little girl who had almost had her shoulder mistakenly amputated and had also seen a news show with Senator Ted Kennedy's son, "the one whose cancerous leg was amputated when he was 12." Leidy remembered wondering while she watched, as she had at other times, whether cancer sites were more prone to occur on places in the body that had suffered some previous trauma. Even though she did not know it as fact, Leidy had it stuck in her head that Edward Kennedy, Jr. had previously broken his leg in a skiing accident. She felt stuck in a peculiar and unresolvable imaginary debate over whether the leg had been made vulnerable to cancer by the break or the break had been potentiated by a silently stalking cancer, an early warning sign that had been missed.

Leidy first described the atmospherics of the dream as "normal" and then "normalizing." No distress was reported, inside or outside its Freudian arborarium. In what was more of a nodding admittance than an "aha" moment, Leidy decided that the diseased shoulder must be a metaphor for the marriage, a traumatized site where bone and sinew were being ravaged by an aggressive but quite familiar intruder. Asked whether she would pursue treatment for the cancer, Leidy said that she had not yet decided at the point when she woke up; in any case it did not seem a substantially pressing concern. She said that she had the vague sense it might be like other cancers of old age: treated, you would live with the uniquely terrible consequences of care; untreated you might just live long enough to die of something else. Not choosing was sometimes the best choice, Leidy decided.

After so many years, she no longer assumed that finding out the "truth" of the cancer (or marriage) – if it could even be determined – would be particularly surprising or at all compelling. At the moment, things were bad but not spreading rapidly. "Anyway, it's like the cancer," she said, "why treat it? There is always the possibility that I might die of something else in the meantime."

I have provided the background information so that you can picture a typical interpretation which might have overtones of the transference, with me being the doctor who strayed from my usual purview (the patient's mind? my own mind?), to investigate a painful appendage (the husband? the therapy itself?), and now was encountering resistance from the patient who stubbornly refuses to take chemotherapy (my toxic treatment?). If you are an interpersonalist, you might follow the patient's associative trail to try to home in on specific characters or images in the dream, or you might pay attention to the way that your interpretative process was itself re-enacting the themes of intrusion and resistance contained within it.

Just to experiment with dream production or the social dreaming matrix, try on the dream as your own, or become an interloper in its action. What is the white room for you? Who is the authority figure? Why is your shoulder in pain? Who do you wish was in the dream that is not? What would be an alternative ending? This kind of riffing opens up the interpersonal space and makes the associative terrain exponentially more fertile. Whether a psychoanalyst chooses to share personal associations is almost secondary to the fact that these techniques encourage engagement with the material in a very intimate way, and help generate images which can be linked to cultural themes that invite political, as well as personal, analysis.

Collective change

I have tried to imagine personal reflection as it might be tied to personal action in a broad sense, and sometimes a political one, and how that sensibility might infuse clinical technique. Samuels (2004) has queried to what extent we have been willing to weave ideas about "political selfhood" into conversations other than those that involve communally shared events like the attack on the World Trade Center. Many therapists responding to a large survey that Samuels performed expressed that they felt unprepared to grapple with such material when clients introduced it and even questioned whether psychotherapy or psychoanalysis was the appropriate forum to engage such issues.

> And when we read most clinical texts, the external world is hardly mentioned. Much therapy still seems (or claims) to take place in a political vacuum. There are several delusional aspects of this virginal fantasy about what we do . . . [one] delusion is that it is not possible to find a responsible way to work directly with political, social, and cultural material in the clinical session.
>
> (Samuels, 2004, pp. 827–828)

The reticence to engage these issues certainly has something to do with the reluctance in psychoanalysis to examine the analysts' own privilege in regard to clients, the power imbalances generated by the clinical situation, and the ways in which clinicians may be recapitulating the oppression that clients experience in the outside world. Besides, talking politics can seem quite distant from the "experience near" focus psychoanalysts favor. It seems more natural to investigate effects of the immediate field than far flung events of questionable relevance. But another way to look at this, as Sullivan (1965) suggests, is to view local experience as merely the point of impingement rather than its essential cause. The understanding of someone's problems in living always comes from working within the "total situation."

> As a student of larger than personal units, [the psychiatrist] may become concerned as to a whole stream of social phenomena arising within an organization of which the affected individual happened to be a significant unit.
>
> (Sullivan, 1965, p. 15)

Sullivan contextualizes all personal psychology and pathology in terms of their many moving parts. Some parts are intensely local: derivatives of character perhaps, or the product of an intermix of what is environmentally attended and internally transformed, or what is completely ignored but still impactful. The further out we get from the hub of our personal activity, the less visible are the emanatory waves that comprise our own effect on the universe. The same is true of the outlying waves that feed the smaller waves that crash against the shores of our intimate lives. The further afield the catalyst of action, the harder to conceive its role in our misery or bliss. Sullivan's use of the term dynamisms (instead of the more Freudian "mechanisms") to describe human patterns of behavior captures both the energy and the complexity of the many moving parts that constitute any single feeling, thought, action, or absence. In "Tensions Interpersonal and International: A Psychiatrist's View" (1950), he explored the political causes and consequences of psychological trauma, affirming that individual impediments to development and deformations of character ultimately played out on a global stage.

Coming from a similar theoretical stance, Boal's therapeutic theater worked not only toward the psychological liberation of the individual but the political liberation of the collective (it came to be called The Theater of the Oppressed). He was greatly influenced by Paulo Freire's analysis of educational pedagogy, which posited that race, class, and gender oppression were sustained through a "culture of silence" that eliminated people's capacity to articulate a critique of their oppressors. For abused women, what happens at the broader social level is exactly what happens in the bedroom. Oppression decimates language and with it, meaning, or at least meanings that refuse to conform to the dominant discourse. Boal, like Foucault, imagines a policing function that is successful once it no longer requires an actual enforcer. Boal personifies this as "the cop in the head," shorthand for the internalized persecutors that sustain the influence of external oppressors. In other words, yes, battered women have a cop in the bed problem. But they also have a cop in the head problem.

Katie Gentile (2010), in a paper on how social activism might influence individual psychoanalytic work with abuse survivors, expands on Freire's idea that critical consciousness cannot be just an intellectual activity but must comprise "praxis, action, and reflection" (p. 1). She tells the story of a student, Lauren, who came alive while volunteering with an organization that educates young people about dating violence:

> For the first time Lauren was surrounded by people who identified domestic violence and men's violence against women as criminal. It was not to be condoned, it was not about losing one's temper, drinking too much, or being provoked by another person. Additionally, this social network developed around action-activism, movement. But coming to life for Lauren, as for many students, had consequences.
>
> (p. 5)

Lauren's new comrades and surroundings invigorated her search for answers and her sense of being an active agent, on the one hand, but also called into question old defensive constructions that allowed her to master trauma by assuming responsibility for her father's violence toward her mother and his sexual abuse of her. As Lauren struggled mightily to maintain her narrative of self-blame, Gentile was able to use Lauren's contemporary experience of activism to highlight inconsistencies in the way she assigned responsibility for maltreatment. For example, Gentile asked whether Lauren's training sessions at her volunteer organization, or texts in her gender studies classes at school, had described children being responsible for their own abuse. Acknowledging that they had not, a new narrative that held victims blameless could begin to be created. Lauren could eventually insert her own experience into that narrative.

Because so many of the subjects in this book came to me through a domestic violence support network, I was able to speak with women about their experiences, not only as members of support groups, but as active educators and advocates for gender justice. For some, the experience of hearing other women tell their stories was profound. Hayal heard a speaker at her school:

> A survivor came in and told her story and I was just moved by it and took her card, and one day I just started going [to the survivor's group]. Because I

didn't know what domestic violence meant. I had never heard of the word. So, and then [the group leader] started going over the calm/control wheel, and I was like, "Oh my god, that's me. I've been experiencing that all along." And um, even though I knew something was wrong with my marriage, um, not having a label to it, you know, made it harder to define what it is so that I can know what remedy to use.

For me, I think it was increasing my self-worth, my self-confidence. I was doing things. You can't do that in isolation. You can't do it if you're isolated and not around people who believe in you and who support you. So for me, I felt like I'm worth something; these people say I'm worth something and just hearing positive, positive, positive stuff, like "you're beautiful." I mean, I thought I was so ugly; I hated the way I looked. You can't imagine the perception I had of myself, like dirty, because of, like, enduring the pain and witnessing my mom's stuff [Hayal's mother was also a victim of domestic violence, as well as a perpetrator] and the molestation. I hated to the look in the mirror. I hated to look in the mirror.

And you know, pampering myself? Why am I gonna go get a manicure? I'm ugly. Why am I gonna go – I mean, just, just being around other women who were like sisters, you know, like, "you're beautiful." You know, just hearing it, I was just like, I started to believe it. Whereas when you just hear so much negativity and so much put-down, you just start thinking that's what you are. So my self-worth had increased. I became more able to realize that it wasn't fair and that I deserved more and I have a right to deserve more and you know, I guess, and yeah, there is a point where there's a sort of switch where you would do anything – you would even lose your life. And at some point, I was like, I don't care if I die. I used to tell my mother, "Kill me, I don't care," because I'd rather die on my feet than live on my knees.

And that's kind of how I felt. I was like, I told them that I would rather die a hero than you know, live a like prisoner. And then, when I finally got divorced, my mom actually kicked my dad out of the house.

Today Hayal is quite active politically around issues of women's rights and safety. She remained in group and individual therapy but, because of her tendency "to overanalyze everything," found herself most comfortable with a therapist who empowered her to act. Sadly, as often happens in social service settings, after two years the agency decided "Look, she's been hanging around for two years, she's made a lot of progress, you know, we have to close the case." Hayal's sessions were terminated but her therapist continues to stay in touch.

She's still a support system. We call each other, we text each other. And I'm actually gonna see her tomorrow. So she's still there. [And] she's an inner voice. She's still an inner voice.

There is no doubt in my mind that the integration of dissociated aggression needs to be part of a therapeutic strategy, certainly for women in violent relationships, but also for women caught in more ambiguous abuse situations. Gwynne smiled so sweetly when she recalled her DV counselor's encouragement in this regard that I commented on it. She described that first intervention as very pragmatic, with a megadose of assertiveness training. This began her odyssey toward greater agency. Although she elected to stay in her marriage, she was able to change many of the abusive dynamics by becoming more willing to assert herself, even when that felt unnaturally aggressive. Later Gwynne moved on to a more psychodynamic therapy, where she has continued to work on seeing herself as the "grown woman" her first therapist had invited in, the one who can do things even without "permission."

> There was a book I read about whacking the problem, knowing what you are asking for and checking to see if it's understood. So it's some assertiveness training . . . thinking through interactions more productively . . . what I want out of them . . . [and that] it's perfectly fine for me to say "no."

From anger to agency to activism (Bunny's story)

> My therapy was to do what I'm doing now. It's like to do the advocacy, to talk to the people in the community.
>
> *And that's therapeutic?*
>
> Yeah, for me. I tell them [I am] turning my pain into power. Because what I want to do is just to tell my daughter and everybody else, you know, about the other face that people don't see. And for me, telling them that story is my therapy. Because I do believe that talking to someone, I will have the opportunity to express what is inside. So I use what is inside to educate people. I will tell them that when people talk about culture, I can use that to tell them what is happening . . . I can use that to tell them how, when you are working with [my culture's] men and women, make sure that you look at this man being present every day with this woman. Men beat and abuse as a way of protecting this woman sometimes. I live that life where someone will hold my hand but holding my hand is, for me, not be able to go. It's to go to *this* direction. He's not holding my hand because he loves me so much. He's holding my hand because it's like, "I arrest you." For me, it was holding my hand. Or someone bringing me to my job every morning can be something beautiful for people. But you know, taking me to the job can be, for someone, a way of [saying] "I put you in that place and I come back at four to take you from that place."
>
> So people can see it as, "Oh you are lucky to have such a man come to the job in the middle of the day," and I can tell them, "No, I was not that lucky. It was someone stalking me." Someone will tell me, "Oh, your man will call you five times, six times a day. Oh, it's love." I can tell people, "No, it doesn't

mean that calling five and six times, it's something good." Ask this woman if she's happy about it – if she has a right to say, "You don't have to call me." Then you can say, oh, that's something good. Because sometimes when you ask, if you ask me at this time, if I'm happy about my ex-husband calling me six, seven times, I will tell you, no, he's bothering me. Someone bothering me. Why? I feel like someone was controlling me, had their eyes on me, and always accusing me of something. But people from the outside will tell me that's love.

So in this way, I use my experience to talk. But not to even think about past memory. For me, it's not that painful now. I was angry at myself first. How can I get in *that* relationship? You know, I talk to myself. I was being so smart. So in that sense, with this pushing, I didn't think I was so smart to choose. That's the blaming of myself: "You did not see that he is this way." And then when things happen in the relationship, I start thinking of bad behavior before we get married and I make the connection. Because some of the signs, I should – if I was that smart, I should see that he did that before. But of course he did that before. But before things had escalated, you don't do the connection.

Yes, you know, people will say, "They're a happy couple." No one asked me. No one knew what was going on. That was inside, inside. That's when things escalated, people said, "Oh, what is happening? They were such a lovely couple!" The first day she may say, "Yes, yes, I'm happy," because it's hard to sit with you when – it's hard. It was not easy for me to sit and explain to people. I don't know what to say. But talking to someone day after day, and interacting. Then, if she feel open enough, she can tell you. Because my experience – the first time – I couldn't talk to people, tell them my story.

I don't want to say that people here are lucky, but I want people to think that other people in the world are worse, you know, in that area of women rights and women issue. Because when I came here and I, you know, that, oh, things happen and you can call 911 in the middle of the night and – in my country, things happen, there was no 911 you can call at night.

And there is no organization where a woman can – the only woman organization are the church, you know. And then they say the same idea . . . your man is the boss. But [in America] there are organizations where women can stand up and talk with women about struggle and violence.

I mean because I listen to other people story, I kind of imagine – first of all, some of them, I didn't think it was abuse at the beginning. Oh, OK, that's – the word "emotional abuse"? We don't use that. I feel bad but I cannot express it as emotional abuse. It's like I didn't know. Now I can categorize. I do, I go and study advocacy, human rights, and things. But before I can say only that bad things happen to me.

A lot of bad things of that type happened to me, but I just change it and make it *powerful*. I mean, I probably thought that I will die from all this atrocity. But I didn't die from this atrocity. I go and study human rights advocacy. Just because I want to help people not to be in that situation. Not only for domestic violence. Any abuse. What if [people] don't know what to look for, or they don't think it's an issue? Something somewhere is wrong. I want to tell people. Of course, it's an issue. A real issue.

Epilogue

I began working with Phoebe during the course of a post-doctoral fellowship at a psychoanalytic institute. At around the two-year mark in our relationship, the laws governing practice and licensing for psychoanalysis changed in my state. Because of my full-time teaching and research commitments, I elected not to continue at the institute. I explained the situation to the handful of patients I was seeing and offered to refer them on to colleagues who were remaining in the program, but they chose instead to continue working with me in a new arrangement. I remained very close to my colleagues at the psychoanalytic institute, who have been a continuous source of support and wisdom. They have provided a respite from the political machinations of academic life, as well as an intellectual salon where I can test out my ideas. I have made it a kind of personal mission to bring the insights of psychoanalysis, and particularly the work of Harry Stack Sullivan, to bear on issues of perpetration and victimhood in the forensic arena, where I do the majority of my work, and where I preach Sullivan's (1947) most enduring sermon: we are all much more simply human than otherwise (p. 7).

Phoebe may have terminated by the time this book comes to print. Maybe it is just my own laborious journey toward the final chapter of the book that is making me feel a sense of closure around the gender-related issues that dominated the conversations with Phoebe for so many of the last few years. We have worked together for a long time and rarely talk about men anymore, at least not the way we once did. She has been in a loving, stable, relationship of equals for a while and, so, has the energy to complain about other things: her job, her friends, and that perennial favorite of people on the couch everywhere, her mother. I remember so much of our dialogue as occurring in the dark: two blind women feeling different parts of the male elephant, trying to compose a meaningful narrative from the negligible information that our mutual dissociation supplied. Or perhaps I just remember the days as dark because the office in which we met for many years had no window, a fitting metaphor for the airlessness of Phoebe's life at the time and my own difficulty in spelling out how the things that happened in the room could be made relevant to the world outside.

At around the same time that I began the work with Phoebe, a colleague from my college started a feminist theory reading group, to which I was dragged kicking and screaming, but in whose membership I signified much unformulated material that seemed impervious to psychoanalytic ministration. We wrestled over what was political and what was personal, what constituted our subjectivity, and whether female agency was achievable in conditions of patriarchy.

At the time Phoebe and I met, I had not yet figured out my own personal and professional relationships with men. Although I did not discuss my private life with her, every word Phoebe said spoke volumes to me about how I was complicit in my own subjugation to the phallic enterprise that Man made and Freud enshrined. I identified with Phoebe's rage and the inability to express it. I became sensitized to every apology I uttered when I had done nothing wrong and every time I seemed to be saying yes when I meant no or, worse, said no but somehow capitulated to someone else's desire, need, or whim anyway. No surprise; patients often needle the defensive structure of clinicians, forcing them to re-litigate their own conflicts. In countertransference enactments, empathy is briefly forsaken and replaced with a pungent set of affects and thoughts that, if they are not disclaimed, can motivate deeper reflection (Kantrowitz, 1997).

> To be truly engaged is to allow oneself to be vulnerable to another. The relationship benefits the analyst beyond the cognitive recognition and clarification of personal issues. Once engaged, the interaction that occurs between patient and analyst provides the analyst an opportunity to change.
>
> (p. 145)

Because I could see what Phoebe was dissociating, I started to fathom what I too distanced or disowned. We enacted, on the scaffold of a slowly developing ambivalence, a play about agency that presaged a reversal in both our fortunes. We engaged, and were sometimes seduced by, the aggressive parts of ourselves. We acted our way into good thinking. Fascinated by the shift in our mutual awareness around issues of gendered trauma, dissociation, and agency, I decided to devote my research agenda at the college to victims of domestic violence. Like the work with Phoebe, and my prior investigations of violent crime from the perpetrator's vantage point, the study turned out to be, at least in part, a self-study.

One day, Phoebe and I delightedly discussed a sexcapade in which Phoebe had demonstrated complete ownership of her sexuality. I flashed without warning on her darker days. Almost instinctively, the lifeguard in me knew something was missing and in the two seconds that save an utterance from being an enactment, I purposely decided to ask whether she was using birth control. To say I ruined the mood is a severe underestimation.

Before we could venture much further conversationally, a very loud and peculiar grinding noise seized our attention. At first, it seemed to be emanating from the bathroom, which adjoined the east wall of the office. Then we realized it was coming from the closet that separated the two rooms. "A mouse!" Phoebe guessed. Tentatively, I opened the closet. (At this point, let me add that the office was a sublet. I had no idea what I might find.) A red light notified us that the paper shredder had turned itself on and was suddenly working overtime. I tried but could not find the off switch. I looked at Phoebe quite helplessly and she launched off the couch, reaching past me to slide something near the LED indicator to the left, stopping the monster in its tracks. Failing to wait the aforementioned requisite two seconds to think about what to say, I instead blurted out "You saved us!" Or perhaps it was the even less professional "You saved our lives!"

I did not mean to say it. Granted, it was extreme, as the language of enactment often is. On the other hand, such extended parapraxes always contain an element of truth. I am really different now from when I started work with Phoebe, and immeasurably changed from when I began interviewing women for this book. Looking at violence in the lives of women made me recognize that, while there is much outside of our control, there is also much that we have the ability to change. The idea, if women embrace it, may indeed save a lot of lives.

References

Note: *S.E.* = *Standard Edition of the Complete Psychological Works of Sigmund Freud*, trans. J. Strachey. London: Hogarth Press and the Institute of Psychoanalysis.

Alexander, C. (2010), *The Creative Space of Play: D.W. Winnicott.* http://onluminous-grounds.wordpress.com/2010/09/19/the-creative-space-of-play/. Retrieved 11/12/12.

Alexander, F. and French, T.M. (with staff members of the Chicago Institute for Psychoanalysis) (1946), *Psychoanalytic Therapy: Principles and Application.* New York: Ronald Press.

Allison, C.J., Bartholomew, K., Mayseless, O., and Dutton, D.G. (2008), Love as a battlefield: Attachment and relationship dynamics in couples identified for male partner violence. *Journal of Family Issues*, *29*, 125–150.

Almeida, R. and Durkin, T. (1999), The cultural context model: therapy for couples with domestic violence. *Journal of Marital and Family Therapy*, *25*(3), 313–324.

Almeida, R.V. and Lockhard, J. (2005), The cultural context model: A new paradigm for accountability, empowerment, and the development of critical consciousness against domestic violence. In Natalie J. Sokoloff (ed.), *Domestic Violence at the Margins: Readings on Race, Class, Gender, and Culture* (pp. 301–320). New Brunswick, NJ: Rutgers University Press.

Almeida, R.V., Parker, L., and Dolan-Del Vecchio, K. (eds.) (2008), *Transformative Family Therapy: Just Families in a Just Society*. Boston: Pearson.

Amado, G. (2009), Psychic imprisonment and its release within organizations and working relationships. *Organisational and Social Dynamics*, *9*(1), 1–20.

—— (1968), *Diagnostic and Statistical Manual of Mental Disorders* – II. Washington, DC: American Psychiatric Association.

American Psychological Association (1996), *Violence and the Family: Report of the American Psychological Association Presidential Task Force on Violence and the Family*. Washington, DC: American Psychological Association.

Araji, S.K. and Bosek, R.L. (2010), Domestic violence, contested child custody, and the courts: Findings from five studies (chapter 6). In M.T. Hannah and B. Goldstein (eds.), *Domestic Violence, Abuse, and Child Custody: Legal Strategies and Policy Issues.* Kingston, NJ: Civic Research Institute.

Arias, I. and Pape, K.T. (1999), Psychological abuse: Implications for adjustment and commitment to leave violent partners. *Violence and Victims*, *14*(1), 55–67.

Arias, I., and Street, A.E. (1996), Children of psychologically abused women: Effects of maternal adjustment and parenting on child outcomes. Presented at the 8th International Conference on Personal Relationships, Banff, Canada.

Arias, I., Street, A.E., and Brody, G.H. (1996), Depression and alcohol abuse: Women's responses to psychological victimization. Presented at the American Psychological Association's National Conference on Psychosocial and Behavioral Factors in Women's Health: Research, Prevention, Treatment, and Service Delivery in Clinical and Community Settings. Washington, DC.

Asch, S.S. (1976), Varieties of negative therapeutic reaction and problems of technique. *J. Amer. Psychoanal. Assn.*, *24*, 383–407.

Ayers, Mary Y. (2011), *Masculine Shame: From Succubus to the Eternal Feminine.* London and New York: Routledge.

Azundris (2008), Pretty in pain: Beauty and the art of female destruction. Azundris.com/output/femme. Retrieved 6/12/12.

Baly, A.R. (2010), Leaving abusive relationships: Constructions of self and situation by abused women. *Journal of Interpersonal Violence*, *25*(12), 2297–2315.

Bancroft, L. and Silverman, J.G. (2005), *The Batterer as Parent: Addressing the Impact of Domestic Violence on Family Dynamics*. Thousand Oaks, CA: Sage.

Barvosa-Carter, E. (2001), Strange tempest: Agency, poststructuralism, and the shape of feminist politics to come. *International Journal of Sexuality and Gender Studies*, *6*(1/2), 123–137.

Basch, M.F. (1976), The concept of affect: A reexamination. *Journal of the American Psychoanalytic Association*, *24*, 759–777.

Bateson, G. (1972), *Steps to an Ecology of Mind: Essays in Anthropology, Psychiatry, Evolution, and Epistemology*. Northvale, NJ: Jason Aronson.

Bell, C.C. and Mattis, J. (2000), The importance of cultural competence in ministering to African American victims of domestic violence. *Violence Against Women*, *6*, 515–532.

Bell, M. (2005), A woman's scorn: Toward a feminist defense of contempt as a moral emotion. *Hypatia*, *20*(4), 80–93.

Benjamin, J. (2004), Beyond doer and done to: An intersubjective view of thirdness. *Psychoanalytic Quarterly*, *73*, 5–46.

—— (1988), *The Bonds of Love: Psychoanalysis, Feminism, and the Problem of Domination*. New York: Pantheon Books.

—— (1983), Master and slave: The fantasy of erotic domination. In A. Snitow, C. Stansell, and S. Thompson (eds.), *Powers of Desire: The Politics of Sexuality*. New York: Monthly Review Press.

Berandt, C. (1966), *The Third Reich of Dreams*. Chicago: Quadrangle Books.

Bierce, A. (1911), *The Devil's Dictionary*. New York: Neale.

Bion, W.R. (1961/1991), *Experiences in Groups and Other Papers*. London: Routledge.

—— (1958), On arrogance. *Int. J. Psycho-Anal.*, *39*, 144–146.

Bisson, M.A. and Levine, T. (2009), Negotiating a friends with benefits relationship. *Archives of Sexual Behavior*, *38*, 66–73.

Blatner, A. (2007), Morenean approaches: Recognizing psychodrama's many facets. *Journal of Group Psychotherapy, Psychodrama, and Sociometry*, Winter, 159–170.

Bloom, S.L. (2005), Neither liberty nor safety: The impact of fear on individuals, institutions, and societies, part iii. *Psychotherapy and Politics International*, *3*(2) 96–111.

Boal, Augusto (1996), *The Rainbow of Desire : The Boal Method of Theatre and Therapy* (reprinted. ed.). London: Routledge.

Bollas, C. (1987), *The Shadow of the Object: Psychoanalysis of the Unknown Thought.* New York: Columbia University Press.

Boonzaier, F. (2008), "If the man says you must sit, then you must sit." The relational construction of women abuse: Gender, subjectivity, and violence. *Feminism and Psychology, 18*, 183–206.

Bowkers, L. (1983), *Beating Wife Beating*. Lexington, MA: D.C. Heath.

Bowlby, J. (1969), *Attachment and Loss, Vol. 1: Attachment.* London: Hogarth Press.

Bromberg, P.M. (2008), Shrinking the tsunami: Affect regulation, dissociation, and the shadow of the flood. *Contemporary Psychoanalysis, 44*, 329–350.

—— (2006), *Awakening the Dreamer: Clinical Journeys.* Mahwah, NJ: Analytic Press.

—— (2003). Something wicked this way comes: Trauma, dissociation, and conflict: The space where psychoanalysis, cognitive science, and neuroscience overlap. *Psychoanalytic Psychology, 20*(3), 558–574.

—— (1998), *Standing in the Spaces: Essays on Clinical Process, Trauma, and Dissociation.* Mahwah, NJ: Analytic Press.

—— (1994), "Speak! That I May See You": Some reflections on dissociation, reality, and psychoanalytic listening. *Psychoanalytic Dialogues, 4*, 517–547.

Bucci, W. (2002), The referential process, consciousness, and the sense of self. *Psychoanal. Inq., 22*(5), 766–793.

Buechler, S. (2008), *Making a Difference in Patient's Lives: Emotional Experience in the Therapeutic Setting*. New York: Routledge.

Buie, D.H., Meissner, W.W., and Rizzuto, A. (1996), The role of aggression in sadomasochism. *Canadian J. Psychoanal., 4*, 1–27.

Bunch, C. (1997), *The Intolerable Status Quo: Violence Against Women and Girls.* UNICEF Annual Report: The Progress of Nations. New York: UNICEF.

Bureau of Justice Statistics (2006). *Intimate Partner Violence in the U.S. 1993–2004.* Washington, DC: Bureau of Justice Statistics.

Bureau of Justice Statistics (2003). *Intimate Partner Violence in the U.S. 1993–2001.* Washington, DC: Bureau of Justice Statistics.

Bureau of Justice Statistics (1995). *Violence Against Women: Estimates from the re-designed survey, August 1995*. Washington, DC: Bureau of Justice Statistics.

Campbell, A. (2007), Attachment, aggression and affiliation: The role of oxytocin in female social behavior. *Biological Psychology, 77*(1), 1–10.

Camus, A. (1992), *The Rebel: An Essay on Man in Revolt*. New York: Vintage.

Caplan, P.J. (1984), The myth of women's masochism. *American Psychologist, 39*(2), 130–139.

Celani, D.P. (1994), *Illusion of Love: Why the Battered Woman Returns to her Abuser.* New York: Columbia University Press.

Chancer, L.S. (1992), *Sadomasochism in Everyday Life: The Dynamics of Power and Powerlessness*. New Brunswick, NJ: Rutgers University Press.

Chasseguet-Smirgel, J. (1991), Sadomasochism in the perversions: Some thoughts on the destruction of reality. *Journal of the American Psychoanalytic Association, 39*, 399–415.

Chesler, P. (1986), *Mothers on Trial: The Battle for Children and Custody*. Chicago: Lawrence Hill Press.

Chewter, C.L. (2003), Violence against women and children: some legal issues. *Canadian Journal of Family Law, 20*(1), 99–178.

Children Now/Kaiser Permanente poll, December 1995.

Chodorow, N. (2002), Gender as a personal and cultural construction. In M. Dimen and V. Goldner (eds.), *Gender in Psychoanalytic Space: Between Clinic and Culture* (pp. 237–262). New York: Other Press.

—— (1974), Family Structure and Feminine Personality. In M.Z. Rosaldo and L. Lamphere (eds.), *Woman, Culture and Society* (pp. 43–66). Stanford, CA: Stanford University Press.

Collins, G. (1985), Women and masochism: Debate continues. *New York Times*, December 2.

Coontz, S. (2012), The M.R.S. and the Ph.D. *New York Times*, February 11.

Currie, J. and Tekin, E. (2006), Does child abuse cause crime? Research paper series, working paper 06-31, Andrew Young School of Policy Studies, Department of Economics. http://aysps.gsu.edu/publications/2006/index.htm. Retrieved 12/8/10.

Dahlin, B. (2009), On the path toward thinking: Learning from Martin Heidegger and Rudolf Steiner. *Studies in Philosophy and Education*, *28*, 537–554.

Damasio, A. (1999), *The Feeling of What Happens: Body and Emotion in the Making of Consciousness*. New York: Harcourt.

Davies, J. (1998), Repression and dissociation: Freud and Janet. In N. Skolnick and D. Scarff (eds.), *Fairbairn Then and Now* (pp. 53–69). Mahwah, NJ: Analytic Press.

De Beauvoir, S. (1952; reprinted 1989), *The Second Sex*. Trans. H.M. Parshley. New York: Vintage Books.

—— (1949/1989), *The Second Sex*. New York: Vintage Books.

De Mijolla, A. (2005), Editor: Alain de Mijolla: *The International Dictionary of Psychoanalysis*. New York: Macmillan Reference USA.

De Sade, Marquis (1966), *The Complete de Sade*. Los Angeles: Holloway House Publishing.

—— (1791), *Justine or The Misfortunes of Virtue*, vol. I, pp. 47–206.

—— (1795), *Philosophy in the Bedroom*, vol I, pp. 207–319, digitized version.

—— (1797), *Juliette*, vol II, pp. 9–164.

Deleuze, G. (1989), *Masochism: Coldness and Cruelty and Venus in Furs*. Cambridge, MA: Zone Books/MIT Press.

Devereux, G. (1978), *Ethnopsychoanalysis: Psychoanalysis and Anthropology as Complementary Frames of Reference*. Berkeley: University of California Press.

Diamond, M.A. and Allcorn, S. (2004), Moral violence in organizations. *Organisational and Social Dynamics*, *4*(1), 22–45.

Dickinson, E. (1924), *The Complete Poems of Emily Dickinson*. Boston: Little, Brown. Bartleby.com, 2000. www.bartleby.com/113/. Retrieved 1/2/2013.

Dimen, M. (2011), *With Culture in Mind: Psychoanalytic Stories*. New York: Routledge.

Dohrn, B. (1995), Bad mothers, good mothers, and the state: Children on the margins. University of Chicago Law School Roundtable. Keynote address.

Dorey, R. (1986), The relationship of mastery. *International Review of Psychoanalysis*, *13*, 323–332.

Dragiewicz, M. (2010), Gender bias in the courts: Implications for battered mothers and their children (chapter 5). In M.T. Hannah and B. Goldstein (eds.), *Domestic Violence, Abuse, and Child Custody: Legal Strategies and Policy Issues*. Kingston, NJ: Civic Research Institute.

Dunn, J.L. (2005), "Victims" and "Survivors": Emerging vocabularies of motive for battered women who stay. *Sociological Inquiry*, *75*(1), 1–30.

Dutton, D.G. and Painter, S. (1993), Emotional attachments in abusive relationships: A test of traumatic bonding theory. *Violence and Victims*, *8*(2), 105–120.
EAP Digest November–December 1991.
Ellis, H. (1940), *Studies in the Psychology of Sex, Volume 3*. New York: Random House.
Eng, D.L. (2000), Melancholia in the late twentieth century. *Signs*, *25*(4), 1275–1281.
Erickson, N.S. (2010), Fighting false allegations of parental alienation raised as defenses to valid claims of abuse (chapter 20). In M.T. Hannah and B. Goldstein (eds.), *Domestic Violence, Abuse, and Child Custody: Legal Strategies and Policy Issues*. Kingston, NJ: Civic Research Institute.
Evans III, F.B. (1996) *Harry Stack Sullivan: Interpersonal Theory and Psychotherapy*. New York: Routledge.
Ewing, C.P and Aubrey, M. (1987), Battered women and public opinion: Some realities about the myths. *Journal of Family Violence*, *2*(3), 257–264.
Fairbairn, W.D. (1954), *An Object Relations Theory of the Personality*. New York: Basic Books.
Feimberg, H. (2005), *The Telescoping of Generations*. London: Routledge.
Fischer, K., Vidmar, N., and Ellis, R. (1992–1993), Culture of battering and the role of mediation in domestic violence cases. *Southern Methodist University Law Review*, *46*, 2117–2174.
Foer, J. S. (2005), *Extremely Loud and Incredibly Close*. New York: Houghton Mifflin.
Follingstad, D.R. and DeHart, D.D. (2000), Defining psychological abuse of husbands toward wives: Contexts, behaviors, and typologies. *Journal of Interpersonal Violence*, *15*(9), 891–920.
Fonagy, P., Gergely, G., Jurist, E.L., and Target, M. (2002), *Affect Regulation, Mentalization, and the Development of the Self*. New York: Other Press.
Forte, J.A., Franks, D.D., and Rigsby, D. (1996), Asymmetrical role-taking: Comparing battered and non-battered women. *Social Work*, *41*(1), 59–115.
Foucault, M. (1995), *Discipline and Punish: The Birth of the Prison*. 2nd ed. New York: Vintage.
Franks, D.D. (1989), Power and role-taking: A social behavioral synthesis of Kemper's power and status model. In D.D. Franks and E.D. McCarthy (eds.), *The Sociology of Emotions: Original Essays and Research Papers* (pp. 153–177). Greenwich, CT: JAI Press.
Freire, P. (1970/2000), *Pedagogy of the Oppressed*. New York: Bloomsbury Academic.
Freud, S. (1925), Some psychical consequences of the anatomical distinction between the sexes. *S.E.*, XIX, 241–258.
—— (1924), The economic problem of masochism. *S.E.*, XIX.
—— (1918), From the history of an infantile neurosis. *S.E.*, XVII, 1–122.
—— (1917/1963), Mourning and melancholia. In *General Psychological Theory*, ed. Philip Rieff, 164–79. New York: Collier.
—— (1908), On the sexual theories of children. *S.E.*, IX, 209–26.
—— (1896), The aetiology of hysteria. *S.E.*, III, 191.
Friedkin, W. (director) (1973), *The Exorcist*. Warner Bros.
Fuller, A.K. (1986), Masochistic Personality Disorder: A diagnosis under consideration. *Jefferson Journal of Psychiatry*, *4*(2), 7–21.
Gardner, R. (1992), *Parental Alienation Syndrome: A Guide for Mental Health and Legal Professionals*. Creskill, NJ: Creative Therapeutics.
Gentile, K. (2010), Women's centers + gender studies = social justice. Feminist Pedagogy November Conference, New York: CUNY Graduate Center.

Gentile, K., Raghavan, C., Rajah, V., and Gates, K. (2007), It doesn't happen here: Eating disorders in an ethnically diverse sample of economically disadvantaged, urban college students. *Eating Disorders: The Journal of Treatment and Prevention*, *15*(5), 405–425.

Ghent, E. (1990), Masochism, submission, surrender, 1: Masochism as a perversion of surrender. *Contemporary Psychoanalysis*, *26*, 106–136.

Glick, P. and Fiske, S.T. (2001), An ambivalent alliance: Hostile and benevolent sexism as complementary justifications for gender inequality. *American Psychologist*, *56*, 109–118.

Golding, J.M. (1999), Intimate partner violence as a risk factor for mental disorders: A meta-analysis. *Journal of Family Violence*, *14*(2), 99–132.

Goldner, V. (2004), When love hurts: Treating abusive relationships. *Psychoanalytic Inquiry*, *42*, 346–372.

—— (2002), Toward a critical relational theory of gender. In M. Dimen and V. Goldner (eds.), *Gender in Psychoanalytic Space: Between Clinic and Culture* (pp. 63–87). New York: Other Press.

—— (1999), Morality and multiplicity: Perspectives on the treatment of violence in intimate life. *Journal of Marital and Family Therapy*, *25*(3), 325–336.

—— (1998), The treatment of violence and victimization in intimate relationships. *Family Processes*, *37*(3), 263–286.

Goldner, V., Penn, P., Sheinberg, M., and Walker, G. (1990), Love and violence: Gender paradoxes in volatile attachments. *Family Processes*, *29*(4), 343–364.

Goldstein, B. and Hannah, M.T. (2010), Introduction. In M.T. Hannah and B. Goldstein (eds.), *Domestic Violence, Abuse, and Child Custody: Legal Strategies and Policy Issues*. Kingston, NJ: Civic Research Institute.

Gordon, R. (1987), Masochism: The shadow side of the archetypal need to venerate and worship. *Journal of Analytical Psychology*, *32*, 227–240.

Gremillion, D.H. and Kanof, E.P. (1996), Overcoming barriers to physician involvement in identifying and referring victims of domestic violence. *Annals of Emergency Medicine*, *27*(6), 769–773.

Grossman, W.J. (1986), Notes on masochism: A discussion of the history and development of a psychoanalytic concept. *Psychoanalytic Quarterly*, *55*, 379–413.

Guerin, C. (April 6, 2012), Brushstroke Series #59: Cupid Chastised. Zealotry of Guerin: http://christopherguerin.blogspot.com/2012/04/cupid-chastised-bartolomeo-manfredi.html. Retrieved 1/15/2013.

Hannah, M.T. and Goldstein, B. (2010), Introduction. In M.T. Hannah and B. Goldstein (eds.), *Domestic Violence, Abuse, and Child Custody: Legal Strategies and Policy Issues* (pp. xxvii–xxxvi). Kingston, NJ: Civic Research Institute, Inc.

Hannah, M. and Waller, G. (2008), Battered mothers' custody conference. www.youtube.com/watch?v=5viwjaIorU8

Harris, A. (2002), Mothers, monsters, mentors. *Studies in Gender and Sexuality*, *3*(3), 281–295.

Hart, B.J. (1996), Rulemaking and enforcement/Rule compliance and resistance. In B. Sipes and E.J. Hall (eds.), *I Am Not Your Victim: Anatomy of Domestic Violence* (pp. 258–263). London: Sage.

Herman, J.L. (1992a), *Trauma and Recovery: The Aftermath of Violence from Domestic Abuse to Political Terror*. New York: Basic Books.

—— (1992b), Complex PTSD: A syndrome in survivors of prolonged and repeated trauma. *Journal of Traumatic Stress*, *5*(3), 377–391.

Hockenberry, S.L. (1995), Dyadic violence, shame, and narcissism. *Contemp. Psychoanal.*, *31*, 301.

Holtzworth-Munroe, A., Smutzler, N., and Sandin, E. (1997), A brief review of the research on husband violence, Part II: The psychological effects of husband violence on battered women and their children. *Aggression and Violent Behavior*, *2*(3), 179–213.

Hornsby, T.E. (2010), Do judges adequately address the causes and impact of violence in children's lives in deciding contested child custody cases? In M.T. Hannah and B. Goldstein (eds.), *Domestic Violence, Abuse, and Child Custody: Legal Strategies and Policy Issues* (7-2 thru 7-30). Kingston, NJ: Civic Research Institute, Inc.

Howell, E. (1997), Masochism: a bridge to the other side of abuse. *Dissociation*, *10*(4), 240–245.

Hughes, M., Morrison, K., and Asada, K.J.K. (2005), What's love got to do with it? Exploring the impact of maintenance rules, love attitudes, and network support on friends with benefits relationships. *Western Journal of Communication*, *69*(1), 49–66.

Hyden, M. (1999), The world of the fearful: Battered women's narratives of leaving abusive husbands. *Feminism and Psychology*, *9*(4), 449–469.

Iliffe, G. and Steed, L.G. (2000), Exploring the counselor's experience of working with perpetrators and survivors of domestic violence. *Journal of Interpersoanl Violence*, *15*, 393–412.

Izard, C.E. (1977), *Human Emotions*. New York: Plenum.

Jaggar, A. (1989), Love and knowledge: Emotion in feminist epistemology. In A. Garry and M. Pearsall (eds.), *Women, Knowledge, and Reality: Explorations in Feminist Philosophy* (pp. 129–155). Boston: Unwin Hyman.

James, W.H., West, C., Deters, K.E, and Armijo, E. (2000), Youth dating violence. *Adolescence*, *35*, 455–465.

Janet, P. (1889/1973), *L'Automatisme Psychologique*. Paris: Alcan.

Johnson, M.P. (1995), Patriarchal terrorism and common couple violence: Two forms of violence against women. *Journal of Marriage and the Family*, *57*(2), 283–294.

Johnston, J.R., Lee, S., Olesen, N.W., and Walters, M.G. (2005), Allegations and substantiations of abuse in custody disputing families. *Family Court Review*, *43*, 283–284.

Josephs, B. (1982), Addiction to near death. *Int. Journal of Pyschoanalysis*, *63*, 449–456.

Jung, C. (1916), Wandlugen und Symbole der Libido. Yearbook III (*Pyschology of the Unconscious. A Study of the Transformation and Symbolism of the Libido. A Contribution to the History of the Evolution of Thought*). Trans. B.M. Hinkle. London: Kegan Paul Trench Trubner.

Kant, I. (1797), *The Metaphysics of Morals*. (2nd ed.), ed. and trans. Mary J. Gregor, intro. Roger J. Sullivan. Reprint, Cambridge: Cambridge University Press, 1996.

Kantrowitz, J.L. (1997), A different perspective on the therapeutic process: The impact of the patient on the analyst. *J. Amer. Psychoanal. Assn.*, *45*, 127–153.

Kelly, J.B. and Johnston, J.R. (2005), The alienated child: A reformulation of parental alienation syndrome. *Family Court Review*, *39*(3), 249–266.

Kernberg, O.F. (1988), Clinical dimensions of masochism. *J. Amer. Psychoanal. Assn.*, *36*, 1005–1029.

Kernic, M.A., Monary-Ernsdorff, D.J., Koepsell, J.K., and Holt, V.L. (2005), Children in the crossfire: Child custody determinations among couples with a history of intimate partner violence. *Violence Against Women*, *11*(8), 991–1021.

Kerr, J. (1993), *A Most Dangerous Method: The Story of Jung, Freud, and Sabina Spielrein.* New York: Vintage.

Khan, M.R. (1981), From masochism to psychic pain. *Contemp. Psychoanal., 17,* 413–421.

—— (1979), *Alienation in Perversions.* New York: International Universities Press.

Kimerling, R., Alvarez, J., Pavao, J., Kaminski, A., and Baumrind, N. (2007), Epidemiology and consequences of women's revictimization. *Women's Health Issues, 17,* 101–106.

Kimmel, M.S. (2002), "Gender symmetry" in domestic violence: A substantive and methodological research review. *Violence Against Women, 8,* 1332–1363.

Kindler, R.C. and Gray, A.A. (2010), Theater and therapy: How improvisation informs the analytic hour. *Psychoanal. Inq., 30,* 254–266.

Kohut, H. (1972), Thoughts on narcissism and narcissistic rage. *Psychoanalytic Study of the Child,* 27, 360–400. New York: Quadrangle.

Krystal, H. (1988), *Integration and Self-Healing: Affect, Trauma, Alexithymia.* Mahwah, NJ: Analytic Press.

Laing, R.D. (1959), *The Divided Self.* London: Tavistock.

Laitinen, I. (2006), Book review: Introduction to Social Dreaming. *Psychoanalytic Psychotherapy, 20,* 122–136.

Lansky, M.R. (1999), Shame and the idea of a central affect. *Psychoanalytic Inquiry, 19*(3), 347–361.

Laughlin, R. and Sher, M. (2010), Developing leadership in a social care enterprise: Managing organizational and individual boundaries and anxiety: An action learning approach to leadership development. *Organisational and Social Dynamics, 10*(1), 1–21.

LaViolette, A.D. and Barnett, O.W. (2000), *It Could Happen to Anyone: Why Battered Women Stay.* Thousand Oaks, CA: Sage.

Lawrence, G. (2000), The social dreaming phenomena. Presented at the Harry Stack Sullivan Society Lecture, February 23.

Lawrence, W.G. (2005), *Introduction to Social Dreaming: Transforming Thinking.* London: Karnac.

Layton, L. (2012), "You can't be neutral on a moving train": The psychosocial connection between patient and analyst. *Psychoanalysis, Culture and Society, 17*(1), 58–63.

—— (2007), What psychoanalysis, culture, and society mean to me. *Mens Sana Monogram, 5,* 146–157.

Leo, J. (2005), Behavior: Battling over masochism. *Time,* June 21.

Levenson, E.A. (1988), The pursuit of the particular: On the psychoanalytic inquiry. *Contemp. Psychoanal., 24*(1), 1–16.

Lewin, K. (1935), A dynamic theory of personality. New York: McGraw-Hill.

Lifton, R.J. (1999), *The Protean Self: Human Resilience in an Age of Fragmentation.* Chicago: University of Chicago Press.

Lionells, M. (2000), Sullivan's anticipation of the postmodern turn in psychoanalysis. *Contemp. Psychoanal., 36,* 393–410.

Lippmann, P. (1998), On the private and social nature of dreams. *Contemporary Psychoanalysis, 34*(2), 195–221.

Liss, M.B. and Stahly, G.B. (1993), Domestic violence and child custody. In M. Hansen and M. Harway (eds.), *Battering and Family Therapy: A Feminist Perspective* (pp. 175–187). Thousand Oaks, CA: Sage.

Madsen, L.H., Blitz, L.V., McCorkle, D., and Panzer, P.G. (2003), Sanctuary in a domestic violence shelter: A team approach to healing. *Psychiatric Quarterly, 74*(2), 155–171.

Marshall, L.L. (1996), Psychological abuse of women: Six distinct clusters. *Journal of Family Violence, 11*, 379–409.

Mason, M. (2003), Contempt as a moral attitude. *Ethics, 113*, 234–272.

McCauley, J., Kern, D.E., Kolodner, K., Dill, L., Schroeder, A.F., DeChant, H.K., Ryden, J., Bass, E.B., and Derogatis, L.R. (1995), The "battering syndrome": prevalence and clinical characteristics of domestic violence in primary care internal medicine practices. *Annals of Internal Medicine, 123*(10), 737–746.

McNulty, F. (1977), *The Burning Bed: The True Story of Francine Hughes, A Beaten Wife Who Rebelled*. San Diego, CA: Harcourt.

Meltzer, D. (1975), Adhesive identification. *Contemp. Psychoanal., 11*, 289–310.

Menaker, E. (1953), Masochism: A defense reaction of the ego. *Psychoanal Q., 22*, 205–220.

Mencken, H.L. (1956), *Minority Report: H.L. Mencken's Notebooks*. New York: Knopf.

Meyersfeld, B. (2008), Domestic violence, health, and international law. *Emory International Law Review, 22*, 61–112.

Miccio, K. (1994–1995), In the name of mothers and children: Deconstructing the myth of the passive battered mother and the "protected child" in child neglect proceedings. *Albany Law Review, 58*, 1087–1107.

Miller, S.L. (2001), The paradox of women arrested for domestic violence: Criminal justice professionals and service providers respond. *Violence Against Women, 7*(12), 1339–1376.

Mills, L.G. (1998), Mandatory arrest and prosecution policies for domestic violence: A critical literature review and the case for more research to test victim empowerment approaches. *Criminal Justice and Behavior, 25*(3), 306–318.

Mitrani, J.L. (1994), On adhesive pseudo-object relations. Part I: theory. *Contemp. Psychoanal., 30*, 348–366.

Modell, A.H. (1965), On having the right to a life: an aspect of the superego's development. *Int. J. Psychoanal., 46*, 323–331.

Moreno, J.L. (1987), *The Essential Moreno: Writing on Psychodrama, Group Method, and Spontaneity*. New York: Springer.

Morgan-Jones, R. (2006), The management of risk of recycling trauma in the context of conflicting primary tasks: An analysis of the use of group dynamic of incohesion basic assumption activity. *Organisational and Social Dynamics, 6*(1), 22–41.

National Clearinghouse for the Defense of Battered Women (2005), *The Impact of Parental Kidnapping Laws and Practice on Domestic Violence Survivors*. www.vaw.umn.edu/documents/pkreport/pkreport.html#id496966. Retrieved 7/19/12.

National Institute of Justice (2000), *Prevalence, Incidence, and Consequences of Violence Against Women: Findings from the National Violence Against Women Survey*. Washington, DC: National Institute of Justice.

National Institute of Justice (2004), *Violence Against Women: Identifying Risk Factors. Research in Brief*, November 2004. Washington, DC : National Institute of Justice.

Novick, K.K. and Novick, J. (1987), The essence of masochism. *Psychoanal. St. Child, 42*, 353–384.

Nylen, L. and Heimer, G. (1999), Sweden's response to domestic violence. *FBI Law Enforcement Bulletin*, November 1999.

—— (1989), On the concept of an autistic-contiguous position. *Int. J. Psychoanal.*, *70*, 127–140.

Palahniuk, C. (2002), *Choke*. Harpswell, ME: Anchor.

PDM Task Force (2006), *Psychodynamic Diagnostic Manual*. Silver Spring, MD: Alliance of Psychoanalytic Organizations.

Peled, E. (1993), The experience of living with violence for preadolescent witnesses of woman abuse. Unpublished doctoral dissertation, University of Minnesota, Minneapolis.

Peled, E., Eisikovits, Z., and Enosh, G. (2000), Choice and empowerment for battered women who stay: Toward a constructivist model. *Social Work*, *45*(1), 9–25.

Peter, T. (2006), Domestic violence in the United States and Sweden: A welfare state typology within a power resources framework. *Women's Studies International Forum*, *29*(1), 96–107.

Pizzey, E. and Shapiro, J. (1982), *Prone to Violence*. Middlesex, UK: Hamlyn Paperbacks.

Pollock, L. and Slavin, J.H. (1998), The struggle for recognition: Disruption and reintegration in the experience of agency. *Psychoanal. Dial.*, *8*, 857–873.

—— (1994), *The Transtheoretical Approach: Crossing Traditional Boundaries of Change*. Malabar, FL: Krieger Publishing Company.

Prochaska, J.O. and DiClemente, C.C. (1982), Transtheoretical therapy: Toward a more integrative model of change. *Psychotherapy: Theory, Research, and Practice*, *19*, 276–288.

Psychodynamic Diagnostic Manual: PDM Task Force (2006), 1st edition. Silver Spring, MD: Alliance of Psychoanalytic Organizations.

Quindlen, A. (1998), *Black and Blue: A Novel*. New York: Dell.

Réage, P. (1954), *The Story of O*. New York: Ballantine, 1977.

Reich, W. (1949), *Character Analysis*. Rangeley, ME: Orgone Institute Press.

Reik, T. (1972), *Masochismus und Gellenschaft*, Hamburg: Hoffman and Campe.

—— (1941), *Masochism In Modern Man*. New York/Toronto: Farrar and Rinehart.

Renn, P. (2012), *The Silent Past and the Invisible Present: Memory, Trauma, and Representation in Psychotherapy*. New York: Routledge.

Reza, Y. (2009), *God of Carnage*. London: Faber and Faber.

Rigas, D. (2008), Silent dialogues in the analytic relationship. *Int. Forum of Psychoanalysis*, *17*, 37–43.

Ringstrom, P. (2007), Principles of improvisation relevant to relational psychoanalysis. Presented at meeting of International Association for Relational Psychoanalysis and Psychotherapy (IARPP), Rome.

—— (2001), Cultivating the improvisational in psychoanalytic treatment. *Psychoanalytic Dialogues*, *11*(5), 727–754.

Roth, P. (1969), *Portnoy's Complaint*. New York: Bantam.

Rozin, P., Lowery, L., Haidt, J., and Imada, S. (1999), The CAD triad hypothesis: A mapping between three moral emotions (contempt, anger, disgust) and three moral codes (community, autonomy, divinity). *Journal of Personality and Social Psychology*, *76*(4), 574–586.

Ruddick, S. (1989), *Maternal Thinking: Towards a Politics of Peace*. New York: Beacon Press.

Sacher-Masoch, L. von (1870/2008), *Venus in Furs*. Tark Classic Fiction. http://openlibrary.org/publishers/Tark_Classic_Fiction

Safran, J.D. (1993), Breaches in the therapeutic alliance: An arena for negotiating authentic relatedness. *Psychotherapy*, *30*(1), 11–24.

Samuels, A. (2004), Politics on the couch: Psychotherapy and society – some possibilities and some limitations. *Psychoanalytic Dialogues*, *14*(6), 817–834.

Saunders, D.G., Faller, K.C., and Tolman, R.M. (2011), *Child custody evaluators' beliefs about domestic abuse allegations: Their relationship to evaluator demographics, background, domestic violence knowledge, and custody visitation recommendations*. National Institute of Justice, US department of Justice, October 31, 2011.

Scheff, T.J. (1987), The shame–rage spiral: A case study of an interminable quarrel. In H.B. Lewis (ed.), *The Role of Shame in Symptom Formation* (pp. 109–149). Hillsdale, NJ: Lawrence Erlbaum Associates.

Searles, H.F. (1960), *The Non-Human Environment in Normal Development and in Schizophrenia*. New York: International Universities Press.

Seligman, M.E.P. and Maier, S.F. (1967), Failure to escape traumatic shock. *Journal of Experimental Psychology*, *74*, 1–9.

Sharfstein, S.S. (1998), Harry Stack Sullivan: Interpersonal theory and psychotherapy. *The American Journal of Psychiatry*, *155*(6), 852–852.

Shengold, L. (1989), *Soul Murder: The Effect of Child Abuse and Deprivation*. New York: Ballantine.

Sievers, B. (2009), "Pushing the past backwards in front of oneself": A socio-analytic perspective on the relatedness of past, present, and future in contemporary organizations. *Organisational and Social Dynamics*, *9*(1), 21–42.

Silverman, J.G., Mesh, C.M., Cuthbert, C.V., Slote, K., and Bancroft, L. (2004), Child custody determinations in cases involving intimate partner violence: A human rights analysis. *American Journal of Public Health*, *94*(6), 951–957.

Socarides, C.W. (1958), The function of moral masochism: With special reference to the defence processes. *Int. J. Psychoanal.*, *39*, 587–597.

Spelman, E. (1989), Anger and insubordination. In A. Garry and M. Pearsall (eds.), *Women, Knowledge, and Reality: Explorations in Feminist Philosophy* (pp. 263–273). Boston: Unwin Hyman.

Spielrein, S. (1994), Destruction as the cause of coming into being. *Journal of Analytical Psychology*, *39*, 155–186.

Spivak, G. (1988), Can the subaltern speak? In C. Nelson and L. Grossberg (eds.), *Marxism and the Interpretation of Culture* (pp. 24–28). London: Macmillan.

Stark, E. and Flitcraft, A. (1988), Violence among intimates: An epidemiological view. In V. Van Hasselt, R.L. Morrison, A.S. Bellack and M. Hersen (eds.), *Handbook of Family Violence* (pp. 293–318). New York: Plenum.

Stein, A. (2011), The utility of contempt. *Contemporary Psychoanalysis*, *47*(1), 80–100.

—— (2010), Dreams as historical artifacts. *Journal of Psychohistory*, *38*(2), 125–132.

—— (2007), *Prologue to Violence: Child Abuse, Dissociation, and Crime*. Mahwah, NJ: Analytic Press.

Stein, A., Lewis, D.O., and Yeager, C.A. (1993), The juvenile justice assessment instrument. *Juvenile and Family Court Journal*, *44*(3), 91–102.

Steiner, J. (1990), Pathological organizations as obstacles to mourning: The role of unbearable guilt. *Int. J. Psychoanal.*, *71*, 87–94.

Steiner, R. (1894/1916), *Die Philosophie der Freiheit* (The Philosophy of Freedom), translated from the German edition of 1894 by Mr. and Mrs. R.F.A. Hoernle. London and New York: G.P. Putnam's Sons.

Stern, D.B. (2010), *Partners in Thought: Working with Unformulated Experience, Dissociation, and Enactment*. New York: Routledge.

—— (2009), *Partners in Thought: Working with Unformulated Experience, Dissociation, and Enactment*. London and New York: Routledge.

—— (2003), The fusion of horizons: dissociation, enactment, and understanding psychoanalytic dialogues. *International Journal of Relational Perspectives, 13*(6), 843–873.

—— (1997), *Unformulated Experience: From Dissociation to Imagination in Psychoanalysis*. New York: Routledge.

—— (1990), Courting surprise: Unbiddden perceptions in clinical practice. *Contemporary Psychoanalysis, 26*, 452–478.

Stirner, M. and Byington, S.T. (1845/2010), *The Ego and His Own*. New York: Creatspace.

Stone, L. (1977), *The Psychoanalytic Situation: An Examination of Its Development and Essential Nature*. Madison, CT: International Universities Press.

Strindberg, A. (1907/2004), *The Ghost Sonata*. Amsterdam: Amsterdam University Press.

Sullivan, H.S. (1970), *The Psychiatric Interview*. New York: Norton.

—— (1965), *Personal Psychopathology, Early Formulations: The Changing Social Scene and Its Effect on the Incidence of Mental Disorders*. New York: W.W. Norton.

—— (1964), Tension interpersonal and international: A psychiatrist's view. In *The Fusion of Psychiatry and Social Science: Collected Works, Vol. II* (pp. 293–331). New York: Norton.

—— (1956a), *Clinical Studies in Psychiatry*. New York: W.W. Norton.

—— (1956b), *The Interpersonal Theory of Psychiatry*. New York: Norton.

—— (1953a), *The Interpersonal Theory of Psychiatry*. New York: Norton.

—— (1953b), *Clinical Studies in Psychiatry*. New York: Norton.

—— (1950), Tensions interpersonal and international: A psychiatrist's view. In Hadley Cantril (ed.), *Tensions That Cause Wars: Common Statement and Individual Papers by a Group of Social Scientists Brought Together by UNESCO* (pp. 79–138). Urbana, IL: University of Illinois Press.

—— (1947), Conceptions of modern psychiatry. The first William Alanson White Memorial Lectures. Washington, DC. William Alanson White Psychiatric Foundation.

Taft, C.T., Resick, P.A., Panuzzio, J., Vogt, D.S., and Mecahnic, M.B. (2007), Examining the correlates of engagement and disengagement coping among help seeking battered women. *Victims and Violence, 22*(1), 3–17.

Thibaudier, V. (2005), The mystique of masochism. *Cahiers jungiens de psychanalyse, 115*, 13–23.

Thompson, C. (1974a), "Penis Envy" in women. In Jena Baker Miller (ed.), *Psychoanalysis and Women* (pp. 52–57). New York: Penguin.

—— (1974b), Cultural pressures in the psychology of women. In Jena Baker Miller (ed.), *Psychoanalysis and Women* (pp. 69–84). New York: Penguin.

—— (1974c), Some effects of the derogatory attitude toward female sexuality. In Jena Baker Miller (ed.), *Psychoanalysis and Women* (pp. 58–68). New York: Penguin.

—— (1964), *On Women*. New York: New American Library.

Tjaden, P.G. and Thoennes, N. (2000), *Full Report of the Prevalence, Incidence, and Consequences of Violence Against Women: Findings from the National Violence Against*

Women Survey. Washington, DC: US Department of Justice, Office of Justice Programs, National Institute of Justice.
Tolman, R.M. (1999), The validation of the Psychological Maltreatment of Women Inventory. *Violence and Victims*, *14*(1), 25–37.
Topliffe, E. (1991–1992), Why civil protection orders are effective remedies for domestic violence but mutual protective orders are not. *Indiana Law Journal*, *67*, 1039.
Twemlow, S.W. (1995), The psychoanalytic foundations of a dialectical approach to the victim/victimizer relationship. *Journal of the American Academy of Psychoanalysis*, *23*, 545–561.
Uebel, M. (2002), Masochism in America. *American Literary History*, *14*(2), 389–411, quote at 395.
US Department of Housing and Urban Development (2011), Memorandum February 9, 2011: www.hud.gov/offices/fheo/library/11-domestic-violence-memo-with-attachment.pdf. Retreived 7/13/12.
van der Kolk, B.A. (1989), The compulsion to repeat the trauma: Re-enactment, revictimization, and masochism. *Psychiatric Clinics of North America*, *12*(2), 389–411.
van der Kolk, B.A., Roth, S., Pelcovitz, D., Sunday, S., and Spinazzola, J. (2005), Disorders of extreme stress: The empirical foundation of a complex adaptation to trauma. *Journal of Traumatic Stress*, *18*(5), 389–399.
Voices of Women (VOW) Organizing Project (May, 2008), Justice denied: how family courts in NYC endanger battered women and children. Executive Summary.
Von Krafft-Ebing, R. (1886) *Psychopathia Sexualis*. New York: Rebman Publishing Co. (Open Library).
Waits, K. (1998), Battered women and their children: Lessons from one woman's story. *Houston Law Review*, *35*, 29. www.omsys.com/kw/waits_houston.htm#Rkw29640. Retrieved 2/26/13.
Waldrop, A.E. and Resnick, P.A. (2004), Coping among adult female victims of domestic violence. *Journal of Family Violence*, *19*(5), 291–302.
Walker, L.E. (2009), *The Battered Woman Syndrome* (3rd ed.). New York: Springer.
—— (1994), *Abused Women and Survivor Therapy: A Practical Guide for the Psychotherapist*. Washington, DC: American Psychological Association.
—— (1979), *The Battered Woman Syndrome*. New York: Springer.
Walker, L.E.A., Brantley, K.L., and Rigsbee, J.A. (2004), A critical analysis of parental alienation syndrome and its admissibility in the family court. *Journal of Child Custody*, *1*(2), 47–74.
Wallerstein, J. (1977), Book notices. *J. Amer. Psychoanal. Assn.*, *25*, 725–744.
Warshaw, C. (1989), Limitations of the medical model in the care of battered women. *Gender and Society*, *3*(4), Special Issue: Violence against Women, pp. 506–517.
Weems, R.J. (1995), *Battered Love: Marriage, Sex, and Violence in the Hebrew Prophets*. Minneapolis, MN: Fortress Press.
Westlund, A.C. (1999), Pre-modern and modern power: Foucault and the case of domestic violence. *Signs*, *24*(40), 1045–1066.
Williams, O.J. and Becker, R.L. (1994), Domestic partner abuse treatment programs and cultural competence: The results of a national survey. *Violence and Victims*, *9*(3), 287–296.
—— (1993), The location of cultural experience. In Peter L. Rudnytsky (ed.), *Transitional Objects and Potential Spaces: Literary Uses of D.W. Winnicott* (pp. 3–12). New York: Columbia University Press.

—— (1971), *Playing and Reality*. London: Tavistock.

Winnicott, D.W. (1965), *The Maturational Processes and the Facilitating Environment: Studies in the Theory of Emotional Development*. The International Psycho-Analytical Library, 64 (pp. 1–276). London: The Hogarth Press and the Institute of Psycho-Analysis.

Young, G.H. and Gerson, S. (1991), New psychoanalytic perspectives on masochism and spouse abuse. *Psychotherapy*, *28*(1), 30–38.

Zorza, J. (2010), Batterer manipulation and retaliation compounded by denial and complicity in the family courts (chapter 14). In M.T. Hannah and B. Goldstein (eds.), *Domestic Violence, Abuse, and Child Custody: Legal Strategies and Policy Issues*. Kingston, NJ: Civic Research Institute.

Index

abandonment: and attachment 95; of children 116–17; fear of 35, 54, 71–2, 79, 82, 92
Abraham Lincoln (painting by Dali) 61
abusive relationships: costs 100, 102; Emotional Empowerment Project 15–17; and love 3, 4, 6–7, 46, 84, 107, 125; psychological effects 118; staying in 2–3, 6, 20, 97, 146. *see also* aggression; attachment; child abuse; escape from abusive relationships
acceptance/normalization of childhood abuse 72–3, 100
acquiescence 61. *see also* collusion; complicity
activism 159–61
adaptations to trauma 11, 24, 68, 70, 72–3, 75, 85–6, 128
adhesive states 89. *see also* attachment; fusion with the aggressor
advocacy 159–61
aesthetic space 146–9
affect, dissociation. *see* dissociation of negative affect
agency 1–2, 8, 25, 159–61; and anger 131–2; consciousness raising 22, 23, 73; fear of 82; gendered expectations 145; Gwynne 159; Hayal 66; learned helplessness 78; Phoebe 33, 34, 98, 163; psychoanalytic theory 43; and psychological violence 138; renegotiating 104; and victim self-states 70
aggression 1–2, 71, 74, 131, 152; and attachment 34–8; collusion with 73, 84; cycles of 53; denial 4–5; female 33–4; institutional dissociation 127; intermittent 19; passive 36, 74; psychological 136–44, 159–60. *see also* abusive relationships; anger
Almeida, R. 24
alter ego, Naggy Maggie 91. *see also* self-states
amnesias, dissociative 108
analysis. *see* psychoanalytic perspectives; psychotherapy
analytical theater 25. *see also* psychodrama
anger: and agency 131–2; engagement 8–10, 26–7, 37; Phoebe 37; repression 2. *see also* aggression; dissociation of negative affect
anorexia 5
anthropology, theatrical 25
anxiety 1, 8, 11, 19, 103; annihilation 130; and appraisals of others 144; avoidance 79, 127, 145; separation 35, 89
approval-seeking 144
assertiveness 8–10, 26, 73, 159
attachment 101; and abandonment dynamic 95; and aggression 34–8; costs 100, 102; defensive 4–8; learned helplessness 79–80; mother–child 121, 124, 125; oscillating 48, 53, 69; paradoxical 19; psychoanalytic theory 43, 69; sadomasochistic 3, 101–2; and self-esteem 81; traumatizing 53, 68, 83; victim self-states 61, 79; *see also* abusive relationships; love
authenticity 148
automatisms, dissociative 18, 108, 132
autonomy 33
avoidance 54
awakening 42, 48, 73
Ayers, Mary 45, 46, 105

The Ballad of Francine Hughes (Hardy and Herbert) 1
Bancroft, Lundy 119
Bateson, G. 44
battered women's syndrome (BWS) 113–14
batterer/victim binary 74
bearing witness 150–1
benevolent sexism 10
Benjamin, Jessica 22–3, 73
Berandt, Charlotte 151
betrayal 4, 5, 41, 80, 98; denial 108; institutional 127
Bettleheim, Bruno 151
bias, gender 115–26, 129–30, 143–4
Bierce, Ambrose 38
biological determinism 83, 85
Bion, W.R. 83, 129
Black and Blue (Quindlen) 7
Boal, Augusto 25, 26, 146–7, 156–7
body language 82
Bollas, Christopher 80, 124
bonding, traumatic 53, 68, 83. *see also* attachment
The Bonds of Love: Psychoanalysis, Feminism, and the Problem of Domination (Benjamin) 22
boundaries, personal 53, 68, 70, 74, 78, 96
Bowlby, J. 83
brainwashing children 114–16
Bromberg, P.M. 13, 41, 141
brutality. *see* abusive relationships; aggression
Buechler, S. 30
Bunny's story 132; agency to activism 159–61; dissociation of anger 63–4; escape from abusive relationships 116–17; institutional dissociation 121–2, 123; psychological violence 144
The Burning Bed (McNulty) 1
business trips 139–40
BWS (battered women's syndrome) 113–14

CAD triad (contempt, anger, and disgust) 39
Camus, Albert 105
Caplan, Paula 86
Care of the Soul (Moore) 126
case studies. *see* Bunny; Doris; Gwynne; Hayal; Ileana; Janice; Lauren; Leidy; Marta; Millie; Misty; Paula; Phoebe *and* Rosalie's stories
Cézanne, Paul (artist) 45
Chancer, Lynn 101
change 145–6; collective 155–9; and poiesis 99–104; psychotherapy for 145–6; self-creation 146–9; and staying the same 41; transtheoretical models 26
child abuse, by violent partners 115, 118–19
Child Advocacy Services 105
child custody. *see* custody of children
childhood abuse 53–4; acceptance/normalization of 72–3, 100: and child custody 120–1; Emotional Empowerment Project 17–18; Phoebe 40; re-enactment 5–6, 7, 52–4, 103, 108. *see also* trauma; *and see individual case studies*
childhood defenses 34
children, brainwashing 114–16
Chodorow, N. 23
choice, staying in abusive relationships 146
church 90, 160
coercion 32. *see also* abusive relationships; aggression
collective change 155–9
collusion with violence 73, 84
communalizing narratives 103
complementarity 61
complicity in oppression 10, 22, 60, 75
consciousness raising 2, 21–7, 48, 73–6, 157
constructivism 135, 145
contempt 29–31; and childhood abuse 54; countertransference reactions 95; Phoebe 31, 34, 37, 38, 42, 47, 48; psychoanalytic theory 38–40; self-states 61
contempt, anger, and disgust (CAD triad) 39
conversion symptoms 108, 155
Coontz, Stephanie 83
costs of romantic attachment 100, 102
countertransference: institutional dissociation 130; masochism 94–9; Misty 92; Phoebe 97–9. *see also* transference
criminal justice system, goals 127–8. *see also* legal perspectives
critical consciousness 2, 22, 26, 48, 157. *see also* consciousness raising
cultural: perspectives 20–1, 24, 25, 95–6; pressure 73; scripts 10, 34, 71, 74
culture: institutional 143–4; of silence 156–7

Cupid Chastised (poem) vii
Cupid's knife 4
custody of children 17, 131–2; bias against mothers 115–19, 120–6, 129–30; and childhood trauma 120–1; custody evaluators 118–20; legal perspectives 105–6, 114–18, 120–1; unsupervised visitations 114, 118
cycles of violence 53

Dali, Salvador 61
data collection, Emotional Empowerment Project 10
death instinct 87
defense mechanisms 2; childhood 34; institutional 107, 127; relational masochism as 100–1
defensive attachment 4–8
definitions: emotional abuse 16; masochism 68
Deleuze, G. 70
denial of abuse aggression 4–5; legal perspectives 112–13; societal 106, 108
dependence: adaptations to trauma 73; sadomasochistic attachment 83, 101
depersonalization 40, 131
depression 19; and custody of children 119; learned helplessness 80; Phoebe 31, 32; and psychological violence 138–40; and unacknowledged resentment 81
desire, erotic 89
de Sade, Marquis: Justine 77, 79 Juliette 77
DESNOS (Disorders of Extreme Stress Not Otherwise Specified) 73
destructive intimacy 60
detailed inquiry 13; psychological violence 137–8; rule-making/following 142–3. *see also* interview methods
devaluation of girls 71
developmental models 83–4, 99
Devereux, George 61
Diagnostic and Statistical Manual of Mental Disorders 9, 85–7
diagnostic criteria: masochism 85–7; PTSD 73
Dickinson, Emily 134
disavowal 44, 48, 56, 73
disbelief, societal 106, 108
disengagement strategies 54
Disorders of Extreme Stress Not Otherwise Specified (DESNOS) 73
dissociated enactment 25, 53, 70–1, 76, 146; Doris 62–3; Ileana 56, 59–60
dissociation of negative affect 1–2, 4, 5–10; Bunny 63–4; and contempt 30, 40; and depression 81; Doris 62–3; eliciting dissociated material 136–45; engendered self-states 52–4; Hayal 64–6; integration 159; Leidy 153; Misty 92; as normal brain function 108; Phoebe 42, 47; political consciousness raising 22–3; psychoanalytic theory 11–12; role in inducing/maintaining abuse 54, 62, 71, 74; symptoms 18–19, 54, 108. *see also* institutional dissociation
distancing, psychological 40, 53
divine existence 90
divorce mediation 114
doctors, institutional dissociation 109–11
doing nothing 147
domestic violence. *see* abusive relationships; aggression
dominant/submissive binary 74
domination. *see* oppression
Doris' story 9, 62–3
double binds 143
drama therapy 25, 26, 37, 146–9, 156
dreams 110–11, 150–5; social dreaming 25, 26, 151–2, 155
dynamisms 156

'The Economic Problem of Masochism' (Freud) 88
education 159
eliciting dissociated material 136–45
emotional abuse 16–17. *see also* psychological violence
Emotional Empowerment Project: data collection 10; dissociative signs/symptoms 18–19; domestic abuse section 15–17; emotional range 19–20; history of childhood maltreatment 17–18; interview methods 13–15; subjects 12–13
emotional range 19–20
emotions: lack of 4, 18, 35, 43, 52; uncanny 6, 30, 53, 54, 132. *see also* dissociation of negative affect
empowerment 2, 27, 75, 101; and contempt 30; through psychotherapy 145–6
enabling environments 52
enactment: aggression 34; new self 148; psychoanalytic 49. *see also* dissociated enactment; re-enactment

Eng, D.L. 80
engagement of anger 8–10, 26–7, 37
engendered self-states. *see* self-states
erotic desire 89
escape from abusive relationships 42, 47, 52, 54, 58, 101–2, 107, 149–55; Bunny 116, 117; and murder 20, 27, 28, 67; Penny 149, 150; Phoebe 38
Eternal Feminine (painting by Cézanne) 45
ethnicity/race 20–1, 95–6
Ethnopsychoanalysis journal 61
evaluators, custody 118–20
evolutionary biology 83, 85
The Exorcist (film) 34
expectations, gendered 145
expression of dissociated aggression 71. *see also* dissociated enactment
externalized rage 9, 12, 103. *see also* aggression; anger

failure to protect 113–18, 120, 126–31
false allegations of abuse 115, 118, 119
fantasy structure, masochism 86
feelings, lack of 4, 18, 35, 43, 52. *see also* dissociation of negative affect
feet 38
feminine masochism 85–6, 88
femininity 70; scripts 102. *see also* stereotyping
feminist perspectives 22–3, 60–1, 68, 75, 135
fight and flight response 79
financial considerations 27, 107, 119
flashbacks 18, 108
flatness of affect 4, 18, 35, 43, 52. *see also* dissociation of negative affect
forgiveness 79–80
Foucault, M. 136, 157
Franks, David 32
freedom. *see* escape from abusive relationships
Freire, Paulo 24–6, 157
Freud, Sigmund 44–5, 81, 84–8
friends with benefits 2, 32
Fromm, Erich 84
frozen shoulder, Leidy 154–5
fugues, dissociative 108
fusion with the aggressor 33. *see also* adhesive states; dependence

Gardner, Richard 114–15
Gender and Violence Project, Ackerman Institute 69
gender: bias 115–26, 129–30, 143–4; expectations 145; inequality 10, 21, 73; neutrality 111; roles 23, 45, 62, 102; swapping 25–6
Gentile, Katie 150, 157
The Ghost Sonata (Strindberg) 4
Gladys Ricart Memorial March 132
Goethe, Johann Wolfgang von 29
Goldner, Virginia 23, 69
growth 149. *see also* change
Guerin, Christopher vii
guilt 7; institutional dissociation 130; Phoebe 51, 80–1
Gwynne's story 139–40, 142, 159

Haaken, Janice 8, 23
Hardy, Lyn 1
hatred 4; loving 125
Havelock Ellis, Henry 84
Hayal's story 64–6, 157–8
helplessness 78–83, 114
Herbert, Donna 1
Herman, Judith 53, 70, 75
history of childhood maltreatment 17–18
hopefulness 78–83
hostility triads 39, 42
hotlines, domestic violence 140
Hughes, Francine 1
Hume's guillotine 49
humiliation 2, 3, 5, 32, 39, 40, 46, 47, 50; of love 100; and pride 56; and shadow self 90
hypervigilance 11, 73, 128

identity 3, 7; adhesive states 89; confusion 18; invalidation 39, 103; relational 82; renegotiating 104; victimhood 82
Ileana's story 9, 55–61, 72, 125
'The Illusion of Personal Individuality' (Sullivan) 144
imaginary scripts 137
imagination, moral 42–5, 48
immigrant women 20–1, 95–6
imperviousness to danger 52
imprisonment: abusers 93–4; Doris 13, 63; internal 136–7
improvisation, psychodrama 148–9
income 27, 119
indignation 54
inner: critics 144; voices 158
insight 145

institutional: contexts 20–1, 26; culture 143–4; defences 107, 127
institutional dissociation 107–9; bias against mothers 115–19, 120–6; custody evaluators 118–20; failure to protect 113–18, 126–31; legal perspectives 111–13; medical staff 109–11
integration: aggression 8; dissociated affect 8, 48, 71, 73, 75, 108; self 147
internal working models 99. *see also* role models
internalization 69; learned helplessness 80; others' appraisals 144. *see also* victim self-states
interpersonal sphere: masochism 89–90; political consciousness raising 21–7
interpretation: dreams 150; and psychodrama 149
interview methods 13–15. *see also* detailed inquiry
intimacy, destructive 60
invalidation 39, 32

Jaggar, A. 30
Janice's story 120, 124, 129
jealousy 33–4
joint custody arrangements 118
Jung, C. G. 89–90

Kant, I. 39
Khan, Masud 88, 98, 103–4
killings, of women leaving 20, 27, 28, 67
Klein, Melanie 83, 128
knowing and not knowing 4, 45, 121–2
Kohut, H. 39
Krafft-Ebing, Richard Freiherr von 84, 85

language/talking cures 145
Lauren's story 157
Lawrence, W.G. 25, 151, 152
Layton, Lynne 23, 33, 144
learned: helplessness 78, 114; hopefulness 78
legal perspectives 105–7; custody of children 105–6, 114–18, 120–1; failure to protect 113–18; goals 127–8; institutional dissociation 111–13; masochism 87
legislative theater 25
Leidy's story 152–5
Lewin, Kurt 147
life history questions 13
Lifton, R.J. 24
loss 82. *see also* abandonment
love, abusive 3, 4, 6–7, 46, 84, 107, 125. *see also* attachment

magical thinking 57, 125, 128
malevolent transformations 53
Marta's story 72
martyrdom 90
Masculine Shame (Ayers) 105
masochism 68–70, 74, 76–8, 87, 100–1; costs of romantic attachment 100, 102; countertransference reactions 94–9; developmental reasons for 83–4; as externalized rage 103; and helplessness/hopefulness 78–83; interpersonal sphere 89–90; medicalization of 85–7; Misty 90–4; Phoebe 37; psychoanalytic theory 84–5, 87–9; transformation/poiesis 99–104
masochistic (self-defeating) personality disorder 85–6
mass hysteria 108
medical staff, institutional dissociation 109–11
medicalization of masochism 85–7
Messler-Davies, J. 149
metaphor of frozen shoulder 155
The Metaphysics of Morals (Kant) 39
Meyersfeld, Bonita 21
Millie's story 67–8
mindfulness 73
mirroring, analytic 149
missed appointments, Phoebe 35–6
Misty's story 90–4, 100
Moore, Thomas 126
moral imagination 42–5, 48
moral masochism 87, 88. *see also* masochism
Moreno, J. L. 25, 26, 37, 147, 150–1
Morgan-Jones, R. 130
mother–child attachment 121, 124, 125
motherhood, Ileana's story 57–9
mothers, societal bias 115–19, 120–6, 129–30
mourning 80, 81–2
Mourning and Melancholia (Freud) 81
multiple-self theory 24, 25, 74, 135. *see also* self-states
murder, of women leaving 20, 27, 28, 67
The Myth of Masochism (Caplan) 86

Naggy Maggie (alter ego) 91
needs 49; and rights 146

negation 44–5, 71
negative affect. *see* dissociation of negative affect
no, saying 91
normalization of childhood abuse 72–3, 100
not-me self 31. *see also* self-states
not knowing, and knowing 4, 45, 121–2
novels, romantic 83
numbing 81. *see also* dissociation of negative affect

obsessive behaviour 126, 139, 140
Oedipal triangles 23, 45, 56, 85, 88
oppression: complicity in 10, 22, 60, 75; cultural perspectives 25, 156–7; embracing 82; Hayal 64; Phoebe 33; political consciousness raising 22–3. *see also* power relations; subservience
organizational dissociation. *see* institutional dissociation
outlaw emotions 39
oxytocin 83

pain 99, 100, 102, 103, 104
panopticon 136
paper shredder example 163–4
paradoxical: attachment 19; resistance to brutality 102–3
paralysis 52
paranoid–schizoid position 128
parataxic distortions 14
parental alienation syndrome (PAS) 114–15, 118
participant-observer models 26
passion, and self-destruction 89–90
passive aggression 36, 74
passivity 1–2, 9, 26, 34, 62; politics of 73–6
patriarchal: norms 118, 119, 120; terrorism 7
Paula's story 117–18, 122–3, 131–2
PDM (*Psychodynamic Diagnostic Manual*) 87
Pedagogy of the Oppressed (Freire) 24–5
penis envy 45, 56, 71, 88
Penny's story 140–2, 149–50
personal reflection 24
Phoebe's story 2, 10, 162–4; attachment/aggression dynamic 34–8; contempt 31, 34, 37, 38, 42, 47, 48; countertransference reactions 97–9; guilt 80–1; integration of dissociated affect 71; learned helplessness 80; masochism 77–8, 84, 89; middle stage of analysis 40–2; moral imagination 42–5, 48; psychodrama 149; resolution 49–51; shame/guilt 46–7, 51, 104
physical abuse, Emotional Empowerment Project 15–16. *see also* abusive relationships; aggression
Pizzey, Erin 7
play 43–4, 146–9
pleasure principle 87
poiesis 99–104
policing of domestic abuse 112–13
political consciousness raising 21–7, 26, 48, 73–6
politics of passivity 73–6
possessiveness 6, 64
post traumatic stress disorder (PTSD) 19; diagnostic criteria 73; Ileana 60, 72. *see also* childhood abuse
Power Politics (Atwood) 77
power relations 3, 19, 49, 60, 74; analytic 156; countertransference 96; renegotiating 101, 103. *see also* empowerment; oppression
powerbroking 25
pregnancy, Ileana 57–9
pride/humiliation dynamic 56
projections: aggression 34; contempt 30; and mother–child attachment 124; paralyzing 20; Phoebe 36, 41
projective identification 36, 83
Prologue to Violence (Stein) 2
protection: failure 113–18, 120, 126–31; orders 112
protective feelings towards partners 54, 62
psychic change. *see* change

psychoanalytic perspectives: Phoebe 33–4; and political consciousness raising 21–7; resistance 97, 145, 155; reverie 148
psychodrama 25, 26, 37, 146–9, 156
Psychodynamic Diagnostic Manual (PDM) 87
psychodynamic therapy 159
psychoeducation 37, 48, 75
psychological distancing 40, 53
psychological violence 136–44, 159–60
psychosocial subject 61–2
psychotherapy: empowerment through 145–6; and institutional dissociation 109–11

PTSD. *see* post traumatic stress disorder
punishment 7, 17, 19, 53, 70, 79, 90, 102; divine 104
pursue-y-ness 139

Quindlen, Anna 7

race/ethnicity 20–1, 95–6
ragdoll metaphor 126
rage, externalized 9, 12, 103. *see also* aggression; anger
The Rainbow of Desire (Boal) 146–7
The Rebel (Camus) 105
re-enactment of childhood abuse 5–6, 7, 52–4, 103, 108, 125. *see also* repetition compulsion
reflection, personal 24
Reich, Wilhelm 85
Reik, T. 88
relational: identity 82; masochism. *see* masochism; role models 74–5, 96, 99, 125
relationships, abusive. *see* abusive relationships; aggression
religious perspectives 90, 160
repetition compulsion 7, 23, 48, 74; masochism 83; Phoebe 33, 99. *see also* re-enactment
repression of anger. *see* dissociation of negative affect
repressive relational structures 136
resentment, unacknowledged 81. *see also* dissociation of negative affect
resistance: analytic 97, 145, 155; to brutality 68, 74, 155; paradoxical 102–3
responsibility for abuse 33, 47, 69, 78, 84, 157
revenge 25, 39, 61. *see also* dissociated enactment
reverie, analytic 148
revictimization of women 120
reward/punishment dynamic 19, 53
rights, and needs 146
Ringstrom, Phil 148–9
risk-taking behavior 91
ritual 25, 101, 125, 142. *see also* rule-making/following
role models, relational 11, 74–5, 96, 99, 125. *see also* re-enactment
role-taking 33
romance novels 83
romantic scripts 104. *see also* love
Rosalie 112–13, 119, 124–6, 130, 132; custody of children 105–6, 131
rule-making/following 15, 25, 43, 121, 149; and psychological violence 136, 139, 142–3

Sacher-Masoch, L. von 84
sadomasochism 9, 10, 46, 60. *see also* masochism
safe spaces 25, 47, 149
safety 12, 27, 40, 65, 71, 73, 75; countertransference reactions 95; and psychodrama 148–9; and victimhood 79
Samuels, A. 155–6
Saunders, D.G. 118
Schindler's List (film) 46
scripts: cultural 10, 34, 71, 74; femininity 102; imaginary 137
self-creation 146–9. *see also* change
self-criticism 54
self-destructive behavior 86, 89–90
self-esteem 102; and attachment 81; collective change 158; Misty 91; Penny 142; and psychological violence 138
self-fulfilling prophecies 139–40
self-states 13, 48, 52–4; Ileana 55–60; masochism 100; psychoanalytic theory 11–12, 43; psychosocial subject 61–2; victim role 9, 66–73, 79; working with 60–1. *see also* multiple self theory
self transcendence 89–90
separation anxiety 35, 89. *see also* mourning
sex, and masochism 84
sexism, benevolent 10
sexual abuse 17, 115
sexually transmitted diseases 17, 57
shadow self 67, 90
shame 16, 19, 20, 76; Ileana 56; institutional dissociation 130; Phoebe 36, 45–9, 51, 104
Shapiro, Jeff 7
Simpson, Nicole Brown 153
social: change 155–9; dreaming 25, 26, 151–2, 155; liberation 26; masochism 88
societal dissociation. *see* institutional dissociation
sociometry 147
sociopolitical perspectives 21–7
Spielrein, Sabina 89
Spivak, Gayatri 22
splitting. *see* dissociation of negative affect
spontaneity, of psychodrama 148–9

stalking 139, 159
statistics: custody of children 106; domestic abuse 20; United States intimate partner violence 27–8
status: deprivation 32–3, 36; of marriage 142, 145
Stein, Abby 162–4
Steiner, Rudolf 42–3, 48
stereotyping 3, 37, 45, 62, 88, 96, 111, 115. *see also* gender roles
Stern, Donnel 70
Stirner, Max 127
subjects, Emotional Empowerment Project 12–13
submissiveness 3, 74, 83, 85, 88, 89, 102
subservience 19, 39, 70, 82. *see also* oppression
substance abuse 80
suicidality 80
Sullivan, Harry Stack 1, 6, 11, 24–6, 48, 53, 56, 162; contempt 30, 31, 39; detailed inquiry 137; dreams 150, 152; fight and flight response 79; interview methods 13, 14; others' appraisals 144; psychotherapy for psychic change 145; total situation 156; truthiness 138
survivor therapy 75
survivors 60, 69
Sweden 21
symptoms: conversion 108, 155; dissociative 18–19, 54, 108

Taft, C.T. 54
talking cures 145
'Tensions Interpersonal and International: A Psychiatrist's View' (Sullivan) 156
terror of confrontation 82
theater, therapeutic 25, 26, 37, 146–9, 156
'Theater of the Oppressed' (Boal) 25
theatrical anthropology 25
theory, psychoanalytic 10–12; contempt 38–40; masochism 84–5, 87–9
therapeutic theater 25, 26, 37, 146–9, 156
therapy. *see* psychoanalytic perspectives; psychotherapy
Thompson, Clara 86, 88
total situation 156
transcendence of the self 89–90
transference 14; institutional dissociation 130; Leidy 155; Phoebe 35. *see also* countertransference
transformation/poiesis 99–104. *see also* change
transgenerational repetition 125. *see also* re-enactment
transtheoretical models of change 26
trauma: adaptations to 11, 24, 68, 70, 72–3, 75, 85–6, 128; and childhood abuse 52–4; and dissociation 54, 62, 71; undoing 107. *see also* post traumatic stress disorder
traumatic bonding 53, 68, 83. *see also* attachment
triggers: depression 31; dissociated enactment 48, 51, 53, 68, 70; shame/guilt cycles 47; violence 15, 39, 136
truthiness 138
Twemlow, Stuart W. 68

uncanny emotions 6, 30, 53, 54, 132
unconscious repetition. *see* re-enactment
United Arab Emirates 21
United States, statistics of intimate partner violence 27–8

van der Kolk, B.A. 73
venereal infections 17, 57
Venus in Furs: Sacher-Masoch, Leopold von 84
verbal abuse, Emotional Empowerment Project 16
Verleugnung (disavowal) 44–5
victim self-states 9, 66–73, 79. *see also* self-states
victimhood 3, 61, 77, 79
victimization 52, 68
victims as survivors 60
victim/victimizer dialectic 68
violence; *see* abusive relationships; aggression; dissociated enactment

Wallenstein, Judith 114–15
Winnicott, D.W. 43, 92
wishful thinking 54
withdrawal 54
witnessing 150–1
working models 99. *see also* role model